Enjoc
Love + ĭ
K

C000254949

LOVE
BEYOND
LINDISFARNE

Kimberley Adams

Shy Bairns Publishing

ISBN: 978-1-7385717-0-3

For my amazing auntie Emma
and my beautiful niece Bella.
I love you both beyond words xx

Dear Reader

It's me, Kim, writer of Love Beyond Lindisfarne, a follow on to my debut romcom, Love Lindisfarne, which was released late autumn 2023 in time for Christmas.

I adored writing Love Lindisfarne, and it seems that a lot of readers enjoyed it too. Whilst I didn't have it in mind to write another, I didn't take much persuading to return to the gorgeous Holy Island with the characters I'd come to know and love.

So, for those of you who didn't read LL, I wanted to bring you up to speed on who is who. Of course, it's still out there available if you want to read the books in order, but no pressure. Hopefully you will quickly tune in after reading this.

Ellie Montague was living in London and was unceremoniously dumped by boyfriend Matt at the office Christmas party. A chance meeting with Lord Bamburgh, patron of a dog rescue charity, led her to packing in her job and taking a month-long volunteer role on Lindisfarne, a small tidal island off the coast of north Northumberland. Ellie's role was to help look after what turned out to be a range of furry and feathery rescue animals. Her arrival on the island was fraught, and it was thanks to the gorgeous Zen, her rescuer, that she was saved from near drowning. Ellie and Zen are now taking the first steps into a love at first sight relationship as Ellie decided to stay on Lindisfarne with her gorgeous new man. For the moment, Ellie is living above the Love

Lindisfarne gift shop owned by Imogen who we don't meet in this book.

The people you need to know about other than Ellie and Zen are her inner circle friends from London – bestie Sophie and her fiancé Jake, former work colleague Tara and her husband Toby who are awaiting the arrival of their first baby, and Peckham's finest coffee makers Stanislaw and Aleksy who hail from Poland.

Ellie forges many new friendships on Lindisfarne. Meg and Bert, who she stayed with when she first arrived, are caretakers of Lindisfarne Castle and are now like grandparents to her. Zen's sister Aurora runs the village café and is married to Jack a fisherman. Then we have the cantankerous but loveable rogue, Ethel, from the village, oyster farmer Maurice and the various members of the Crafty Lindisfarners craft group.

Last and very much not least, as they form a big part of this story, are Aidan, second son of Lord Bamburgh, and Isla, commonly referred to as the witch, or poison Isla… you get the picture!

You will also meet a range of adorable animals, but I will let you find out about them for yourselves, and I hope you enjoy your spring to summer break on Lindisfarne and beyond…

Love and stotties, Kim x

Prologue

April. Was it really four months since I had been rescued from near drowning on the causeway as I made my way onto Lindisfarne for the first time? I'd arrived from London after a chance meeting led me to the island to help look after rescue animals belonging to Lord and Lady Lindisfarne, or James and Grace, as I now know them. I hadn't really known where Northumberland was, let alone the tiny Holy Island, but even though I hadn't been here very long in the grand scheme of things, I'd come to love the place, its eclectic residents, the hilarious bunch of reprobate animals and, of course, Zen, my rescuer, who I knew from the very first time I'd seen those gorgeous coffee bean eyes, was the one for me.

Life had been pretty peachy since then – the freezing cold Northumberland winter weather excepted – but today the big spring sun was shining, bathing the newly emerging green landscape in warmth. Swathes of heavy headed daffodils were following on from delicate snowdrops and dancing on the gentle breeze; crocuses were popping up like splodges of colour on an artist's paint palette, adding splashes of vibrancy across the ground – it should have been the kind of day to be glad to be alive. Except it wasn't. In the midst of all the new life emerging around me, we were in death. Lindisfarne had lost one of its own...

CHAPTER 1

One day in early March, after I'd finished doing my yard duties, I called into Meg and Bert's cosy cottage to thaw out and catch up on the gossip. This was a lovely ritual that had fallen into place and was always conducted with the huge brown teapot filled to the brim and a plate of whatever biscuits Meg had in stock. We referred to them as our mood biscuits, and they were chosen specifically to mark how we were feeling on any given day.

'Here Ellie, listen to this. I've had an email from Spain. It's from Ethel. She's still out there on her winter warmer as she calls it, with her cousin, like she does every year, and I normally don't hear a peep out of her until she wants picking up from the airport. Someone must have shown her how to send messages, or maybe wrote it for her. I don't recognise the name of the sender, Squidney69, whoever they might be. I'll read it out to you.

Dear Meg

I'm having a canny time in Benidorm. It's a heck of a lot warmer over here and there's a drink promotion every night called OAPeed, where us pensioners get Two for One, or you spin a wheel, but I'm sure that's rigged. I won a bottle of 'Champagne' the other day but I'm sure it was Lambrusco with the label changed. Anyway pet, I have been well pee'd. I am at the minute as it happens. And I got talking to our Sybil, and she said I should be thinking about what happens when I go, and she didn't just mean back to Lindisfarne. I told her I had no intention of that happening for a long time yet, but she's always been organised has Sybil (boring old fart) and she said if I drink much more then it will be sooner rather than later. So pet, I've decided, what I want is for you to organise my wake for me. I

2

want it in the Crab; I want Eric and Dean singing the Geordie songs; I want everyone to be up dancing, drinking, and having fun. No sadness hinny. No dark mizza clothes (tell Ellie to wear that fluorescent jacket – that'll brighten the place up.) Get Maurice on the still and have a few barrels of hooch on the bar but tell him I don't want any of his slimy oysters. Ask Aurora to take care of the food – she can make it as fancy as she likes but no healthy nonsense. Invite the whole island. I'm very popular you know, so they will be out in force – I want a party that will go down in island history.

My solicitor will give you the money back for the expenses.

Hope it's not for a long-time pet, but now you know. Right, I'm off for the cocktail of the day, a double Beni Banga, see you in a month.

Love Ethel xxx

'What do you make of that Ellie?'

'Typical Ethel.' I smiled. 'Suppose it makes sense but it's not something I want to happen any time soon.'

'I've known Ethel since I was a girl, Ellie. She's older than grass but got more energy than most people I know. She's a cantankerous so and so, but you can't help admiring her zest for life...' And at that Meg burst into tears.

'Oh Meg, come here,' I said hugging her. 'Ethel will probably outlive us all. She's like Teflon, so just put the letter somewhere safe and forget all about it for now.'

'You're right, pet, I will. Go and pop the kettle on and we'll have a nice cup of tea – unless you fancy getting OAPeed.' She guffawed.

3

'Think I'll stick with tea. Biscuits don't taste that good with gin, and definitely not at this time of the day. I'm here to help Bert so better keep a clear head or he'll be giving me one of his famous bollockings!'

'Ignore him pet. He's like a bear with a sore head at the moment. It's the pain in his hip, and the frustration of not being able to do everything he wants to do, but hopefully it won't be too long now before he's put right.'

We sat at the kitchen table nursing our tea and making inroads into the pile of biscuits in front of us.

'I can't believe you've been on the island for four months now Ellie – time flies. You look the picture of health and happiness, you bonny lass. I take it you made the right decision?'

'You know I did, Meg. I can't believe how much my life has changed in the last few months either. Leaving London, coming to Lindisfarne and meeting Zen.'

Zen, my gorgeous boyfriend who I had met when I first crossed the Causeway on to the island. Zen, with his unruly dark curls, eyes like dark roast coffee beans with twinkling shards of golden demerara sugar as they caught the light, his impossibly high cheekbones and those kissable lips…I sighed dreamily before returning to the conversation.

'Oh, and everyone else of course,' I added hastily. 'I've loved every minute of living in Imogen's flat, and the best thing is that Zen is two doors down, so it works perfectly for us. We are getting to know each other, yet I still have space for me to adjust to my new life, and he is able to continue building the coffee empire. It's love you know,' I whispered looking at Meg and hoping for her approval.

'Lass, that's nothing to whisper about. You can shout it from the castle roof for me. I am so pleased for the pair of you. That is, I hope Zen feels the same?'

'I'm sure he does Meg. We haven't said the words yet, but you just know, don't you? My bestie Sophie told me I would know when it happened, that everything in the world would feel like it had fallen into place. I think it was love at first sight you know. But it's one of those things until afterwards, when time has passed, that you actually believe it to be true. Tell me, was it love at first sight for you and Bert?'

'Eeh Ellie you're going back since pussy was a cat. Bert and I have known each other all our lives, both of us being born on the island. He's a year older than me as you know, but we went to school together. All the children, no matter what age, shared the classroom back in those days. Can you believe there were eighteen in our class compared to the six there are now?'

'That just shows how life on the island has changed over the years,' I responded as I took yet another biscuit.

'He was a proper little ragamuffin was Bert. His family were poor. His Dad had been injured in the war and found it hard to get work but Cissy, his mam, was a grafter and made sure all the bairns were fed and clothed, even if it was in hand-me-downs.'

'Bert must have inherited his work ethic from her,' I smiled.

'From being a young boy though, Bert had his sense of humour and gentle ways, and we were there for each other. He would come

5

to our house and my mam would feed him up and find him odd jobs so he could earn a few pennies. She really loved Bert,' said Meg, a faraway look in her eyes, probably thinking about her long-gone mam.

I squeezed her hand.

'Our friendship continued into our teens when we became a couple. We were married at seventeen, offered a rented cottage on the estate, and we both started working for the Lindisfarnes. A few years later we jumped at the chance of moving here to Courtyard Cottage and becoming more involved with the castle. He's always been the one for me Ellie, belligerent old so and so that he is at times, but if I had my life all over again, I wouldn't change him... Hmmm... unless it was for Roger Moore maybe!'

'Who's that? But more to the point... did he Roger Moore?' I grinned.

'Eeh, you are as bad as Ethel, you are. He had an eyebrow, you know.'

'Who did? Roger? I hope he had two.'

'Yes Ellie, of course he had two.' She tittered. 'But he used to raise one of them and look all suggestive, so maybe that's where he got his name.'

Meg attempted to raise one eyebrow, unsuccessfully, and we both burst out laughing.

'He was very suave and sophisticated, and terribly handsome. Aidan Bamburgh has a bit of a look about him, come to think about it. He was James Bond long before you were even a twinkle in your mammy's eye.'

'Ah, I think I might know who you mean, but I'll Google it.' My search history was looking random these days thanks to the older inhabitants of the island.

At that, little Nacho and Flo the collie, who were both lying under the table, eyes fixated on us in the hope of biscuits dropping their way, suddenly jumped towards the door barking, tales wagging furiously, and the subject of our conversation came into the cottage. Flo was beside herself with joy at his arrival and tiny terrier, Nacho, did his thing of patting him on the foot furiously with his paw to remind him of his presence.

'Look at you two gassing like fishwives as if there was nothing better to do.' He smiled at us both. 'Eeh, I need to take the weight off; this hip is giving me gyp. As soon as they make me into the six-million-dollar man the better. Any tea left in that pot?'

'Bert, young Ellie here won't have a clue who you mean.' Meg turned to me. 'It's a bionic man, pet, made out of used car parts or something like that.'

'Err right,' I said, nodding like I knew what she was talking about – another one to Google.

'I've been showing Ellie Ethel's email, Bert.'

'Aye lass, I know it's upset you but, for once in her life, Ethel's actually trying to do what's best. Not before time mind. She's less organised than a Fishing Club Shindig. We will do what we have to, when the time comes, but knowing her, she'll outlive us all. Ethel hasn't got blood running through her veins – it's pure alcohol!'

'This is just too sad, Zen,' I said, clutching his hand. We walked down Main Street to the Crab. It didn't seem possible that, less than a month ago, Meg had shown me Ethel's email. Now, here we were, on the very day she was meant to be coming home from Benidorm, going to her wake, or party as she would have preferred it to be called.

He stopped, folded me into his arms and gently took the tissue from my hand. He dabbed at my eyes and gave me *the* look, the Zen coffee bean eye look, which made everything in the world feel better and my insides turn to mush.

'It is sad Ellie, but Ethel had a good life, and all her friends will be there today to remember her in the way she had asked, It's up to us to make sure that her wishes are granted. She didn't want anyone to be sad; that just wasn't her. She was always the life and soul of the party and that is how she would want today to go.'

'Oh, I know you're right, but I feel cheated. I only got a couple of months with her before she went over to Spain, so I feel I never even got to know her properly. She was such a character. I really liked her sharp wit, and even though her tongue could have cut through the cliffs on Greater Reef, I loved spending time with her. She will be such a miss.'

'Knowing Ethel, she'll be hovering around us somewhere. Her star will never leave this island.' He smiled, kissing me on the top of my head.

'And by the way, you could have put that jacket through the wash – it stinks!' he said, referring to the communal fluorescent yellow hi-vis coat, worn to clean out the animals, that Ethel had specifically requested I wear to the wake.

We walked into the Crab and the place was full to bursting. It seemed like all the islanders had come to say their fond farewells to Ethel. Hardly surprising, as her family had lived on the island for generations and sadly, she was the last in line. Other than her cousin in Spain, she had no family. Meg had followed Ethel's instructions to the letter and Dean and Eric were in the corner, livening up proceedings with some sea shanties. There was a barrel of the famous Fishing Club hooch on the bar counter and a buffet table groaned with enough food to feed an army, made by Aurora and her staff at Northern Lights and Bites. Bert and Meg were at the door greeting people as they came in.

'Thanks for coming, pets,' said Meg dabbing her eyes. 'She would have liked all this.' She gesticulated around the room.

'She would that,' said Bert, looking a little glassy eyed.

'You okay Bert?'

'Aye, Ellie lass. I'm more than all right, in fact I'm tip top. I've had two glasses of hooch, and I can't feel my dicky hip anymore. Might just sneak a barrel home.'

'Oh no you won't, Bert, and no more today, otherwise we'll be scattering you with Ethel,' said Meg.

'When are her ashes coming back from Spain? It was awful it happening over there the way it did, and just after you got her email. That was such a shock, and to be holding this wa... erm... I mean party today on the same day she was due to come back, well

9

that is even sadder,' I said. 'It was as well her cousin was there to organise everything. Talking of, is that her over there in the corner? I don't recognise her.' I glanced at a woman clad from head to toe in black, with sunglasses so big that most of her face was covered.

'It must be,' said Meg. 'I haven't had the chance to go over yet. She's obviously in mourning wearing all that black.'

Zen's sister Aurora came over. I could see she had been crying, as her eyes were red, but she pasted on a smile and offered us a vol au vent from a platter.

'Ethel's favourite, Crab and Marmite, love it or hate it she always used to say. I'm going to miss the old girl. Loved Ethel to bits.' She sniffed, put the platter down and gave me a hug. 'Anyway, how goes it, *sis in law*?' She smiled.

'Hey, not quite there... yet,' I winked. 'But tell me now you're three months in, how is married life for you?'

'The best, Ellie, apart from him being so untidy and constantly wanting to watch fishing stuff on the telly. I feel like I know that Bob and Paul from *Gone Fishing* personally! Sorry that I've hardly seen you or Zen, other than when I wave at him in the shed from the kitchen window. Things are just hectic preparing for the season.'

'I know, sorry too. I haven't been in to see you recently. It's just been so busy, what with the shop and the animals. Bert's been really struggling with his hip lately, so I've been going over every day, but hopefully Imogen will be back soon. Fingers crossed it won't be too long until Bert gets sorted, although his recuperation will take a while. Oh, and did you hear? I've got myself a part time job as seasonal Team Leader at the castle, working with the volunteers. Plus, Grace said she might want my help with some marketing stuff, so honestly Aurora, I feel like everything is falling into place. Well, apart from having to say goodbye to Ethel, of course.'

Aurora's attention turned to the woman in the corner.

'Is that Ethel's cousin over there?'

'She's got some head of hair for an older woman,' I said, looking at her jet-black bouffant style hair.

'Do you think she's got a visual impairment?' asked Bert.

'Ethel never used to talk about Sybil, other than when she was going over to Benidorm. She would say she was staying with her, but I know nothing about her. I'm not even sure which side of the family she's from, so got no idea about her eyesight, but have you seen the rhinestones on them goggles? A little over the top, and her hair looks quite familiar,' mused Meg, staring intently at the woman.

'Just a blinking minute!' Meg suddenly pushed her way through the pub towards the woman, Aurora and I following behind, desperate to be in on whatever Meg was up to.

Meg stood in front of the woman, hands on her hips, looking her up and down, a look of distain on her face.

'Meg whatever's the matter? Be kind to her,' I whispered. 'Remember she's been through a lot; she's just lost her cousin.'

'A lot? She'll be going through a lot more soon. I knew I recognised the hair. It's Pelvis Presley.'

'Sorry Meg, have you been drinking the hooch as well?'

11

The next minute, Meg grabbed the woman's hair and pulled a wig off her head, quickly followed by the sunglasses.

'Ethel! I knew it! You wore that to the village fancy dress just last year. What the heck are you playing at? We all thought you were dead. I've gone through a box of blooming expensive tissues and the poor Crafty Lindisfarners are distraught. They've got fingers like ham hocks through crocheting black poppies by the dozen – at your behest I might add.'

By this point the music had screeched to a halt, drinks were put down, and all eyes focused on the corner where Meg, wig in hand, was glaring at a very sheepish but delighted, living and breathing Ethel. I bent down and threw my arms around her and all I could manage to say was, 'You're alive!'

Ethel stood up and looked around the room.

'Listen you lot, I've never ever missed a party on this island in all my years, so you don't think I was going to miss the biggest and last one that was all about me, do you? There's no show on Lindisfarne without Ethel!' She cackled.

'And don't worry, I'll be paying you all back for this, and the next round of drinks are all on me as well. I had a little win in Benidorm, had to guess how many ping pong…'

'Enough Ethel,' shouted the group of Crafty Lindisfarners in the other corner, all staring at her like she was Marley's ghost, a mix of emotions on their faces.

'What the Beejeezus,' exclaimed Linda, taking off her specs and polishing them on her jumper to get a better look.

'Has she come back to haunt us already?' muttered Muriel, a look of pure terror on her face.

'You're meant to be dead Ethel,' gasped Dora. 'We made sausage rolls especially for you.'

Ethel smiled coyly.

'Okay, I'll say no more so come on lads and lasses, let's get this party started. Will someone please bring me a glass of hooch and one of me favourite volly vonts?'

'Tell me you old devil, was your cousin Sybil in on this?' demanded Meg.

'Erm, well actually, there is no Sybil. I've been going to Benidorm for years to meet up with Sid, my gentleman friend from Barnsley.' She gave a lascivious wink, and I thought Meg was going to choke.

'You what? Squidney69 by any chance?' retorted Meg, who then burst into tears, threw her arms around the older woman, and gave her a big kiss on the cheek.

'Never ever change, my pet. We love you just the way you are.'

The band struck up playing their version of 'You're the Devil in Disguise.' Chatter increased and a seat was placed next to the inglenook for Ethel who resided like Queen Victoria in mourning, the Elvis Presley wig lopsidedly placed back on her head. She received her guests as one by one the villagers lined up to welcome her back to the land of the living. It was one fabulous party, and the best bit was that we still had our Ethel – potty mouth, and all!

CHAPTER 3

The next morning, I bumped into Bert as he was coming out of the Post Office.

'Ellie lass, please get yourself over and see Meg. She's desperate to show you something.'

'I'm on my way there now Bert. Is everything okay? I got a text off her earlier, but I was sorting stock out in the shop waiting for Harriet to get back to open up.'

'Well, depends on how you look at it.' He winked. 'We're all fine, but I know she wants a chat.'

I quickly walked across the bay, past the fishing huts and up the hill to the castle, which looked as stunning as ever, sitting on top of its commanding hilltop position looking out to sea. A big sign at the bottom of the hill informed people that it would be open for the season in a week's time, when I was due to start my new seasonal job.

'You took your time,' said Meg as I pushed open the door.

'What's happened? Is everything okay? Bert was very vague.'

'Men. They don't get stuff like this but look, I couldn't wait to show you. It's not out in the shops yet but Dora found this copy. There was a pile of them when she was cleaning at the hotel.'

Before I had time to take my coat off, Meg shoved a copy of *YI* Magazine in my hand. It was the county magazine, the glossy that celebrated the great and the good of Northumberland – of which neither description reflected the characters featured on the cover.

Exclusive! The Honourable Aidan Ettrick Bamburgh celebrates engagement to daughter of Lindisfarne hoteliers, supermodel Isla Rose Thompson.

'Oh my God, Meg! Surely not. He's kidding, isn't he? And what's with the supermodel, eh? Super bitch more like.'

'Doesn't look like he's kidding, pet. Look at her. She's like the cat who got the blinking cream. This will not end well, believe you me, but at least they'll be in London or occasionally Bamburgh; although we might be graced with the odd royal visit if they go to see Elspeth and Gordon at the hotel.'

'Look at the size of that ring,' I gasped. 'It's as big as a gull's egg. It's exactly what you would imagine Isla choosing – totally over the top.'

The ring was one massive oval cut diamond and looked like it was weighing her hand down.

'She'll never get her fleecy gloves over it, that's for sure,' said Meg, as practical as ever.

'I bet there are some gorgeous antique rings over at Bamburgh from throughout the ages that she could have chosen; but no, Isla would have to have new, and I don't think she'll be too worried about the gloves Meg.' I replied, laughing.

After Christmas, Aidan Bamburgh had returned to London, quickly followed by Isla. It was such a relief to see the back of her that I didn't think too much about what was happening to the pair of them. My life on the island was perfect as it was, and I hadn't given them a second thought. Apart from the odd joke on WhatsApp, I hadn't had any communication from Aidan, so this had all come as a bit of a shock. Aidan and I had parted on good terms as friends after a very brief flirtation, and I was fond of him, as was Zen. Even though he was a chancer, he had a kind heart, unlike Isla whose own heart was made of stone.

'Do you think she's bribing him, Meg?' Isla had a track record of using bribery to get whatever she wanted, and I pondered this possibility.

'Who knows with that trollop, but she's got exactly what she wanted all along. Fame and wealth. Although, Aidan isn't going to inherit the lion's share. It's family money so if she thinks she's going to be able to get her hands on it then she must get through Lord B and Aidan's older brother, Lance, first. That said, she'll never have to worry about money ever again. Aidan isn't exactly on the breadline. I wouldn't mind being a penny behind him that's for sure.'

I leafed through the twelve pages of pictures taken in the state rooms and grounds of Bamburgh Castle, a place I'd not yet been to. Dislike of Isla aside, I couldn't help but gaze in awe at the pair of them, the golden couple. They looked so good together, Isla far more tastefully dressed than she had been when I'd first met her. The multitude of outfits she was wearing in the photos had obviously been chosen by a top stylist and she looked almost regal as she posed in the stunning castle. I started to read the syrupy sweet article but even after one line it had me as hooked as everyone else on the island would be when they saw it.

The couple – who will wed in June posed for a photo shoot together at Aidan's ancestral home, the majestic Bamburgh Castle in glorious Northumberland, with a series of images proving just how in love they are.

Yuk...

Aidan and his beautiful fiancée, Isla Rose, sit on an antique chaise longue from the French renaissance period with the supermodel gently holding her partner's hand, as he gazes into her eyes.

Double yuk...

Wearing a vintage Dior black and scarlet dress with a crystal embossed bolero and a ruffled taffeta skirt, Isla looks incredible, every inch the supermodel.

More tasteful than she has ever looked before, I suppose...

Taken on the castle parapet with the amazing views of the wild ocean behind, Isla and Aidan snuggle together as he adorably wraps her in his cashmere coat to protect his pretty bride-to-be from the North Sea chill.

Just one little push and she'd be over the edge...

A close up shot of Isla's slender hand shows off her dazzling engagement ring, believed to be designed by the model herself in partnership with top royal jewellers, *Garrards,* as she grins coquettishly at her future husband.

Laughing all the way to the bank no doubt...

Bamburgh Castle shared the pictures with us at *YI* magazine as they felt that Northumberland should be the first place to know about this joyous news, and we are so proud to bring you this incredibly happy and exclusive announcement.

I'll give it a year and he'll not be seeing that engagement ring again...

Isla has been welcomed to the family by Lord and Lady Bamburgh. Isla's parents Mr and Mrs Gordon Thompson, hoteliers from Lindisfarne—

They own one hotel on a tiny island, they are hardly flipping Hilton International...

—attended the castle for a family engagement dinner.

And a thrashing out of the dowry no doubt...

Aidan was snapped driving his future wife back to London in a black Range Rover with the pair no doubt chatting excitedly about their forthcoming nuptials on their return to the capital.

Enough already, pass the bucket...

Once finished, I lay the magazine down on the table, took off my coat and pointed to the biscuit cupboard as I went to put the kettle on the Aga.

'Double chocolate Hobnobs today, Meg. We need them.'

'You're not wrong, pet. Let's have a quick cuppa and then I'll go and milk Nanny – that goat has more personality than Isla Thompson will ever have!'

CHAPTER 4

Tea drunk, Meg and I left the warmth of the cottage. It was late morning, and the sun was already high in the sky making a valiant effort to break through and give us some long-awaited spring sunshine. I'd shivered my way through winter. It was far colder here than London and whilst I was now fully kitted out with clothes to keep me warm, the season had been long and very chilly, and we were all desperate for a glimpse of spring. The upside was that I'd had Zen to keep me warm through the long icy nights.

Even just thinking about my gorgeous Zen gave me a glow from head to toe like I'd been plugged into the mains. It had been a very convenient excuse for us to stay with each other on the freezing winter nights, citing the cold as a reason not to go home! It was hard to believe we had been together for over three months. The time had just flown, and I couldn't imagine my life without him in it. He really was the kindest and most handsome man in the world, and we seemed so compatible – in every sense of the word.

All four dogs were mooching about the yard as we crossed to see to the goats. They were a very eclectic bunch, from the three-legged ex racing greyhound that was Tri, Flo the odd-eyed Collie, Robson the Bedlington Terrier who resembled a small lamb, and of course my Nacho, the tiny terrier who had been instrumental in me coming to the island in the first place.

Nanny McPhee was eager to get on to her milking bench the minute she saw Meg, and there in the stall snuggled up to her was our latest arrival, the prettiest little black Pygmy goat who had quickly become Nanny's best friend. We had rescued her from a couple in Lowick on the mainland who were moving into a retirement apartment, and whilst they had wanted to take her with them, keeping a goat, even a miniature one, was definitely not allowed in the lease.

'It's good to see that Holly Goatlightly has settled in well Meg. She's gorgeous with all that dark fur – definitely the Audrey Hepburn of the goat world – and Nanny looks happy with her company. I still think you need to take that pearl collar off her mind. Nanny will get an inferiority complex!'

'Nanny does like her, and thankfully Holly doesn't need milking, although Nanny still blooming does. Neither of these are having any more kids – too much like hard work.'

Jenny the donkey was alone in her stall next to the goats. After Christmas, Bert had found another donkey to keep her company, but she had showed total disinterest, much preferring the company of Nanny McPhee and Holly Goatlightly. Our resident male donkey, Wonky, had taken an immediate dislike to the newcomer named Magic Mike by Grace and me because, in the words of Bert, he was a "randy little sod." Meg did enquire why he was named after a magician, but I left that one to Grace to explain. Mike, formally known as Derek, was a much younger donkey, full of youthful enthusiasm for the ladies and Wonky was not for sharing, especially when it came to Wilma, our other newish acquisition with whom he was absolutely smitten. We had held a board meeting around the kitchen table, and it was agreed that Mike/Derek would go to a new home. He is now extremely happy strutting his stuff around the ladies of the Asses and Lasses Sanctuary across on the mainland near Morpeth.

'Any sign of Colonel Sanders, Meg?' I asked about our missing Cockerel, as I swept out the goat's stalls.

'No, none, thank gawd. I hope he's found someone else to wake up at silly o'clock.'

I left Meg to it and took the dogs down to the paddocks to see what feed was needed, doing my usual thing of standing on the cinder path and gazing at the view in front of me. The landscape had changed from a blanket of dull browns to patchwork shades of vivid greens, and vegetation was breaking through from its winter hibernation, popping up to welcome spring. The bird chatter was increasing too, as we headed towards breeding season, and even though I had loved living in the castle's guest apartment, it was far quieter in Imogen's flat above the Love Lindisfarne gift shop. One sound that was missing was Wonky's serenade across to Wilma's former home on the farm. Peace had ensued now that they were together at last. This ritual, as I stood and did some breathing exercises that I'd learned from my Yoga class in London, was my version of meditation. I never got time for the real thing. Zen's mam, Simone, was forever trying to persuade me to join her in her early morning practice, but the idea of getting up at sunrise and having to get Zen to sail me over to the tiny conservation island of Greater Reef on the Lady Eleanor, tired me out before I started. This for me was the compromise, and I always felt better after taking a few minutes to be at one and reflect on the gratitude for what I now had in my life.

***

Later that day, I called in to the café to grab some lunch. I hadn't seen much of Aurora since Ethel's living wake, and she had arranged

21

to take her break with me. The topic of conversation, of course, was Aidan and Isla. It was the hot subject on the island, and, apart from Gordon and Elspeth, her parents, who had apparently taken their previous snobbery to a whole new level, no-one was exactly thrilled by the union.

'What the hell is Aidan thinking? He had his choice of all those gorgeous girls like you see on *Made in Chelsea*, and he picks poison bloody Isla. There must be a rabbit off somewhere.' Aurora grinned.

'What rabbit? She's good in bed you know. I heard her telling Zen that once...'

'You what?' She spluttered, interrupting me.

'Hey, keep your hairnet on! It was at the Gansey party at Christmas, and I overheard them talking, but Zen was having none of it. You don't think they'd ever come back up here, do you?' I asked, munching on a deliciously different type of flapjack.

'Mmm this is good, what kind is it?'

'Rhubarb and custard. I'm thinking of branching out and making them for retail to go with Zen's coffee. I've got my business plan ready – going to call it Flapjackius and sell them along Hadrian's Wall.'

'Haha, that's very good and this is scrummy. You amaze me Aurora, running this place, your jewellery, helping across the island. I don't know how you fit it all in. You'll be on Dragon's Den next.'

'Not sure about that, but thanks. Anyway, back to the more interesting stuff. No, I don't think they'll come back up here. Imagine Isla having to live in an estate house over at Bamburgh.

Remember, Aidan's the spare and not the heir. No castle for them, so no incentive to come North. I seem to remember Meg telling me that the Bamburghs own a spectacular house in London and that Aidan was living there as the second son, so that would suit the poisonous cow much better.'

'Nearer Harrods and Harvey Nicks, I suppose,' I laughed.

'Do you think any of us will get invited to the wedding?' she mused, finishing her latte, and standing up.

'Not if Isla's got anything to do with it, and I wouldn't go anyway.'

'Nor me,' she said, laughing. 'Next wedding I'll be going to is yours and Zen's!'

'Ooh talking of weddings, that's made me think about Sophie and Jake. I have told you that the gang are coming up and hiring Muriel's holiday house, haven't I?'

'Only about a thousand times Ellie, but it's great, and we look forward to meeting them. I can see how excited you are about it.'

'I am – can't wait for you to meet them, show them the island and to take them to all the places I've not yet got to in Northumberland, so this is the perfect excuse.'

'I know, we never did manage to get far when you first arrived, thanks to all the drama. Hopefully, you will make up for it with your friends.'

'The boys and Sophie and Jake are staying for two weeks, but Toby and Tara are staying on longer as Toby has managed to get on to a voluntary archaeological dig over in Bamburgh. That means

Tara can put her feet up before the baby arrives. And Toby will be in his element – digging up tin cans, probably.'

'Hey, I'll have you know that a unique sort of Roman-British roundhouse was discovered in Bamburgh. Not to mention the dozens of Anglo-Saxon burial sites which helped reveal a very diverse population. When you get to Bamburgh, look at the crypt under St Aidan's. You can read the story.'

'I will. Toby's longing to meet James too; I hadn't realised what a big cheese he was in the world of archaeology and to Toby it's like meeting your favourite rock star. By the way, you'll have to give me tips about juggling lots of things, because I start my seasonal job next week. I'm really looking forward to it.'

'You'll be great as a castle guide, Ellie, and helping support the team. You were so quick learning bits of history, and you can just ask any of us if you get stuck. Top tip, some of these tourists think they know more than us, and some do, of course, but we always just nod and thank them for their input. One fella, PhD in stupidity, was in the café the other week and told me all about how the Vikings had built the castle. He was only about 750 years out.'

'No, he didn't!'

'Yes, he did and was totally serious. Just don't get into a debate with anyone Ellie. Smile and move on.'

'I will, thanks. James and Grace are just wonderful, aren't they? I'm so pleased that I got to meet them thanks to staying on Lindisfarne. Grace and I get on well when she comes to help with the animals.'

'Actually, Ellie,' said Aurora, her face suddenly serious. 'I'm a bit worried about Grace. She was looking really pale when I saw her yesterday in the village. She had to go back to the castle as she wasn't feeling well, and that really isn't like her.'

'Funny, Meg said the same thing. She's going to go and see her today.'

'Ah, well, if you hear anything let me know.'

'Will do. Anyway, best get off. I think Maurice is coming over later to help with some of the heavier stuff – if we can get him detached from Peggy Brannigan that is.'

'Maurice is like a pig in muck.' Aurora laughed. 'It's all he ever wanted, a woman in his life, because when his mother passed, he didn't have a clue how to look after himself.'

'Are you telling me it's more of a practical arrangement than being able to make the most of his aphrodisiac oysters?'

'Bit of both, or so I hear, but I reckon Maurice is more talk than action in the bedroom department. And on that thought – that I wish I could unthink – back to the kitchen for me. See you soon.'

'You will,' I said laughing. 'I'll try and keep my face straight when I see Maurice later!'

'I've just had lunch with Aurora,' I said to Meg, as I got back to the cottage. 'She sends her love and also said to tell Grace she's asking after her when you go to see her.'

And just at that Bert's phone rang.

'Oh no, James...will do...yes, Meg will be over right now...and don't you worry, Ellie and I will sort the animals and get them up to the yard away from the noise. You concentrate on Lady Grace.'

He disconnected the call quickly and looked at us, his face etched in concern.

'Meg pet, Grace has taken proper poorly. James thinks she might have had a stroke—'

'A stroke? Oh my God,' gasped Meg, immediately rushing towards the door.

'The Air Ambulance is on its way. Time is of the essence and the tide is in, so Ellie lass, you come with me, and we'll get the animals back up to the yard, away from the noise of the helicopter when it arrives.'

Bert and I quickly headed towards the paddocks. Just like that, in a split second, things on Lindisfarne had changed, and this time not for the better.

I ran down to the paddocks and systematically brought the animals up the cinder path, handing them to Bert who was waiting at the top of the hill to take them into their respective stalls. Then I ran back down to get the next lot. It was a bit like déjà vu as I remembered back to Christmas, when Aidan and I had struggled in the storm to bring the donkeys and alpacas up to safety. At least the weather was bright today. Once I'd got all the animals away from the paddocks, the hum of a helicopter approaching could be heard.

'I'll go down and greet them, Ellie. You get your breath back lass. You've been up and down that hill about four times.'

'Are you sure Bert?' I gasped. 'Is your hip okay?'

'I'll take my time Ellie; it's going to be a few minutes before it comes in to land.'

Bert went off and I pulled my phone out of my pocket and rang Zen.

'Zen, it's just the most awful news...'

'Ellie, what's wrong? I can hear a helicopter from the roastery. Oh my God, it's Bert, isn't it?'

'No chick, Bert and Meg are fine. It's Grace.' My voice faltered. 'She might have had a stroke.'

'Oh my God. On my way.'

I looked over the five-bar gate from my vantage point in the yard, to see that there was a crowd of islanders and tourists watching proceedings at a distance, from the designated landing spot on the flat scrubland, just beyond the paddocks. I could see Zen, in his role of local coastguard volunteer, helping keep people back at a respectable distance, and I guessed that word had spread quickly across the island.

The Great North Air Ambulance landed, and it was all systems go. The critical care team on board jumped out and straight into the waiting coastguard truck, to drive up the hill to the castle car park. Bert met them at the gate and showed them the back steps leading up to the Lindisfarne's apartment.

'Eeh lass, this is a right rum do,' said Bert, as he joined me back at the gate, puffing with exertion. 'Meg just gave me a quick ring from the castle. It's not looking good Ellie, pet.'

A tear rolled down his lined face, which suddenly looked much older.

'Oh Bert.' I grabbed his hand and gave it a squeeze. 'Let's hope they've arrived in time. Grace is an extraordinarily strong woman, and you know yourself how determined she is which has got to help, surely. Let's go back to the cottage and I'll make us a cup of tea.'

'I'll wait outside until they bring her out,' he said, as we walked back to the cottage. 'I might manage to get a quick word with James.'

'Okay, Bert. I'll put the kettle on.'

From the porch, I heard the team coming down the castle stairs, giving instructions to each other as they gently carried a stretcher, an ashen faced James following behind.

When they were gone, there was no sign of Bert, so I went back to the far end of the yard to the gate and looked across as the truck pulled up. They loaded the stretcher into the helicopter. James must have been given permission to go with Grace to hospital by the crew, as he climbed in too. The noise from the whirring rotor blades as they began to spin in preparation for take-off was loud, even from this distance, and I could see the gulls out on the shoreline turn and fly away from the source of the sound and the backdraft. Very quickly, the green, yellow, and white helicopter took off, swooped around in the direction of the coast, and flew towards the mainland and hospital.

I returned to the cottage and was soon joined by Meg. She looked like the stuffing had been knocked out of her as she slumped down in her chair at the farmhouse table, her head in her hands.

'Oh, Ellie lass,' she said, her voice thick with emotion. 'I've never seen anyone so vibrant look so…so…' She faltered, not knowing what to say, but I knew exactly what she meant.

'Oh Meg, It's just awful. I can't quite believe it myself. Grace is just so, well, alive. She's fit though, you know, so surely that will help, don't you think?'

'I don't know, Ellie; I don't know what to think. She didn't even look like our Lady Grace anymore.' And at that she broke down.

Bert came in, followed by Zen. They went and sat either side of Meg and grabbed a hand each. I noticed Flo creeping under the table and laying a protective head on Meg's knee.

'Now, Meggie my love, we need to think positive. I know it's hard, but let's try and wait to hear what James has to say when they get to hospital and Grace has been examined, then go from there. We need to keep strong.'

'I know you're right, Bert, but you didn't see her.'

I saw Bert and Zen exchange a surreptitious look. I knew at once that they had both seen Grace and were just as worried as Meg but didn't want to exacerbate her fears.

'You've had a nasty shock sweetheart. Zen lad, get the medicinal brandy. Bugger the tea today – we need something much stronger.'

CHAPTER 6

The mood in the cosy cottage was sombre.

'What do we do now?' I asked, looking at Bert.

'Well lass, we continue as normal until James tells us otherwise. I'll go across and check the castle, switch everything off and lock up. Hopefully there will be some good news later. Zen, you'll be wanting to get back to your posh shed. That coffee doesn't grind itself. So, tell you what, give Meg and Ellie a lift over to the café.'

'I'm not going anywhere, Bert,' said Meg.

'Listen pet, all your friends will be over there, and it will do you good to have a chinwag and take your mind off things here.'

'It's a good idea, Meg, and I know Aurora was making some Ginger Parkin. It's your favourite. Come on, let's go and see Ethel and the others. I'll send round a group chat for us all to meet up. They'll want to see you,' I said, smiling at her.

'Oh, okay then. I suppose I'd just be sitting here mithering otherwise. Mind, Bert – you ring me the minute you hear anything.'

'I promise, lass. Now get your coat, and you leave things here to me.'

As Meg went to sort herself out, Bert whispered to me.

'Ellie, you'll take care of her, won't you? She's had a big shock, and she's not as young as she used to be. It's times like this when you remember how old you are; although look at Grace, she's not even sixty, she's still a lassie and...' He broke down.

'None of us know what's around the corner Bert, no matter what age we are. But don't you worry, I'll look after Meg and bring her back home when she's ready. She's a very special woman to us all, and I know the others will look after her too.'

***

Later that night, Zen and I were lying in his bed under the attic eaves, our arms wrapped around each other. I looked at his gorgeous pale face as he lay with his eyes closed, the dark curls fanned across the pillow. A strand of hair lay across his cheek, so I gently brushed it aside, then followed the curve of his cheekbone with my finger, trailing it down to his lips, as always mesmerised by his beautiful face. His thick, dark eyelashes fluttered open at my touch, and we silently stared at each other in the dusk of the room, our eyes reflecting our longing. From the moment our eyes had locked on the causeway when we first met, there was an immediate clicking into place whenever we looked at each other. We both began to speak at the same time.

'You first,' I whispered.

'Ellie, what I learned today is that you need to say what you feel the minute you feel it, otherwise you may never get the chance. I should have spoken out ages ago, but I thought you might think it was too soon. I love you,' he said without any hesitation or faltering in his voice. 'I want you to know that. I feel I'm the luckiest man on Lindisfarne, if not the earth.'

'Great minds think alike.' I smiled. 'I was going to say the same. I love you too: think I have ever since the moment we met. Those stars were right you know, and I *know* I'm the luckiest woman in the whole universe, not just the world.'

32

'I know it's early days Ellie, but I hope we grow old together – as old as Ethel.' He laughed. 'We can take over from Ma and Pa when they retire and move onto Greater Reef with our six kids.'

'Six kids? I doubt I'll ever be ready for life on Greater Reef. Seriously though, I do want children eventually.' I could imagine what Zen's baby would look like – all dark curls and huge coffee bean eyes – and I was smitten already.

'I'm joking about Greater Reef Ellie, but I'd live anywhere with you, and I want a child or children with you too, if we are lucky enough. Seeing Grace like that today was a wakeup call. Life can change in the blink of an eye, and, as Ma is always telling me, live in the present. She is an incredibly wise woman is my ma.'

'Well then, maybe our next step is that I move in with you when Imogen gets back, just to make sure that we actually can live together. It might turn out that we are incompatible. I mean, I prefer tea, and you coffee.'

'Well, that is a deal breaker for me.' He smiled. 'But I will get you to change your mind!'

'We'll see,' I said smiling. 'Does that sound good to you, though?'

'I can't think of anything I want more... except this,' he murmured, drawing me towards him.

I felt the need for him more than ever after the day we'd had, and as he kissed me and I kissed him back, my heart at once began to beat faster in anticipation of what was to come. The traumatic events of the day melted into the heat of the night, and for a while everything in our world was back to being beautiful – our focus only on each other and the here and now. Tomorrow would take care of itself.

***

The next morning, I woke to the gorgeous aroma of coffee. Zen was standing in front of me, clutching a tray, his bed hair making him look like a castaway from a desert island. He had a tea towel slung over his shoulder, which did little to cover his naked torso, and as I looked at him, all thoughts of coffee immediately disappeared from my mind – there were far more exciting ways to wake me up. He obviously knew what I was thinking.

'No can-do, Ellie, much as I want to climb back in there with you. We need to get going. We'll go across and do the full round for Bert and Meg between us today so that they can have a break, and we can find out if they have news. It's early, but it means I can get back to the roastery as I've got a lot on today after not being there much yesterday.'

He placed the tray next to me. There was a mug of coffee, a daffodil which he must have gone outside and picked as it was still wet, and a wrinkled apple that had seen better days.

'Best I could do at short notice.' He laughed. 'But it was made with love just for you.'

'Tell you what, Meg has a teapot as big as a watering can and that apple isn't even fit for Han, so why not move that tray, and come back in here with me for five teensy minutes. We can have breakfast at the cottage when we've, erm, built up an appetite...' I smiled suggestively, patting the bed.

'Ellie Montague, you're catnip.' He laughed, before grabbing the daffodil, placing it between his teeth, then jumping onto the bed and waking me up with a big smile on my face!

CHAPTER 7

It was just before 8.00 am when Zen and I walked hand in hand across to the castle, stopping every few metres to wait for Nacho to catch up. He was in his element, scenting the wild rabbits that inhabited the scrubland near to the fishing huts. When we went into the yard, Bert was just coming out of the cottage.

'Any news Bert?' asked Zen. 'We've wanted to ring you since last night but thought it would be best to come across.'

'I was just going to sort the dogs out, as I'm expecting a call from James,' replied Bert. 'He said he'd ring this morning, and Meg wants to listen in.'

'You go back inside, stay with Meg, and wait for the call. Tell her mine's the usual egg butty and I'll have tea – I suppose if I must – just this once mind!'

'Hoy, you young whippersnapper, you'll get what you're given.' He winked at Zen.

'Bert, we're doing the works this morning, the milking included, so just go and be with Meg and you can fill us in with the news when we're done,' I said.

'Thanks Ellie, and how would you like your eggs?'

'Err, cooked would be good!' I quipped. It was great to see Bert's face break into a broad grin as he went back inside the cottage.

Zen and I worked through the chores at record speed and hurried back to see if there had been any news.

'Take a pew you two. Help yourselves to tea and I'll get your breakfast,' said Meg quietly, and by the look on her face, we knew that they hadn't heard anything good.

'No, you come and sit-down Meg. Forget breakfast for now. I can see you're upset. How bad is it?'

Meg sat down at the table, and I could see her lip quivering. She was close to tears.

'Well, lass,' said Bert, 'it's not great, I'm afraid. Grace hasn't had a mini stroke like we thought. She's had a bleed on her brain. It's got a medical name, but I can't remember what James said... something starting with an H I think.'

'Oh no, is it, err is she...' I tailed off.

'She's critically ill, Ellie. We're praying she's going to get through, although I have a feeling that it's going to be a long road ahead – if she makes it,' said Bert, his hands clasped, white knuckles showing.

'She will Bert,' said Meg, trying to muster up positivity. 'She will. These things affect everyone differently, but Lady Grace will surprise us all.'

I turned to Zen who looked even paler than he normally did. He had known Grace since he was a small child, and I could see this was upsetting him as much as it was Bert and Meg. His eyes were glassy with tears he was struggling to hold back.

'Right,' he said in a croaky voice. 'On a practical level, what can we do to help?'

'You're helping just by being here,' said Meg, looking fondly at Zen. 'Lord B is in London apparently but is making his way back today and will be going straight to the hospital to be with his sister. I'm going to go into the apartment and gather up some things for Grace. Even though she may not need them yet, she will eventually,' said Meg, trying to put a positive spin on things – which was just about impossible.

'Good idea lass, and maybe a few bits for James too. He may be in the hospital for a while and it's not like he can just pop back here from the city and manage the blooming tides. I've a feeling he may find somewhere to stay near Newcastle. His brother lives at Corbridge, so that isn't too far for him to travel from. They know everything here will be fine, so that's one less worry.'

'Ellie and I will be over here more, and I know the islanders will be lining up to help too, so listen up,' he said looking at the older couple. 'You concentrate on being there to help James, and you are not to worry about the animals. It will do your hip good to have a rest anyway, Bert.'

'Zen, I appreciate your help lad, as I will when everyone else comes over to offer support, as I know they will, but it'd drive me blooming mad just sitting around waiting for phone calls. I need to do something to keep occupied.'

'The castle is meant to be opening to the public next week. I was supposed to be starting my job... Ooh sorry, that sounded like I was thinking about myself, which I promise I'm not. I was just wondering what might happen. That's Grace's usual role to co-ordinate it all, isn't it?' I said.

'Oh, I never even gave that a thought Ellie. I don't know, and James will have far too much on his mind I expect. Let's just wait a few days and see what's what.'

'Good idea Meg. Now then, I'm on cooking duty this morning. Even I can manage some fried eggs, I think.'

But at that Meg got up and made a beeline towards the Aga.

'Ellie, I remember the last time you attempted to fry an egg. It was raw on the top and burnt on the bottom so, rather than us all end up in hospital, I think I'll manage.'

'Ellie is going to be moving into the attic with me when Imogen gets back.' Zen smiled, telling them our news.

'You're going to live over the brush?' Bert winked.

'Well, that's the plan, but not until Meg's taught her how to cook.' He laughed.

'Hey, I'll have you know my toast is legendary.'

'Get him told Ellie. Start as you mean to go on.' Bert chuckled.

'Joking aside you two, that's wonderful news,' said Meg. 'And by the way, Zen, never mind Ellie learning to cook. Whilst you might be able to make a good cup of coffee, when it comes to cooking you could burn water. I'm sure between Aurora and me though, we can lick both of you into shape before you starve, because you can't live on love alone!'

'You're blooming, Tara!' I smiled at my former work colleague on the screen, now six months pregnant. 'I bet you're pleased you've finished your sentence in Randy flipping Parrot.'

'I couldn't wait to get out of the door, Ellie, so left as early as I could. I couldn't stand being in that hot house of an office over the summer. Even frozen faced Anna, the ice maiden, wouldn't keep me cool in there. Tell you the truth, I'm thinking I might not go back. It's not been the same since you left, and both Toby and I are wondering whether we want to bring our baby up in central London, aren't we darling?'

Toby nodded.

'Shove over baby Bee Dee and let the rest of us get a look in – your mummy's tummy is taking up half of the screen!' Sophie grinned, muscling her way into the shot.

We were having our weekly online group get together, and all eight of us, plus Nacho and baby Butler Dunne or baby Bee Dee as he/she was affectionately known, were on screen.

'Not many more sleeps until we come to the island!' yelled Sophie.

'I cannot wait,' said Toby. 'Especially to do the dig at Bamburgh.'

'Anyway, Ellie, how goes it? You're starting your new job at the castle on the First of April, aren't you?' said Tara.

I looked at Zen, willing him to explain to them about Grace.

'We've had some more very upsetting news. I know Ellie told you that Grace had taken ill and was rushed to hospital. We were all just hoping it would turn out to be a mini stroke that was going to be relatively quick for her to recover from.'

'A TIA?' asked Sophie.

'Yes, but it wasn't. We now know that Grace has suffered from something called a Haemorrhagic stroke – a bleed on her brain.'

'The upshot is,' continued Zen, 'that Grace is going to need a lot of rehabilitation. The good news as it stands, is that she's no longer in a critical condition, but she is a very poorly woman and won't be coming back to Lindisfarne for a long while to come. Last time Meg spoke to James he was really concerned about her getting the care she needed on the island, what with our location and the tides etc., so he was looking at other options.'

'So,' I joined in, 'James made the decision to delay the opening of the castle until he can work out the logistics. Hopefully it won't be for too long. But listen guys, the good news is that if the castle re-opening is still delayed by the time you arrive, it means I am going to have much more time to spend with you all. We can go and discover parts of Northumberland that I have only heard about. I still haven't been far, so put your requests in.'

'Vindolanda Roman Fort and excavation site.' Toby grinned.

'Some castle called Chillingham where I hear they have very scary ghosts.' Tara laughed. 'It might help baby Bee Dee come along a bit earlier!'

'St James' Park, naturally.' Jake laughed.

'Err, we just happy to see it all and visit a cafe in each place to assess competition, and maybe sell coffee,' said Stanislaw smiling at Aleksy.

'The Metro Centre is it called?' interjected Sophie. 'Lots of shops.'

'Err Miss Olatunji, soon to be Mrs Winter, there is no way you are going from the shopping capital of the world that is London to spending *our* precious time wandering around yet more shops in Newcastle,' said Jake.

'Err, the Metro Centre's in Gateshead,' murmured Zen, 'but Jake mate, I get your point.'

'You know what, I'm just longing to see you all and don't care where we go, or what we do. Even if we just stay put on the island, it would be good enough for me as long as we're together.' I said.

'It may have to do for me,' said Tara. 'I'm bigger than one of those Orca whales that live beside your island.' She smiled.

'I don't think you'll see many of those around here Tara,' smiled Zen.

'Anyway Ellie Nellie,' said Sophie. 'What's the dress code? I refuse to wear fancy dress like you did when you first got on that island. I've got some nice summer dresses that I thought would be perfect.'

'Soph, just make sure you have plenty of jumpers, some flat shoes or boots, a raincoat and possibly a bobble hat.'

Sophie's eyes bulged with horror.

'You are kidding me. It's going to almost be summer when we come up – can you imagine what I would look like trying to fit all my hair under a bobble hat? It would look like I had a giant tea cosy on my head. No babe, it's just not going to happen.'

'She's not kidding you, Sophie, but bring a couple of nice dresses as well. The island nightclub will be right up your street,' said Zen, discreetly winking at me.

'What's it called?' She asked excitedly. 'Has it got a VIP area? Will I bring designer?'

'It's called the Fishing Club Hut, Sophie. I'm sure I can cordon you off a special area around the lobster pots. Might smell a bit fishy, mind, but just pretend it's caviar. And yes, a nice pair of designer wellies would be just the job.'

'By the way, I read all about your Prince Bunk-Up getting engaged to that cow Poison Ivy,' said Sophie, her face twisting into a scowl.

'Prince who?' asked Zen, his eyebrow raised.

'Just our little name for Aidan.' I laughed, hoping he would never find out how near Aidan had been to living-up to that name with me.

'Oh yes, him with the killer blue eyes. He is sexy, isn't he?' Said Tara.

'Those photos were totally staged,' I said. 'She is truly awful, but good luck to them; we are all still trying to work out why he's marrying her.'

'So, will we get to meet them?' Asked Sophie.

'No, the pair of them will no doubt be sunning themselves somewhere hot and expensive – since they came back to announce the engagement, Isla hasn't stepped foot on the island. We know she hasn't been back to the hotel because if she had, the Crafty Lindisfarners would know all about it!'

CHAPTER 9

A few days later, Meg and I walked slowly across to the café with Amelia, and Pacino and Murray, the alpacas. Amelia and her brother William were island kids who often came to help with the animals and she I had become best friends. Amelia was seven going on seventeen and was delightful. She was her gorgeous chatty self today; the sun was shining, and it was a great stress reliever for Meg listening to Amelia's tall tales.

'Bert and I had a chat with James on your internet thingy where you can see each other. He's as pale as a ghost and a little bit unkempt for James. I've never seen him look anything less than dapper before; even when he's going off on one of his digs, he looks like Indiana Jones. Anyway pet, he has decided to keep the castle closed for now but is going to talk to Lord B and see if they can come up with a plan. Maybe someone experienced from Bamburgh will come over and manage it. I know that's not good news for your job, Ellie, and you aren't the only one that's going to be affected. Apart from the staff and volunteers, there is the knock-on effect to the businesses on the island if the number of tourists drops due to the castle being closed. The other thing James took into consideration when deciding to keep the castle closed for now, is that Bert has finally got his date for his hip replacement.'

'Woo Hoo!' I shouted.

'He's waited a while for this, but between you and me, this couldn't have come at a worse time, and I'm having to insist he goes. You know Bert. He'd put it off in a heartbeat to help, but he needs it done, and done it is going to be.'

'You're so right, Meg. He's struggled for a long time and he's going... we will all see to that.'

'My dad said Bert is getting a new hip. Is there a place you buy them, like Amazon?' asked Amelia.

'Do you want to tell her, or will I?' I laughed.

***

Later that day, I waited as patiently as I could for the gang to arrive. They had set off from London early that morning, and I had frequent messages giving me progress reports, which seemed to consist of a stop at every motorway services thanks to Tara's need to wee frequently.

Nacho and I had gone across to the holiday house, lit the fire and popped a big pan of Northumbrian broth in the kitchen ready to be warmed up when they got there. Zen and I had put together a welcome hamper with all kinds of local goodies, including several types of his coffee, a selection of sweet treats and savoury bakes made by Aurora, some home-made stotties from Meg and not forgetting some Lindisfarne mead and local gin. I stopped short at taking the bottle of Fishing Club hooch offered to me by Maurice, although I was quite sure that the boys would be sampling that as soon as they could.

Eventually, headlights lit the room, and I rushed to the door to be nearly knocked over by Tara who was a woman on a mission.

'Where's the loo?' she shouted. 'What kind of place is this? There's been no motorway services for about the last hour and Bee Dee has been sitting on my bladder since Newcastle.'

'Ellie Nellie!' screamed Sophie, coming into the house. 'Oh My God. I told you it was the back of bloody beyond when we first saw that map – I thought we would never get here. I'm so pleased to see you, though. Come here and let me give you the biggest hug I've got left in my poor little bod, after seven hours of being squished between Stan and Alex – it was like being in Harrod's Beauty Room; those boys spray aftershave like the rest of us use air freshener. Toby really needs to get his travel sickness sorted, so he can't always bag the front seat.'

The boys followed her in, carrying luggage, and it was chaos as we all started hugging and behaving like we hadn't seen each other in years.

'What's all this?' Zen surveyed the scene from the doorway. 'Careful, or there'll be rumours of this place being hired by some swingers club from the big city.'

Zen joined in on the hugs, and Nacho loved every minute of being scooped up, kissed, and passed on like he was in a game of pass the parcel.

'This place, from what we see, it looks so beautiful,' said Stanislaw. 'The road, err Causeway, it felt like magic when we cross.'

'It did.' Aleksy nodded in agreement. 'It looked so exceptionally beautiful. Also, when we pass the Angel of the North, which looked amazing too. We can go back and see from its feet right up to the sky, yes?'

'Err yes.' Zen laughed. 'It's about twenty metres high and when we go to the city we will take a trip over to Gateshead, sit on its feet

47

and look up. Does anyone fancy a pint? Jake mate, you look like you could do with one after that long drive.'

'Lead me to it, squire, if that's okay with the girls. Maybe we can all see the *Crab* for ourselves. We've heard so much about it. Or the Fishing Club?' He winked.

'The Fishing Club isn't open tonight, thankfully – plenty time for that.' I laughed.

'Toby, they do a stellar pint of our local real ale, called Lindisfarne Lil, which might make you feel a bit better; you are looking a little green around the gills.'

'Seven hours in a hot minibus with a really strong curry in the back, Creed being sprayed every two minutes and having to stop every half hour so Tara and Bee Dee could pay a visit – not great for someone who struggles with travel sickness.' He smiled weakly.

'Curry?'

'Yes, Ellie, there's a big pot of your favourite Jalfrezi from Dehlicattesen. Mrs Kapoor made it specially for us and sends her regards. There's a Ukrainian couple and their two children living in our old flat now. I saw Mehmet the barber when I went to pick up the curry and he was telling me all about them – they love it, so that's nice to know.'

'Honestly, Ellie, that curry has overpowered the minibus for over three hundred miles, so it better have been worth it. Toby has had his head out of the window since Watford Gap. Anyway, get the kettle on – we're parched.' Tara smiled.

'Never mind the kettle, get the wine opened.' Sophie laughed. 'As big a glass as you like – I can still taste aftershave. I need something to take that away.'

We were soon all sitting in the lounge, drinks in hand.

'This is an amazing house,' said Tara. 'It's like the country houses you see on Instagram.'

'Wait until you see the views in better light,' I said. 'I'm so excited to take you both around the island. Let's do that in the morning and we can go for coffee and meet Aurora – and don't you be calling her Zoflora, Soph.'

'Promise. Can we go to *Love Lindisfarne* too? I'd love to meet Imogen as well, and I'm sure we'll end up buying half of the shop.'

'Too right,' said Tara. 'I've got a list.'

'Aw, this is so lovely. Like old times – just in better surroundings,' I said.

'I still miss our manky sofa though,' said Sophie. 'I wish I had persuaded Jake to let me take it, although it would have looked out of place in our ultra-modern apartment.'

'You got your date sorted for the wedding yet, Sophie?'

'Give me a chance babe, we've only been engaged a few months. I'm already turning into Bridezilla though; I've destroyed half a rain forest already with the amount of bridal magazines I'm going through. Every copy I read, I change my mind from a Spring, Summer, or Winter Wedding. I see no joy in Autumn. I flit from whether it should be at home in Cambridge, or perhaps somewhere

49

more exotic. Jake says he wouldn't mind a good old fashioned East End wedding.'

'What does that involve?' I asked, laughing.

'Oh, a lot of alcohol, a good old knees up and ending in a bar brawl with someone shouting get out of my pub – just like you see on EastEnders!'

Tara flinched.

'And there goes baby Bee Dee. I seriously think it's a boy – he kicks so well. He can't have got that from Toby as he wouldn't know one end of a football from the other, although I suppose Jill Scott could throw a few good kicks too, so bang goes that theory.'

'You chosen any potential names yet?'

'Well, let's just say that it's a work in progress, Ellie. I haven't really thought of any names that I'm fully sure of. It's difficult, not knowing what name will suit Bee Dee. But Toby, oh my God!' She picked up a cushion and hid her face behind it. 'You will not believe his choices, and he really isn't joking.'

'Tara. Come out from behind that cushion and tell us NOW,' I said grinning.

'Well,' she said, sheepishly lowering the cushion and clutching it to her bump like a shield. 'Please don't shoot the messenger – if it's a girl he wants to call her... erm... I can't believe I'm telling you both this... Boudica!'

Sophie, at this point, just about choked on her wine with laughter, tears running down her face.

'Boudica? Oh babes, that's so Toby.' She continued sliding down her chair, giggling.

'Boudica Butler Dunne has a bit of a ring to it,' I said, trying to put a positive spin on things. 'At least she will be unique.'

Which started Sophie off again.

'And if it's a boy?' She eventually squeaked.

The cushion went back up.

'Oh God, what next? Julius or Caesar perhaps?'

'It can't be worse Tara...can it?' I asked, trying to hold my laugh in.

'I'm not sure I can even say it,' she mumbled.

I pulled the cushion away.

'Big girl pants now. Just spit it out...'

'H...Ho...Horatio,' she blurted out, and then burst into peals of laughter. 'Horatio Butler Dunne!'

CHAPTER 10

The next morning, I walked through the village from the holiday house to the cafe, with Sophie, Stan, and Tara. Zen had taken Jake, Aleksy, and an extremely excited Toby across to Greater Reef. Tara had bailed out of the crossing on baby Bee Dee grounds, Sophie had said she was terrified of being dive bombed by nesting birds, and Stan, well Stan was just itching to get to the roastery.

'It's so pretty here. I can see why you fell in love with the place,' said Tara, looking around the gorgeous main street with its eclectic range of cottages and houses. The colours of spring were everywhere thanks to the profusion of hanging baskets and pots, displaying bright spring flowers in primary colours.

'It is gorgeous,' agreed Sophie. 'I can't wait to see how many likes I'm going to get with my photos on Insta, but where are all the shops, babe?'

'Err...'

'Just joking, Ellie Nellie. You gave me the drill before we came, and I promise I'm going to try and be the new Sophie while I'm here – no longer a slave to consumerism.'

'That'll be the day,' muttered Tara, smiling.

We entered the café garden, and, as it was a bright day with what passed for warmth on Lindisfarne, we opted to sit outside. Stan made a beeline for the roastery.

'I see you later.' He smiled. 'I go and see the mothership, as Zen calls it.'

Aurora came out from the café and, almost immediately after the introductions, it was as if she had been in our circle for ages.

'Pip's in control for the next half hour while I sit with you, so give me your orders for drinks and I'll get her to bring them out to us.'

Aurora disappeared back inside the café to return a couple of minutes later with a big cake, which, amazingly, was shaped like the castle and had 'Welcome to Lindisfarne' piped on a flag flying from the top.

'Aurora, that's amazing. Did you make that yourself? I didn't know you made specialist cakes.'

'I thought you knew, Ellie. I made my own wedding cake.'

I remembered the spectacular boat shaped cake with tiny fishermen, sparkling silver fish, lacy fishing nets and the bride and groom at the helm of the boat, like Jack and Rose, albeit on a trawler and not an ocean liner. The attention to detail had been amazing.

'I am booking you now for my wedding cake.' Sophie grinned. 'You can all help me choose a theme.'

'And my christening cake,' said Tara. 'How are you at historical re-enactments?'

We were so deep in conversation; I didn't see Amelia come into the garden until I felt a tug on my sleeve.

'Oh hi gorgeous,' I said, smiling at my young friend who was looking as cute as ever, her deep red plaits catching the sun and making them shine like burnished gold.

'Let's get you a chair, and you can meet my friends and have some cake with us. Tara, Sophie, this is my best friend Amelia, who I've told you about.'

'Hey, I don't know about that.' Sophie smiled. 'What about me? I thought I was your best friend, Ellie.'

Amelia's face twisted into a frown, her eyebrows meeting together.

'Ellie is *my* best friend,' she said, glowering at Sophie.

'Of course, I am,' I said hugging her. 'You are my Lindisfarne best friend, but Sophie here is my London best friend, and it would be really good if she could be your London best friend too.'

Ignoring Sophie, Amelia looked at Tara and her baby bump.

'*You* can be my London best friend,' she said. 'I like babies and I'll be able to come and babysit with Ellie, and we can maybe get another alpaca so he can walk it.'

'He?' Tara grinned. 'How do you know it's a boy?'

'Because next year he is going to be the baby Jesus. We need a new baby on the island, and it would be better if he is a boy.'

'Amelia, Tara lives in London too, so the baby won't be here to babysit very often or to be in the nativity next year.'

'He will be,' she said with absolute certainty. 'I'm going to write to Santa and ask. He won't be busy now so will have time to read my letter. And it worked last time, didn't it?'

'Erm yes, I suppose it did, seeing as I'm still here,' I said smiling at her. 'Anyway, I think we should all just be best friends.'

'I'll see,' she said begrudgingly, looking Sophie up and down before her eyes settled on the cake and a truce was formed – for the moment.

'Sophie and Tara can walk the alpacas with us, Ellie, and if Murray and Pacino like them both then that will be okay… I suppose.'

'Good plan,' I said, smiling.

'Alpacas?' squeaked Sophie. 'Well, if I must, I really do want to be your friend.'

'Ooh, I like alpacas and I used to have a pony called Poppet when I was your age.' Tara smiled, gaining her immediate entry into the Amelia friendship circle.

Satisfied with her interview plans, Amelia helped herself to another piece of cake and skipped off to write her spring letter to Santa.

'Welcome to the island.' I laughed. 'If you think Amelia is a tough nut to crack, just wait until you meet Ethel!'

***

The boys came back from Greater Reef buzzing. I had told everyone to meet at 2.00pm at the holiday house, because this afternoon was my choice of activity.

'I have never seen so many birds before,' said Aleksy, his eyes shining with joy.

'Your mum and dad are just great,' said Jake to Zen. 'Amazing that they have lived like that for so many years. I think Sophie and I would probably kill each other after a few weeks!'

'It was such a privilege to be given permission to visit,' said Toby. 'The lighthouse is a piece of preserved history and with careful maintenance should be there for many more years to come. It's made me want to meet James even more. When our paths have crossed at lectures, it's been so brief. To have been able to meet him one to one about his conservation work would have been amazing, but maybe not to be this time, sadly.'

I smiled at the mention of the lighthouse. It was where Zen and I got together, shared our first kiss and started our relationship. It would always be special to me, but perhaps not in the historical sense that Toby meant.

'The lighthouse is so special,' agreed Zen, his coffee bean eyes twinkling as they caught mine, and I knew he was thinking the same as me.

'Anyway, Ellie, what are we doing this afternoon? The tide's in... hey, listen to me like a local already... so I'm assuming it's something on the island. Are you taking us for a hike?' asked Sophie.

'As if,' I said laughing. 'Your limit is walking the length of Bond Street. This afternoon, we're going over to the castle, and you're going to meet all the animals. Meg and Bert have gone shopping on the mainland, so we're going to help by doing the afternoon shift and getting everyone sorted for the evening. Basically, you're going to help muck out and get your soft city hands all dirty.'

'Err Ellie, whilst I'm sure they're all lovely,' said Sophie sounding anything like sure, 'you know I'm not great around anything furry, except Nacho of course.'

'Well, that's okay then. I'll put you in charge of the hens and turkeys. They've got no fur.'

'But they peck your eyes out,' cried Sophie, dramatically.

'The closest I've ever got to a horse is at Epsom,' joked Jake, 'but lead me to the job in hand. I might end up owning a racehorse one day.'

'Me and Aleksy like the animals. We once worked in circus in Poland,' said Stan.

'You did?' Zen raised an eyebrow. 'I need to hear more about that later.'

'Stan juggle, I acrobat,' said Aleksy, as if it wasn't anything unusual, 'but used to make us clean out cages.'

'Lions?' asked Sophie, eyes like saucers.

'Even elephant called Gaja.' Stan laughed. 'We needed big bucket!'

'I like *All Creatures Great and Small* if that counts.' Tara smiled.

'Tara, you grew up around horses and ponies, so you don't need any experience. You can be on supervisory duty and be excused from the shit shovelling.'

I saw Sophie's nose wrinkling at the thought.

'Oh, and one more thing, you can decide between yourselves who is going to milk the goat.'

There was a silence and the expression on their faces was probably what mine had been like when I'd first arrived and was faced with the prospect of milking Nanny.

'Just joking, but you can watch... err on second thoughts maybe not.' I laughed, thinking maybe it would lead to mayhem when this lot started on the double entendres.

In fairness to the city slickers, they all literally 'mucked' in and seemed to enjoy the afternoon. Tara was besotted by Stout, the gentle giant shire horse, while Hannibal did his usual thing of more or less saying keep the hell away from me, by flattening his ears and baring his teeth.

'He's a feisty one, but so very, very cute.' Tara nodded towards Han, whilst gently stroking Stout and feeding him carrots.

'You don't know the half of it.' I laughed. 'But he has his uses and I love him dearly.'

Sophie turned all Mother Earth on us. She cleaned out the chicken coop without complaining once, and when she uncovered a couple of big, brown eggs. you'd think she had got six numbers on the lottery. The boys had all gone down to the paddocks, where Stan and Aleksy immediately fell in love with Pacino and Murray, the alpacas, and made Zen promise to let them take them out for a walk before they went back to London.

'I hope you all enjoyed that?' I asked, as we walked back over towards the village.

'Ellie, that place is just so magical.' Stan sighed. 'I love it and want to come back lots to help.'

'Me too,' agreed Aleksy. 'Do you think we can keep an alpaca in our flat?'

'Not even a dog,' replied Stan. 'But we can come back here, yes?'

'Absolutely – whenever you like. Right straight to the *Crab*. First drinks are on me,' I said, striding across the scrubland towards the village, my happy band of trainees following me.

We had a brief photo stop at the upturned boats, and again as we skirted the priory. The cameras began to click, capturing island memories.

'Raj na ziemi,' said Aleksy, gazing around in awe.

'Heaven on earth,' translated Stan, 'and it really is.'

CHAPTER 11

The next morning, I was busy cleaning out the stables, earbuds in, singing along to The Beatles who Zen had introduced me to. I couldn't get enough of them and was totally immersed in the music when I felt a tap on my shoulder, causing me to nearly jump out of my skin. I spun around pulling the buds out.

'You nearly gave me a heart… Aidan! What the heck are you doing here?'

Aidan Bamburgh, as devastatingly handsome as ever, smiled at me, his bright blue eyes flashing. He was casually, but very expensively, dressed. I wondered if I should go in for a hug, but considering the hi-vis hadn't had a hose down in a while. Maybe not.

'Ellie Elf, looking as… well as uniquely gorgeous as one can wearing a refuse collector's coat. How have you been?'

'Great,' I said, 'but I'm just so shocked to see you. You're the last person I expected. You do know that your Uncle James isn't here, don't you?'

'Yes, I do. It's why I'm here as it happens. Are you nearly done? Any chance of popping up to James and Grace's apartment for a coffee and a catch up? I need to discuss something with you.'

'Oh no, has something happened to Grace?'

'No, nothing like that. Just come up when you're ready, Ellie. I'll have the kettle on, unless you fancy a glass of vino?'

I glanced at my phone.

'It's 10.45am. A bit too early for me.' I laughed, before a thought struck me like a sledgehammer as he strolled off.

'Is Isla with you?' I shouted to his retreating figure.

'No, you're perfectly safe. *We're* perfectly safe.' He winked. 'We never did quite get round to our tryst, did we? Oh, and Ellie, please don't mention seeing me to Meg and Bert until we've had a chance to talk.'

I was so intrigued I grabbed the brush and began cleaning at breakneck speed. What on earth could he want to discuss?

Aidan was standing in front of the fireplace in the living room when I went into James and Grace's apartment. It was like déjà vu back to the first time we met, except this time, he was fully clothed.

'The coffee's made,' he said, nodding towards a cafetiere and a couple of mugs. 'Come and sit-down Ellie. I don't bite.' He grinned at me, as I stood looking at him from the doorway, not quite knowing what was going on. 'I'm a betrothed man now, got to behave myself,' he said, bursting into raucous laughter.

'Oh yes, I suppose congratulations are in order,' I began, before stopping. Did I really want to congratulate him on marrying Isla?

'Or commiserations, perhaps,' he said, with a wry smile. 'I haven't seen you since Christmas, and a lot has happened in that time. Ellie, I want to apologise. I didn't behave well the last time we were together, but in my defence, nothing had really happened between us, and I always got the feeling that you weren't that interested. Of course, now I know that was because you were already ga-ga over Chambers, and who can blame you? He's far too good looking for his own good. I meant what I said in my note, though, you and I got… get, I hope… on well, and I hope we can be friends.'

'I hope so too, Aidan, but as we are putting our cards down on the table, I can't say that I understand you and Isla getting married. That's a huge step, and you've only been together a few months.'

'Ellie Elf, let's just say it isn't all about love and leave it there, shall we? I really don't want to discuss it at the moment.' His shoulders slumped dejectedly. 'My life is already complicated and is about to take complication to a whole new level, which is really what I wanted to talk to you about today.'

I was desperate to ask him if Isla was bribing or blackmailing him, but, for once, Aidan's confidence seemed to have deserted him, and I could see he was agitated. He kept sweeping one hand through his dark blonde hair and plucking at non-existent dust on his pristine trousers with the other, so now really wasn't the time to stick my nose in where, quite frankly, it had no business being.

'Aidan, just spit it out. Tell me what you're doing here,' I said, as I eventually sat down on the sofa, taking the mug from him.

'I wanted to tell you first, Ellie, and Pa also asked that I talked to you or Zen before we discussed this with Meg and Bert.'

'Discuss what? What's it got to do with Meg and Bert, whatever it is?'

'Well, the thing is, as you know, James and Grace are going to be away from Lindisfarne for a long time. Grace is going slowly with her recovery, and James has found a clinic in California that specialises in providing rehab care to stroke victims, and, as soon as he gets the green light for her to fly, they are both going over there. Grace will be residential in the facility, and James is going to stay with their eldest, my cousin Octavia, who lives in LA. My other cousin, Allegra, lives in New York, so it will be easier all round for the two girls to visit their mother. Grace will also get to see her grandchild more often, so win, win.

'That all sounds very positive, and I'm so pleased that Grace is going to get the best care, but what's that got to do with you? Oh, sorry Aidan, that sounded very brusque – just, I'm not following.'

'Well Ellie, and quite frankly this is not my idea of fun, but I'm being forced into it. Believe you me, if there was a way out, I would take it, but for reasons I cannot go into, you will just have to accept that this isn't of my choosing,' he garbled, most unlike Aidan.

I was getting more and more worried by the minute.

CHAPTER 12

I took a gulp of coffee before carrying on with the conversation.

'Forced into what? Aidan, you're not making any sense.'

'Sorry, just finding this a tad awks. Now that I'm an engaged man and heading towards thirty – it's my birthday soon – Pa has seen a way of elevating my spare position to that of temporary heir. After talking to James, it has been decided that I will take over the running of the Lindisfarne estate for the foreseeable future. Pa says it will be the perfect role for me and Isla, what with her experience in the hospitality industry, and I will at least temporarily be able to take on a role which none of us in the family ever thought I'd get the opportunity to do. Don't forget the overall estate management at Bamburgh will eventually pass to Lance, my elder brother, and I will be relegated to whatever he deems fit for me at the time.'

I felt my mouth opening and then closing like a hungry goldfish, without any words coming out. He had to be joking. Him and poison Isla coming to the island and taking over the whole of the Lindisfarne estate? It was just about the worst news ever. Maybe not so much about Aidan, as he did have some good qualities; although from what I knew of him, he certainly didn't strike me as being equipped to take on this incredibly special role. As for Isla, well there were no words except expletives to describe my feelings over her arriving at the castle.

'Err, what actual hospitality experience does Isla have, other than living in a hotel and treating everyone like staff at her beck and call? And sorry, but do you have any background in estate management?' I eventually found the power of speech and just blurted out what I was thinking.

'Ellie, I get you're a little shocked, but that's not fair. I have grown up in a family that lives and breathes historical and conservation estate management. I have managed our London portfolio for a long time, and it hasn't gone under – yet. Look, I know you aren't Isla's number one fan, and that you share that view with most of the islanders, but, like it or not, she's going to be my wife and that gives her as much right as me to take on this role. Pa is going to give me full reign, to a point, however he will be no doubt watching over me so I will strive to do a good job; but make no bones about it, I'll be doing things my way. James and Grace have never really got the full potential out of the estate, the castle in particular, and I'm sure that we can come up with some new and improved business ideas. Take Greater Reef for example...'

I could feel the hackles on my neck rising like a tiger on full alert of impending attack.

'What a missed opportunity that is,' he continued. 'Imagine how much we could have made on taking boat trips out to the island and having a gift and coffee shop over there. Unfortunately, James has got that tied up in trust tighter than an A lister's prenup, so no can do, but you get my drift.'

Get his drift? I'd seriously like to see him drifting out to sea on a raft without a paddle, and whilst he's bobbling about on the ocean, maybe he could think about his own prenup, because as eggs are eggs, he was going to need one.

'And what about the conservation of the birds and wildlife, Aidan?' I said angrily.

'Oh Ellie, there's tens of thousands of them. We wouldn't miss a few, so there's room for all of us, don't you think?'

No, I did not think. And thank God the islands were in a trust that would preserve the future of the species they were home to. I was seriously in danger of grabbing Aidan by his expensive cashmere jumper and swinging him around the room until his sleeves stretched like clown's arms. Business? James and Grace not getting the full potential? A café on Greater Reef? Lindisfarne was far more than a business and, from my short experience of living on the island and listening to those who had been here a lifetime, James and Grace had managed it perfectly, their strength lying firmly in involving the local community and doing what was best for the island, and not what would make the most money.

'The last thing Pa wants to do is to bother James with the minutia. He has far too much on his plate thinking about Grace, without having to worry about the estate, and this is the perfect solution. Imagine if he had to bring in strangers. That wouldn't be any better, would it? At least this way, it's keeping it in the family.'

I wasn't sure that keeping it in the family was the best approach. I tried to digest the information, but no matter which way I looked at it, I just couldn't see this working. Red flags were waving in abundance, like at a Manchester United home game. Underneath the posh boy persona, Aidan did have some good qualities, but he had that entitled edge to him. He had told me himself that his role in London was basically schmoozing with clients, and I expected he had a team behind him that did the real hard work. This time, he and Isla would be running the whole show on their own – and with a point to prove.

Another thought entered my head. Isla hated the animals; she had no time for any of them, especially Hannibal, who had taken an immediate dislike to her – and who could blame him? I placated myself with the thought that we would never have to see her. She would probably use the front entrance to the castle as befitted her status of Lady of the Manor and wouldn't step anywhere near the yard or outbuildings, and hopefully just let us get on with our jobs. However, if the castle were to open to the public, that would put me in a tricky position having her as a boss... this all just got worse, and I tried to call a halt to the thoughts that were racing through my head on fast forward.

'So,' I said, detaching from my scrambled brain and back to focusing on a twitching Aidan. 'When is this happening and why do you expect me to break the news to Bert and Meg? As your first duty as island custodian, surely that is up to you?'

Aidan had the grace to look shamefaced.

'Yes, it is my responsibility to talk to them and you might think that I am falling flat in my first challenge Ellie, but seriously, I really am thinking about the old couple. I have nothing but admiration for the way they have worked so hard supporting James and Grace over many years, and that to march in now and tell them that they are getting new management – which includes Isla – even I can see that might be a difficult conversation to have.'

Difficult conversation? He had got one thing right at least.

'I had hoped that whilst I break the news – and I had never envisaged you doing that on your own Ellie – at least you could be there and help ease the situation. In answer to your question, this is due to happen in a few days, the quicker the better. Isla is organising couriering our things up from London, and she has arranged for Elspeth to come to the apartment later today and prepare it for our arrival by packing up some of this old stuff.' He gesticulated around the room. 'And we can inject some modernity into this museum whilst we are staying here.'

'Elspeth, her mother? Isn't this Meg's job?'

'Well, that's another thing Ellie. We, and both James and Pa agree...' he hesitated, suddenly taking a great interest in his feet, 'feel that maybe it's time Meg and Bert started to think about retirement. They work for James and Grace, so it seems an opportune moment to stand them down for now. Isla and I will be bringing two of our London staff with us as our housekeeping team.'

I could hear his words but felt like I was in danger of passing out. Everything had gone a shade of pink as the anger swept over me.

'YOU ARE WHAT?'

'Ellie, we know Bert has had trouble with his hip recently, so this can only be a good thing, and it will give him more time to care for the animals as there is no way on this earth that Isla, or me come to that, will be getting involved with them. That night when I helped you in the storm with the flighty ungrateful beasts was enough for me.

Thank God for small mercies...

'All of the animals are darlings,' I said defensively. 'Maybe they just have a sixth sense over which people are worth investing in.' I glared at him. Then another unwanted thought raced through my mind at the speed of a missile. 'And their cottage? Do not tell me you are kicking them out of that to give to your housekeepers,' I croaked, my eyes filling up with tears that had been threatening since the start of our conversation.

'Hey Ellie, I'm not heartless, I thought you at least knew that. Pa was absolutely insistent that they stay in their home until James and Grace hopefully return, and a decision can be made on their future, and I absolutely agree.'

Even that annoyed me. How dare he insinuate that Bert and Meg's future was in anyone's hands but their own. Oblivious to me about to burst into a heady combo of tears and rage, he carried on.

Cyril and his wife Rosa, who are coming with us, will be staying in your guest apartment – oh the happy memories in there, eh?' He reverted to being Aidan the cheeky charmer for a split second. 'That day might have changed the course of all of this had it gone differently,' he said, the happy mask sliding away. I got the distinct feeling that all was not quite right in Aidan's world.

I felt sick to the pit of my stomach. None of this felt real and there was one person I really needed to be with me, Meg, and Bert, when they heard the news. I got my phone out of my pocket.

'Okay Aidan, I'll come and help you do your dirty work, but I want Zen to be there. He's their grandson in all but name.' Aidan nodded.

'Ellie I'm not a monster, I understand. Please let's not get off on the wrong foot. Call Zen and get him over here. Let's go and do this as gently as we possibly can.'

I pressed Zen's number and, as soon as I heard his voice, I felt overcome with longing for him to be here. I knew that Zen would help make things better. He was the rock I'd always wanted. In that split second, hearing him utter, 'Hi Ellie,' just two little words, was enough to make me realise just how much I loved him.

69

CHAPTER 13

Later that evening, the inner circle sat around the large farmhouse table in the kitchen at the holiday house. Sophie clutched my hand as I sniffed my way through my account of the day's events. Word had already begun permeating across the island, probably thanks in the main to Gordon and Elspeth who wouldn't be able to contain themselves with their bragging about their daughter becoming 'Lady Lindisfarne' – albeit temporarily. I knew that by tomorrow, the island would be in uproar.

'Bert and Meg are devastated, as you can imagine. They're of an age where they don't like change, and Meg especially has had a rough time lately worrying about Grace and Bert. This is just too much for them; they feel useless. In fact, Bert said you might as well put us out to grass with the animals and have done.'

'This is not good. He is bad man, Mr Blue Eyes?' asked Aleksy.

'No, in his defence, I don't think he is all bad. Maybe insensitive and a bit of an elitist prick, but not really bad.'

'It's Isla I'm worried about,' said Zen, who always tried to see the best in people, except for, it would seem, the poison witch. 'Now, *she* can be ruthless.'

'Isla is one from magazine who has face of angel but inside like Szatan? She is mean girl, Ellie?' asked Stanislaw.

'Yes, that's her. She's very mean. Think Cruella de Vil times ten!'

'I think that standing Bert and Meg down temporarily could actually be a good thing,' interjected Tara.

'Tara how could you...' I began.

70

'Hear me out Ellie. Listen, Bert is going to get his hip done soon so would have to recuperate anyway, and there is no way that Meg would want to cow tow to that er… cow on her own.' She laughed at her own joke. 'So, is it not better that they just take things easy for a while, do what they can for the animals with help from all of the rest of you, and keep out of Cruella's way as much as possible?'

'I suppose so,' I conceded, 'but that doesn't stop them feeling redundant.'

'That's where all you islanders, and us while we are here, come in. Let's make sure they don't feel neglected.'

Mine and Zen's phones pinged at the same time. A group text. Zen read his out to me.

'It's a group message to all of us who have ties to the Lindisfarne estate, which basically means almost the entire island. Meeting tomorrow in the Village Hall at 9.30am. Word is most definitely out, and it's understandable that people will be worried by change, even if it is only temporary.'

'But how long is temporary?' I asked. 'Are we talking months, years…? No one really knows.'

Zen pulled me out of my chair and wrapped his arms around me, holding me tight.

'Ellie, we deal with this, we don't have a choice. Let's wait and hear what everyone else thinks tomorrow and what James has to say to Meg and Bert when he rings them tonight and take it a step at a time.'

He kissed me on the top of my head.

'Maybe we will hardly even notice the changes. Let's face it, it will be everything for an easy life with those two,' said Zen, his voice determined, but one look into his coffee bean eyes, which had lost their customary sparkle, told me he didn't believe that any more than I did. 'Right, change of subject. Ellie, we are being terrible hosts. Our guests are here on holiday, and they don't need to be bogged down by island politics.'

'I know who I'd like to bog down,' muttered Sophie, 'in as dark, wet and deep a place as possible!'

'Zen mate, we don't mind. It's understandable, and we will just go with the flow.' Jake smiled.

'Jake's right,' agreed Tara. 'We can amuse ourselves.'

'Absolutely not,' I said, forcing a smile. 'I got stuck on the island when I arrived so that isn't happening again. What's on the list for tomorrow? Whose choice is it?'

'Mine,' yelled Zen. 'My day out at the seaside, so buckets, spades, and towels ready, and as soon as we get out of the meeting, we'll get off. Get the minibus fired up Jake. The tide is out from 10.35am, and we can cross back up to about 7pm.

'Will there be sunbeds and cocktails?' Sophie laughed. 'Joking! I suppose I'd better pack the thermals as well, eh Ellie. Last time I was on a beach was when we were on your holiday in the Maldives. I imagine that this will be a different experience altogether.'

'Oh, it will.' Zen smirked. 'I can guarantee that!'

***

'So, what did you make of that?' I asked Zen the following morning as we walked back to the roastery after the village meeting.

'Much as expected Ellie. Quite frankly, we don't really have any grounds to make demands, as nothing has actually happened. Yes, people are wary, me included, but we just need to give Aidan a chance and hope that James and Grace are back before we know it. Bert and Meg might benefit from the rest, and everything else will hopefully just run as it has done. I mean, what could they actually do?'

'I hope you're right. Just, I've got this feeling, you know, like when I saw the stars, except this time it's a bad feeling ...'

And at that he stopped walking, pulled me towards him and kissed me.

'Hey, listen, whatever challenges we might face, we will face them together, like Dogman and Catwoman, you might say.' He laughed. 'Let's forget about it, go and get Ravi, collect the dogs and get over to the house to start our first day out with the gang – we're officially on holiday!'

When Zen opened Ravi the campervan, I could see that it was full of gear in the back with just enough space for the dogs, their harnesses ready for them.

'What's all that stuff?' I asked pointing at the bags.

'Just a few things for today.' He smiled mysteriously. 'I thought we would take all four dogs seeing as we are going to the beach. You know how much they'll enjoy that.'

'You follow me,' said Zen to Jake when we got to the holiday house. 'We're heading for Bamburgh.'

And so, our little convoy set off.

***

'I thought we would start at the first place in Northumberland you all saw on that initial photo,' said Zen, as we piled out of the two vehicles into the car park.

'Not my first,' said Toby. 'I've been to the county several times but never here to Bamburgh – and just look at that castle,' he said gazing in awe at the huge building which dominated the landscape, towering about 150ft above the sea. 'The earliest records of the castle go back to about AD547 and the Anglo Saxon Kings of Northumbria at the time chose Bamburgh as their capital. It was such an important place.'

'Still is.' Zen smiled.

'I wonder if Lord B is in residence,' I said.

'Is he like the King, and the flag flies when he's home?' Sophie grinned.

'I need the loo,' said Tara.

We hadn't even got out of the carpark!

'There's some just along the road in the village. Maybe you girls want to go and grab some coffees to bring back while we go and get the gear down to the beach and give the dogs a run,' said Zen taking things out of the back of Ravi.

Stan and Alex held on to the four dogs, who were all eager to get to the beach. They were pointing in the direction of the sea, tails wagging, noses in the air like a row of performing seals.

'Good plan,' said Sophie. 'Lead me to civilisation. I'm trying hard Ellie, but it's been two days and I need shops!'

I didn't have the heart to tell her that Bamburgh was not exactly the metropolis she was expecting – she would find that out for herself when she walked the one tiny main street.

CHAPTER 14

'This is so beautiful,' said Tara, gazing at the village street which was chocolate box pretty. There were a few shops and hotels interspersed with some gorgeous cottages. A green filled with trees ran down the middle between the two roads.

'It's small but perfectly formed, just like me.' Sophie laughed. 'Oh okay, I concede, I'm actually feeling the vibe and who needs Selfridges anyway?'

We walked up the street to a gorgeous little deli that did takeaway drinks.

'Listen,' said Tara, 'why don't you two go and have a coffee in that cafe down the street, and I'll get some takeaways for the boys and have a slow walk over? I don't want to drink too much cos baby Bee Dee will remind me of their presence by pressing on my bladder when I'm on the beach.'

'The gear Zen has in the back of Ravi; I wouldn't be surprised if he's got a Portaloo stashed away.' I laughed.

We said goodbye to Tara after pointing the way to the beach and turned towards the café.

'*Tea and Bebbanburg Cake*,' said Sophie, laughing at the shop sign. 'Clever! I hope there's a couple of sexy Vikings in there to ravish us.' She chortled.

'Hey, we have our own Vikings now,' I said, as we walked through to the garden and took a seat at a table tucked away in the corner. 'It's just so good to have time together on our own Soph. It's been ages. I love everyone being around, but I've missed one to one time with my bestie.'

'Me too,' she replied, leaning across the table and grabbing my hands. 'Ellie, can you believe how much our lives have changed in just a few months? Both of us living in new places...'

'How is it living in swanky Chelsea in your fabulous apartment?'

'It's lovely – the views of the harbour are great, the bars and restaurants are good but... there's nothing like the atmosphere in Peckham, eh babe? *Dehlicattesen* for our supper, Stanislaw on tap to provide the caffeine, and the market with all that bustle and gorgeous goodies. Chelsea just hasn't got that community feel, but I do like the apartment. And you on your tiny island, that must have taken some adjusting to?'

'Well, what I miss mainly is you, but I don't miss that dodgy headboard rattling against the wall when Jake stayed over,' I laughed. 'I miss our inner circle, ditto Mrs Kapoor's curries and Stan's cure in a cup. Unlike you, I really don't miss the hustle and bustle,' I said, before taking a sip of my latte. 'I love Peckham, but it felt right to move on. I feel that I can breathe on Lindisfarne. Time seems to move more slowly; you notice the seasons, weather and nature more. Life is kind of rhythmic like the tide – it ebbs and flows.'

'Yeah, suppose the Thames is a bit like that too, babe!'

'And how is it being engaged?' I moved her hand to once again marvel at the tasteful sparkling diamond set in a platinum band. The ring caught the sunlight and shone in myriad colours twinkling like a kaleidoscope.

'Just the best Ellie. I know I've met my soulmate. Jake is so different to me, but we are like the sun and the moon in that without one the other wouldn't survive. Blimey, that's deep for me. I know Jake can be Marmite to some – his tough east end shell is a bit daunting and his job in the city has made him super ruthless over some things – but as you know, he's a pussy cat underneath. Family values mean everything to him, as they do to me. And you? It certainly looks to us that you two are in love. You just seem so... well... happy! You are one lucky woman; your Zen is gorgeous inside and out and has fit into our inner circle like the last bit of a jigsaw – he was always meant to be with us I reckon – the space was waiting.'

I squeezed her hand.

'I do love him Soph, more than I can put into words. He is just the most beautiful human being I've ever met, err... well... apart from you.' I laughed. 'I really do think he is the one. I can't imagine my life without him in it. Like you once said, everything feels brighter in the world when we meet the one and no matter what challenges we face, I know we can do it together.'

'We've both done alright, eh babes. So, we kissed a few frogs along the way but we've both ended up with our princes!'

'Frogs? Frog is far too nice a description for Matt the pratt.' I laughed, thinking about my ex. 'Try a great white shark. But yes, we've done okay and then some. It's still early days for me and Zen but I'm learning to trust again, as is he, and I can't wait to move into his flat and take the next steps.'

'That is so good to hear. I'm really happy for you. Love you, Ellie Nellie.'

'And you too, Miss Olatunji. Now come on, drink up and let's go and see what our Vikings are up to on that beach!'

We walked towards the dunes around an immaculate cricket pitch nestled under the towering walls of the castle.

'Goodness me, Ellie, this place really is something else.'

Sophie looked up and up at the ancient exterior walls of the castle which were bathed in a pink light.

'I've never seen anything quite like this. I mean, I've been to some stately type homes and a couple of castles before when we were at school, but they seemed kind of manicured. Nothing like this. It just looks so rugged. I think you are converting me to country living and old buildings. I'll be buying membership for the National Trust next.'

'I'll buy you family membership for your wedding present.' I laughed.

We stopped to take our shoes off for the last bit of the walk onto the beach through the dunes. The sand was fine, silvery and slid through the toes like the contents of an egg timer. The Marram grass lining the edges of the path was blowing in the gentle breeze, tickling our legs as we walked. It was a bright day, the sky a turquoise blue dotted with fluffy white clouds, and looked just like that first photo of Bamburgh Castle that we had all seen, so much so that we could be in that very picture – Northumberland in spring was certainly putting on quite a show for our visitors.

CHAPTER 15

It didn't take long to spot the gang, who were just a little further along the beach. They had managed to create a scene that wouldn't look out of place at a festival. Zen must have been planning this for ages.

'How fabulous. It's so cute,' shouted Sophie, looking around at the small teepee, the blankets and cushions, a camping chair for Tara – and there was even some bunting strung around the little tent. Zen's guitar was propped against a box which looked like it was full of delicious goodies, and there were some bottles of beer, wine and juice. The dogs were all on their own blanket, tired from a long run along the near deserted beach.

'How long have you been planning this?' I laughed, pulling him in for a hug.

'Just wanted to impress your friends.'

'*Our* friends,' I said, kissing him on the cheek. 'And thank you, it's amazing.'

'Well, since I heard Sophie say it wasn't going to be as nice as the Maldives, I rose to the challenge.' He laughed.

'It's just as nice, in a very different way.' Sophie smiled.

'I think it's even better. Just look at that backdrop,' said Toby, pointing behind us towards the castle which sat majestically on top of the sand dunes. 'It's been occupied since prehistoric times, and you can imagine how much bloodshed and how many battles it's witnessed over the centuries. I can't wait to get started on the dig next week.'

'Ew, imagine what you might find,' said Tara. 'Don't be bringing anything back home unless it's gold or jewels.'

'We never remove anything,' said Toby seriously, 'but if I find an old dinosaur bone then it's coming your way.'

'Okay,' said Zen. 'First things first. Aurora's packed us a picnic, so we'd better build up an appetite before we eat. My challenge, should you choose to accept it – who's up for a dip?'

'Dip? As in swim? You have got to be joking!' exclaimed Sophie.

'Exempt on baby Bee Dee grounds, thank goodness. He or she would object vehemently to being dunked into what amounts to an ice bath challenge.' Tara laughed.

'Us!' shouted Stan and Aleksy in unison.

'Yes, mate, lead me to it,' said Jake, enthusiastically jumping up.

'Err, no swimming trunks,' said Toby, horrified.

'Toby, all boys together?' Zen raised an eyebrow.

'Come on Tobes, live a little,' shouted Jake, waving his arms around and limbering up like he was about to embark on a cross channel swim.

'If I must. Brings back awful memories of boarding school and being forced to swim in the unheated pool in winter.'

'My heart bleeds for you.' Jake laughed. 'Fancy having to go to a school with its own swimming pool. Must have been so tough!'

Stanislaw and Aleksy were first to start off down the beach, closely followed by Zen and Jake, all discarding clothing as if they

81

were performing in the Full Monty. Meanwhile, Toby stood beside the tent and methodically took off his clothes, folded them and laid them in a neat pile on the blanket, placing his glasses on the top.

'Go get 'em tiger,' shouted Tara, as he ran off to catch up with the others.

The five of them hurtled towards the sea, which was at quite a distance to us, as we watched on.

'You fancy joining in, Soph?' I said seriously, whilst winking discretely towards Tara.

'You've got to be joking, Ellie Nellie. Crack open the Prosecco and we can sit back and enjoy the entertainment.'

The boys stopped short of the water, standing in a line, looking out to the cold North Sea, which, whilst a nice shade of deep Oxford blue, would be enough to freeze the feet off a penguin. Then Jake began to take off his underpants.

'Oh my God, they're going commando! Are there any binoculars in that box? They're too far away to see. I can just imagine the convo though. Jake will be saying, ''There's no way I'm ruining these Calvins – do you know how much they cost?'' Sophie smiled.

'And Toby is probably saying, "There's no way I am removing my underpants!" Tara laughed. 'Until he caves into peer pressure which he always does, of course.'

'Stan and Alex will be saying, ''We be first in,'' and I can almost hear Zen, "Let's just let it all hang out and embrace nature," I said, doubled up laughing.

And at that, following Jake's lead, they all discarded their underpants and ran, whooping and hollering, into the sea. They were followed by three dogs, little Nacho having none of it, clearly deciding it was much more fun burying the underpants than getting cold and wet.

We had the most amazing day. The conversation flowed as we enjoyed a fabulous picnic, and afterwards Stan serenaded us on Zen's guitar with some traditional Polish folk songs. The beach was surprisingly quiet, with only the odd dog walker or rambler passing by and saying hello or stopping for a little chat along the way. It was paradise.

'I love this place,' said Aleksy. 'It is good for the erm, how do you say, feet?'

'I think you mean soul.' Toby laughed. 'But I totally agree with you.'

'It's breathtaking,' I said, cocooning myself into a blanket. 'Okay, so it's not warm like the Maldives, but you kind of forgive that.'

'You do indeed.' Sophie nodded, full of bonhomie and not feeling the cold due to copious amounts of Prosecco sloshing around her system.

'And it's not quite over yet,' said Zen. 'We've got a while yet before the tide, so next we're going to the Grace Darling Museum in the village. Then we'll finish at Seahouses so you can see the working harbour, have some fun in the penny arcade and maybe fish and chips, if anyone is hungry enough by then.'

'The perfect drink to go with the perfect day.' Stanislaw smiled, reaching for the flask of Zen's coffee. 'Dzieki everyone.'

'Cheers!' said Aleksy.

＊＊

As Zen and I made our way back to Lindisfarne in Ravi after a fabulous day out, the dogs snoozing in the back, my hand lay on his soft denim clad thigh. I felt like I was floating on air. Maybe it was because I'd had a few drinks, but it was more the euphoria of such a magical day with the people I loved.

'Thank you again. You really pulled a blinder. Everyone has had such a good day, and I can't wait to get you home and thank you properly,' I said, smiling at Zen.

'Ooh, Ellie, I wish we were in something a bit faster than old Ravi here.'

'The best things in life are worth waiting for.' I grinned. 'I think it's done us good to get away from the island drama and switch off for a little while. I haven't given Aidan or Isla a thought.'

'I'm really pleased to hear that Ellie, and whilst I don't want to spoil the day with a crash landing into reality, I did get a text message from Meg earlier, but I didn't want to spoil things by telling you at the time.'

'And?' I asked, my heart already reverting from a steady chilled out classical rhythm to something akin to experimental jazz.

'Let's just say the eagles have landed, and it hasn't got off to a good start, but Meg was insistent we don't spoil our day and for you to go over in the morning. I'll take the dogs back on my own.'

'I want to come with you.'

'We've arranged to spend the evening in the holiday house with the others, so let's just finish the day off on a high, eh? Plenty of time to get all angsty tomorrow. You can drop Meg a text. Besides which, you have just made me a promise, and I'm claiming it,' he said grinning, his hand brushing down my leg. 'In fact, I need to clean up before we go over to the house. I'll drop the dogs while you go and get in the shower, and I'll be straight back to join you. You can scrub my back – I promise I'll make it worth your while.'

'Oh, okay then, I suppose, if I must... now put your foot down!'

CHAPTER 16

Zen and I went straight over to the cottage the next morning, and I popped Nacho into the kennel with his doggie friends.

'So,' I asked, before I'd even taken off my jacket, 'what happened yesterday?'

'And good morning to you too, Ellie.' Meg smiled, although the smile didn't really reach her eyes. She looked very tired, and the usual Meg sparkle had abandoned her, which was hardly surprising.

Bert plonked the big teapot down in the middle of the table with a packet of Jammie Dodgers.

'Plate, Bert. We may be upset, but we still have standards. It's a slippery slope – you'll soon be putting the milk carton straight onto the table.'

You just had to love Meg. Bert winked and went off in search of a plate. Tea in hand, Meg told us the events of yesterday. It transpired that firstly, Elspeth had arrived to sort out the apartment and had kept calling Meg to ask for help in finding things.

'Eventually, even though I didn't want to, I went across to the castle. I could have wept. She had stripped the room of all of James and Grace's personal things and put them in boxes. She had that huge hulk of a concierge from the hotel, and his gormless missus, who allegedly cleans the rooms, with her to help. A lot of the furniture was missing, I presume stored in another room in the castle – I expect Aidan has some of his own things arriving.'

'Well, I can't imagine Madam having anything to contribute, other than clothes and makeup – it will take an articulated lorry to bring all of her gear.' I smiled.

'At least they've been banned from James's office, so that's a blessing. Then later, after tea, I went out to see to the chickens, and there she was, Lady blooming Muck, swanning about the yard like she owned it.'

Meg faltered and I could see tears glazing her eyes which she tried to hide but failed.

'Come on, Meggie lass, don't be getting upset. You're stronger than that.' Said Bert.

'What did she say?' I asked.

'She was her usual charming self,' said Meg sarcastically. 'Basically, she told me to keep my nose out of the castle from now on. That we,' she nodded towards Bert, 'weren't needed anymore, and more or less that she is Queen Bee now and what she says goes.'

'Oh Meg, come here,' I said giving the older woman a hug. 'You and Bert will always be needed. We need you, the animals need you, and all your friends over in the village need you too, so please just ignore that cow. Hopefully she won't set foot in the yard again.'

'Do you want me and Zen to go and talk to the organ grinder and not his performing monkey – that would be okay with you lad? Or maybe I can phone James?' said Bert looking at Zen.

It was the first time I had ever seen Bert lean on Zen in this way, and it confirmed to me just how vulnerable he must be feeling. Zen nodded, but Meg shook her head.

'No way are you to bother James with this, Bert. Do you hear me? He's got far too much on his plate at the moment. I don't want you to talk to Aidan either. Hopefully, I won't have to even see her anymore, and I don't want to stir up trouble. She demanded the castle keys back...'

'She what?' I gasped.

'She told me that all of us, including you two and everyone from the village that helps with the animals, are forbidden from the front of the castle – tradesmen's entrance only for us plebs. Apparently, she's considering changing the passcode on the gate and won't even be giving the new one to us. She says everyone on Lindisfarne knows it, and it's a security risk. So, I think you might just say that's it, me and Bert are officially on the scrap heap.'

The cow. I'd like to put her on the top of a scrap heap, next in line for the crusher to make her into a little cube that we could use as a coffee table...

'Never let me hear you say that again Meg,' said Zen seriously. 'Try and think of the break as a holiday, although the animals will still need looking after. Let's just try and continue as normal, get Bert through his op, and forget all about everything else.'

Whilst I agreed with Zen's sentiment, I thought it would be far easier said than done.

***

Later that morning, we were heading down the A1 on the way to our day out in Newcastle when I got a text.

'It's a message from the castle to all of us staff and volunteers,' I said, hurriedly opening it to read the contents.

'Listen to this Zen but keep your eyes on the road.'

Aidan and Isla invite you to a meeting to discuss the re-opening of the castle at 9am tomorrow (Wednesday) in the Henrietta Room. Everyone is expected to attend. Non-attendance will be interpreted as no longer wishing to support the castle and therefore you will not be needed for the forthcoming season.

'Oh my God, what on earth? That's just ridiculous, giving us only 24 hours to fit in with their, or should I say her agenda, because that message has Isla stamped all over it. What if people genuinely can't attend? Bert told me that some of the volunteers have helped at the castle for years.'

'They have. I used to do it along with Aurora, and we saw it as a great way to get work experience and feel like we were contributing towards the island. That message is just going to alienate people before they even start. Do they not understand that they need loyal volunteers? Getting anyone to the castle from the mainland due to tides isn't easy. There's not really anywhere for them to stay on the island. And the knowledge the locals have is so valuable. Bringing new people in, even if that was possible, would not give the same experience at all.'

But at that my phone pinged again.

'Another message from the castle.'

Thank you for your interest in the paid post of Seasonal Team Leader of Volunteers and Castle Guides. Unfortunately, due to change of management and a re-scoping of the business, you will no longer be required. We hope you find alternative employment soon.

'I've been sacked before I even start,' I said flabbergasted. 'It's Isla, isn't it? Just wanting to show who's boss and put me in my place. I was really looking forward to working with Grace, but quite frankly I've dodged a bullet not having to work for Princess Poison.'

'That's as maybe Ellie, but not the point. How dare they treat you, and everyone else, like this? It will be a miracle if they find enough people to actually open up, and if Isla is taking on the role of Team Leader, then God help those that do go. It's actually incredibly sad, Ellie. I feel like I'm watching the disintegration of many years of a happy, in the main,' he smiled, 'island.'

I tried to take in the information. On a personal level, I was relying on that salary, tiny though it was, to help me through to winter. I'd now have to try and find another job, and they were like gold dust on the island. I suppose I could probably get a few hours in the café and maybe carry on in *Love Lindisfarne* if Imogen could afford to pay me.

'Surely Lord B isn't happy about this. He knows more than anyone about the importance of having a loyal team in place and keeping an estate functioning.'

'I don't suppose he knows, Ellie. And like I said before, at the moment there's nothing concrete that we can take to him. It's not great, but I think we just need to sit back and watch this implode, then we can go to him with our concerns. I do think that most of the old guard will go to that meeting tomorrow, just to see what the score is if nothing else. I feel so grateful that Ma and Pa are not being dragged into it. Greater Reef is their life's work, and if they had been forced out, I can't imagine how they would be feeling.'

'They'd be feeling just like Meg and Bert are I suppose. It's been their life's work too, looking after the castle, and suddenly it's been taken from them. This all stinks, Zen.'

'It does, but let's not dwell on it or tell the others for now. Keep that for later and just enjoy today.'

***

Our day trip to the city was fantastic. We started at the Angel of the North where Aleksy and Stan fulfilled their dream of having their photos taken whilst sitting on the feet of the giant angel, which towered above the main A1 road running through Tyneside. The rusted metal structure was so tall it looked like it was reaching up to the clouds, and its wingspan at fifty-four metres was bigger than some aircraft. Quite frankly, I wondered how it didn't just topple over.

Afterwards, we made our way to the city centre, where Stan and Alex decided to go exploring the historic Grainger Market – a foodie heaven – and the many unique independent coffee shops that were dotted around the city, looking for ideas and maybe some sales.

'Hey, you're on holiday.' Zen laughed. 'Although if I wasn't booked to go with Jake, I'd be coming with you!'

Zen and Jake had opted to go on a tour of St James' Park. Zen told me that Jake had previously let it slip that whilst he had to put on a front of supporting The Hammers, him being an east end geezer, he had always been a closet Magpie. I was sure that getting a behind the scenes tour of Newcastle United was something he'd remember for ever.

Toby went off to search out the city's museums and had texted Tara to say he had found the *Literary and Philosophical Society*, which apparently was the largest independent library outside of London, with some really ancient and priceless books.

'He'll not be seeing any other museums today,' said Tara. 'Once he gets his head stuck in books he won't be seen again until it's time to go back. He says it's an amazing place and I know he will come back full of what we might consider useless information, but for Toby it's gold-dust. I know you two might wonder how he and I are together, but I love how intelligent he is. He's just got the most enquiring mind, and I find that very sexy, quite a turn on – and he's gorgeous even with his specs on. Little Bee Dee here is so lucky to have him as a dad,' she said, gently stroking her bump.

'You know what Tara; I promise I've never ever wondered about you and Tobes being together. It just works, even though you are very different to each other,' I said.

'We love him too,' said Sophie. 'Although, sometimes when he's off on a tangent about the flipping Romans or whatever, it would be handy if there was a mute button.'

Sophie, Tara and I had hit the shops; however, after oohing and aahing over the beautiful baby clothes in *Fenwick's*, Tara's swollen feet demanded a rest, so she had settled in the amazing food hall with a cappuccino and a huge piece of cake. Sophie and I approached our mission to fit in as many shops as possible like it was some retail speed dating challenge.

We all met up at 6pm. To have enough time to do what we wanted in Newcastle, we had chosen to miss out a tide, so the earliest we could cross back to the island was after 9pm. This had given us plenty of time to go for a stroll along the quayside and marvel at the bridges that spanned the River Tyne. We walked across the latest addition, the Millennium Bridge, then came back for a drink in one of Newcastle's oldest pubs called *The Crown Posada*. We rounded off the day at a gorgeous little pizzeria we found on the stunning Grey Street, with its amazing Georgian architecture, Toby pointing out Grey's Monument at the top of the street, reminding us of his costume at my leaving do when he had come covered in Earl Grey teabags as Lord Grey.

Newcastle was a resounding hit amongst us all, and the conversation around the dinner table was buzzing with how much we had enjoyed our day out. It was just so good for the soul to see everyone happy and enjoying the northeast as much as me. I wasn't looking forward to them going back to London at all – not one little bit – and wished they would all just move up here permanently.

CHAPTER 17

The following evening, I walked across to the cottage with Sophie and Aurora. Tara was having a well-earned night in front of the fire with her feet up, after a busy day in Alnwick. Meg had invited us for a girls' night, dispatching Bert to the pub. We had tried to persuade her to meet us in the *Crab* for a bar meal, but she was having none of it. I think she just wanted to keep occupied.

'I'd love to go inside the castle,' said Sophie, looking up at the ancient building as we climbed the cobbled hill to the gate.

'Not much chance of that at the moment,' I said, 'but hopefully if it opens next week, you can pay for a ticket. Mind, you may have to go in disguise if the Lady of the Manor knows you're my friend!'

'Can't wait to meet her,' growled Sophie.

And she didn't have long to wait, because as we went through the door in the big wooden gates, there, looking like something from a *Fairfax and Favor* advert, was Isla, notebook in hand, and what looked suspiciously like a tape measure, which she immediately tried to conceal.

'The sooner I get that entry code changed on that gate the better,' she glowered.

'Good evening to you too, Lady Isla,' said Aurora dipping into a curtsey. 'How lovely to see you looking so happy. I can see that being engaged has really worked its magic on you – not.'

'Are those for me?' She smirked, looking at the huge bouquet of flowers we had stopped off for in Alnwick to give to Meg.

'They're for Meg, to cheer her up after what you've just put her through,' I said through clenched teeth.

'Me? Let me tell you, it was not part of my grand plan to come back to this godforsaken place. I should be in the Caribbean getting a tan in time for the Cannes Film Festival, instead of which I've been forced here because of my fiancé's meddling father. I didn't give Grace that stroke, you know, before you blame me for that as well. But now I'm here, you may well want to put in a repeat order for flowers, because let me tell you, there are more changes coming and I doubt they,' she nodded towards the cottage, 'are going to be happy.'

'Do you ever just shut the f...' I began, and then stopped. No point in making matters worse.

'Anyway, Ellie, this could have been you instead of me, if you had played your cards right and hadn't gone all goo-goo eyed over Saint Zen. I still don't know what either of them saw in you, but Aidan's off the market now, just in case you change your mind, or more likely Zenny gets wise and dumps you. He wanted me, you know, but I had a better offer...'

I could feel the tension rising. Aurora's hackles were somewhere around her neck and Sophie, who had remained quiet up to that point drinking it all in, suddenly marched menacingly towards Isla.

'Oh my God!' I looked at Aurora. 'She may be tiny, but when Sophie gets going there's no stopping her and she's frightened of no one. Brace yourself!'

Isla retreated towards the wall as Sophie approached, stopping just feet in front of her.

'Right, you sanctimonious cow. I've only just met you, but I've heard plenty about you, and none of it was good. I'm just putting it out there, if you hurt my friends, then you hurt me, and I won't tolerate it.'

Isla smirked, looking down at Sophie who was about eight inches shorter than her.

'Ah, you're thinking that I'm not really a threat, aren't you? Just as I like it, because believe you me, when you are least expecting it, I'll be there, lurking in the shadows. I'm telling you now, you self-important pylon in hair extensions, any more of this nonsense and you are going to be sorry, because I'll make you pay.'

'And if she doesn't, I will,' shouted Aurora. 'Don't you ever mention my brother's name again – and the only one that's going to get dumped around here is you. I can't wait for that to happen when Aidan comes to his senses.'

'Maybe I'll just see if I can reach to give you a little taste of what's to come,' sneered Sophie, fully immersing herself into the role of soap opera baddie by limbering up.

'Sophie don't do it, you'll snap her! By the way, Isla, she's a kickboxing champion – small but highly dangerous. She could knock your wig off before you know it.'

I wasn't lying, although the championship status was from when Sophie was fourteen. But before she had the time to see how high she could still kick without dislocating her femur, the gate creaked open, and Ethel and Dora came into the yard.

'Thank God, the Golden Girls to the rescue,' muttered Isla sarcastically.

'It can wait,' said Sophie, 'besides which, I want you to meet Jake because he's even nicer to people like you than me.'

'And what's that tape measure for, the one you're trying to hide?' I shouted at Isla's retreating back.

'Well, that's for me to know and you to find out. You lot have just signed your own death warrants, because if I wasn't going to implement my plans before, I certainly am now.'

And on that cryptic note, she went up the back stairs to the castle, slamming the door shut behind her.

'What on earth is she up to?' I looked at the others, a sinking feeling in my stomach.

'Well, whatever it is, we don't tell Meg. Now turn that frown upside down,' smiled Aurora, 'and get in that cottage. Let's have a great night and forget about it all until tomorrow.'

'You are far more like your brother than you think.' I smiled at Aurora, turning towards the cottage door.

After clinking her way across the yard with what sounded like a party pack in her carrier bag, Ethel looked my bestie up and down.

'Are you Sophie? I've been looking forward to meeting you. Someone said you're just like a younger version of me.'

'I'll take that as a compliment.' Sophie smiled.

'Actually, you know what, after seeing you in action Sophie, I think that's spot on,' said Aurora, laughing. 'You two are like peas in a pod, the granddaughter you never knew you had.'

'Right then, me bairn,' said Ethel linking arms with Sophie, 'let's you and Granny Ethel go and show them how to have fun!'

CHAPTER 18

The next morning, I decided to go to the mainland with Zen, to deliver his coffee orders. The gang were having a quiet day sightseeing around the island, with Ethel as their tour guide, God help them. No doubt it would end in the *Crab*.

My phone started pinging like it was on repeat.

'It seems everyone went to the meeting at the Castle. According to Maurice, it started off frostier than a polar bear's underwear, but it sounds like Aidan saved the day by going on a charm offensive. Listen to this bit,' I said, laughing out loud. 'Isla told them they would have to get dressed up as Vikings.'

I thought Zen was going to swerve off the road.

'She what?'

'She said it would add to the experience, that it was what tourists wanted, and it would be just like *Game of Thrones*. She said she would be dressing the castle to resemble a Viking longhouse.'

'I bet that went down quicker than a leaking longboat.' Zen grinned.

'It did. There was almost an uprising. Apparently, only Maurice was keen as he thought he might look like Jon Snow and impress Nora, but even he saw sense. Anyway, the upshot is that the castle is re-opening next Monday without the plastic horns, and, God help them, Isla is going to manage it.'

'Aidan is going to have his work cut out with her, you know, and the trouble is, he won't always be around to be the voice of reason.'

99

'That's the bit that worries me, Zen. We caught her in the yard last night. I think she thought she was safe to go around as it was getting on for 7pm, and Bert and Meg would usually be done for the day by then.'

'Well, I suppose she's entitled to have a walk,' said the ever-reasonable Zen.

'With a notepad and a tape measure? She's up to something, I just know it.'

'Maybe she was just measuring her IQ!' He laughed.

'Ooh, Zen Chambers, is that a little bit of sarcasm hiding under that gorgeous hair? That's about the most insulting thing I think I've ever heard you say about anyone – but funny. Have to say, though, she wouldn't need a tape measure for that – she'd need a magnifying glass.'

Later that evening, we had all arranged to meet up in the pub. As suspected, the gang's sightseeing trip around the island had ended in the *Crab*. Sophie hadn't even made it back to the holiday house to change, having spent the entire afternoon with her new best friend Ethel. The pair of them were well oiled, tucked away in a corner, cackling like the sorceress and her apprentice.

'Ellie Nellie, we missed you today, didn't we Ethel?' hiccupped Sophie.

'We did. Could have done with some help drinking the wine, although more for us. Eeh Ellie pet, your friend Sophie is just a breath of fresh air.'

There was nothing fresh about the air around either of them at that moment. You could have pickled cabbage with those fumes.

'I was just saying to Ethel how I would love to meet Prince Blue Eyes. What's his name again?'

'Aidan.'

'Oh yes, Adey. Well, I need to meet the cad and bounder and give him a piece of my mind about his delightful finance.'

'It's fiancée Soph, and you're not in an episode of *Bridgerton*. I reckon if you call him Adey, you will be deported from the island.'

'Ah noooo. I love it here, and I love my Granny Ethel,' she slurred, grabbing the older woman's hand and looking at her adoringly.

'You do? Really? I mean Lindisfarne, not Ethel, we all love Ethel.'

'Absobloominglutely. It's great, and I don't want to go back to boring old London. It's much more exciting here.'

'I'm delighted to hear that.' I smiled. 'And if you can manage to focus your wine sozzled eyes over towards that door, you might get to meet Aidan quicker than you expected, because he's coming in now. Please Soph, don't make things more difficult than they already are...'

'Moi? Pinkie promise. I'll be the model of dis...dish...' she said, squinting towards the door. 'Jeez, he's fit. He looked good on the photos, but he's like, well tasty in the flesh, but not as good looking as my Jake,' she added quickly, glancing around to see where her fiancé was.

The tumbleweed had blown in with Aidan. Luckily, the place was relatively quiet, with just us and a few of the locals out for an early mid-week pint, but tensions were running high on the island with everyone wondering what changes might take place and how it could affect them.

'Cooeee Aidan, over here. Ours is a bottle of anything red, if you're buying,' slurred Ethel.

'Ethel don't fraternise with the enemy, you traitor,' I hissed.

'Guys,' said Aidan, surveying the audience. 'Can we just address the elephant in the room? Let me get you all a drink and I'll come round and have a chat with everyone and see that we can start as we mean to go on. I come in peace.'

'You'll be in bloody pieces if you do anything to spoil this island,' shouted one of the fishermen from his barstool at the end of the counter.

'Drinks all round,' said Aidan, 'and a bottle of your finest red for the ladies in the corner. I'll take it across to them.'

Aidan brought over the bottle of wine, put it on the table and pulled up a stool.

'It's Ethel, isn't it?' He smiled his best toothpaste advert smile at her. 'I remember when we went on a date to the fishing club shindig at Christmas.'

'That's right pet, and you got intoshticated on the hooch and lost your trousers.'

Sophie's ears were flapping like a cocker spaniel in a hurricane.

'Uncle James' trousers to be factually correct, but yes, a jolly good night was had by all. I hope there are many more nights like that to come when I'm on the island. Now then, who is this stunning woman?' He turned the megawatt smile in Sophie's direction, his bright blue eyes flashing.

'This is me long lost granddaughter,' said Ethel proudly. 'And that's her finance over there – he's related to the Krays, just so you know.'

That was a new one on me. I knew Jake had east end roots, but no one had ever mentioned notorious gangsters before.

'Very pleased to meet you, Sophie, and you may not believe this, but I think I have met your finance, I mean fiancé, before. He works in the city, doesn't he?'

'Yes, that's right, how on earth... anyway, pleased to meet you Adey, erm I mean Adrian, err Aidan.'

Within five minutes, Aidan had Sophie and Ethel eating out of the palm of his very privileged hand. They were laughing like old friends, and despite me kicking her under the table and reminding her he was the bad guy, it was falling on deaf – or drunk – ears.

'Let's catch up very shoon,' slurred Sophie, as Aidan stood up. 'You and Jake can talk money, and me and your intended can discuss weddings.'

'I shall look forward to it. Perhaps you and Jake could come to the castle for supper one night.' And at that he moved on to schmooze his next target.

'Sophie Olatunji, how could you?' I said, the minute 'Adey' was out of earshot.

'Don't get your big knickers in a twist Ellie Nellie,' she said, tapping the side of her nose. 'I'm going undercover, like a little stealth ninja creeping behind enemy lines. I'll be a spy in the camp, get Poison Pylon on side and find out what's going on. Me and my new granny here had it all planned. Put it there Ethel,' she said, holding up her hand for a high five with the older woman.

'Eeh pet, we're just like Judi Dench, or was it Helen Mirren?' mused Ethel.

Sophie and I looked at each other blankly.

'I think we deserve another drink for that,' continued Ethel. 'You buying, Ellie?'

'Well, I'm not sure you'll get an invite after you made such a good impression on her last night, Soph. She looked terrified of you, and your kickboxing skills.' I laughed. 'But yes, the drinks are on me. You two are both as mad as hatters but flipping hilarious with it!'

CHAPTER 19

The days flew by. Sadly, our hope that Isla was going to keep out of the yard didn't happen.

'Ellie,' said Meg, as I popped in to say a quick hello before starting on the horses. 'I'm not sure how much more I can take of *her*.' She gesticulated towards the castle. 'She's all over the place like a rash, poking her nose into the outbuildings, making notes on that blooming pad she carries about. Mind, she never ventures near when the dogs are loose, but I don't feel comfortable in my own yard anymore. I haven't sat outside with my cuppa since Grace left. I feel trapped in the cottage to keep out of her way.'

'Is she unpleasant to you?' I fumed.

'No, not really. She's just like an itch you can't scratch and drives you mad. But it's worrying me what she's up to. Mind, she hasn't been around for a couple of days, so we've had a little respite.'

'Probably because the castle opened its doors to the public yesterday. It seems that everything went okay according to the village group chat – no one appeared to be screaming blue murder at least.'

A little while later, I was giving Han a quick brush down in the yard. His full name was Hannibal Lecter, and he was called that for good reason. The surly Shetland pony and I hadn't got off to the best of starts. He didn't really like anyone much except for his stablemate Stout, the ex-brewery Shire. Then, for whatever reason, he eventually took to me, and we were now friends, much to the surprise of everyone else who had tried to win him over. He was a gorgeous boy, tiny with huge brown eyes and the longest of eyelashes, like a little cartoon pony.

I heard the back door to the castle slam shut, and there she was, approaching me. Isla with a face like a melted wellie. She marched over, stopping at a distance from the small pony whose ears immediately flattened, and he gave the Chianti smile towards what he hoped was his next victim.

'Is that thing still here?' she spat. 'I thought I'd made it clear when it kicked me at Christmas that it should go to the knacker's yard.'

'What can I do for you, Isla? Come for a friendly chat to tell me about your supper with *my* friends last night?'

'That was Aidan's idea not mine,' she grumbled. 'But there are times when one must put one's personal feelings aside if it is good for business, even if it means spending time with two extras from Eastenders. And stop changing the subject Ellie – back to that barrel on legs.' She nodded at Han. 'It ruined my very expensive *Moncler* coat.'

'Oh, come off it, Isla. It was a tiny mark which could have easily been sponged off, and anyway, it looks like you managed to find new things to wear,' I said, pointing at her outfit, which today, shrieked highly expensive country casual chic, all tweed and cashmere. Even though it pained me to admit, it looked fabulous on her.

'Are you rocking Claudia's *Traitors* look by any chance? That jumper looks familiar.' I gazed in envy at the bottle green cable knit teamed with a mini kilt and black biker boots.

'My stylist, Gigi, the best in the business, works with all the A listers. She sources all my clothes. I must keep up appearances now that I'm in the public eye. Anyway, I didn't come here to talk fashion with you of all people,' she said, disdainfully looking me up and down and taking in one of Bert's boiler suits that I was wearing over my going out clothes to save getting changed later.

'Didn't think so,' I muttered. 'So, what did you come to talk about?'

'I want that washing line removed,' she said bluntly, pointing towards the cottage where Meg's line was strung across the yard. 'It's like looking out on to a yard in a Dickens novel.'

I momentarily got distracted thinking that if she'd read Dickens then I was one of the Brontë sisters.

'I mean, why should I have to look at giant underwear flapping about like I'm in Wishy Washy's laundry?'

Aladdin the pantomime was far more Isla than Dickens...

'Not to mention those ghastly chickens pecking about, and whatever they are with their beady eyes.' She pointed at Sage and Onion, the ancient Turkeys. 'And don't get me started on those broken excuses for dogs who all look like rejects that even the rescue didn't want, careering about and defecating all over the place – ew, it's disgusting.'

Her face had as pinched an expression as the overload of Botox would allow.

'Anyway, back to the washing line. You tell *her* to get it taken down, or I will get the staff to remove it. I mean what's wrong with a tumble dryer? What century are we stuck in here?'

Meg was old school. Did her washing every day to a schedule for lights, darks, and animal related. I knew this as she had drilled me when I first arrived. There was a tumble dryer in one of the outbuildings, but it was only ever used in emergencies. Meg preferred the sweet smell of fresh air and was a woman who followed tradition. It was things like this that started world wars, and Meg was already on the edge. In the normal course of events, I knew that Meg would have stood right up to Isla on this one, but what with worrying about Bert and Grace, and effectively being laid off from a job they loved, this may well have been the final straw.

'Did it ever cross your mind that Meg and Bert might be on a tight budget, or maybe more eco conscious than you? They have lived in that cottage for over forty years, and their washing has never offended James and Grace who are the *actual* owners of the castle. You are only going to be here temporarily...'

'You don't know that, Ellie. James and Grace may decide to stay in the States.'

That didn't bear thinking about...

'Whatever, Isla. You are temporary for now, so I don't think that you have the right to make such demands. Meg is going through enough without your petty third world problems. Bert is going for his operation soon, so I'm asking you, for once in your life, try to be a little kinder and just leave the hell alone for now.'

I knew that trying to appeal to her better side was futile, as she didn't have one.

'Anyway, there's only one tiny window on the landing of the stairwell that looks out over the yard, and I can't imagine you look out of that very much, so what's the issue?'

'I've got people coming. Important people. I will be bringing them around the yard, and there is no way that they are going to have to duck under a line of granny's big knickers.'

'What important people? Why do they need to come into the yard? This is a working area, and the animals have priority, you know that. You can't just bring people around without notification.'

'Oh, I think I can.'

My blood was now boiling. She had lit the touch paper, and I was going to explode. I think Han felt my tension as he began striking at the ground with his tiny hoof, neighing loudly for such a little chap.

'Seems Han needs a bit of a run-around,' I said, as I began to unclip him from the ring on the wall.

Isla took several steps back.

'You wouldn't dare let go of him.'

'Oh, I would, and he could outrun you back to the door. Forget the washing line, Isla. It's hardly top priority. You must have so much more to think about, what with running the castle and your wedding.'

'There are minions you hire called Wedding Planners, Ellie. Don't suppose you will be able to afford one, if Zenny darling ever pops the question that is, which he won't, as he's bound to come to his senses before then. I mean, I know Aidan is handsome, but Zen, well, he's so fit that he's bound to get better offers.'

She licked her inflated lips, clearly enjoying herself thinking about *my* boyfriend.

'All men have a roving eye, it's in their DNA. Woman to woman, you are punching above your weight and believe you me, his eye will be turned by someone more in his league. You will scuttle off back to London, so you may as well do that before he breaks your heart. Maybe that someone will be me. I know he wants me. It's just a matter of time. It would only be for the sex, you understand. He's a very pretty man, but way too boring for me.'

Ouch. The absolute cow! That stung like falling into a giant nettle patch, but I wasn't going to let her see that she had touched a raw nerve. My insecurities, which I thought I'd managed to get well and truly under control, came flooding back, almost taking my breath away, and I suddenly felt lightheaded. I knew with absolute certainty that Zen would never look twice at Isla, but she was right – he was so handsome, he would get offers. When we were out and about, I'd noticed a few women taking far too much of an interest in him and that was when I was by his side, so what would happen when I wasn't there? What if...

'That line has to come down,' she said, interrupting my thoughts and pulling me back into a very unpleasant reality. 'But I'm a fair woman...'

'What?' My concentration was shot, and I could hardly focus on what she was saying. 'You? Fair?' I echoed, eventually catching up.

About as fair as a rainy St Swithin's Day...

'So, I'll give you a few days to sort it out,' she went on. 'It needs to be gone by Thursday evening so that the yard is clear on Friday. That's my last word on the subject.'

She crept her way down the yard, her back to the wall, keeping an eye on Han, as she pushed her way through a row of Bert's boiler suits hanging proudly on the washing line. I rather hoped she would garrot herself in the process and hang there like the witch she was, but unfortunately, she didn't, and she bolted back to the safety of the castle stairs. I scratched Han's ears as I unclipped him and led him back into the stable.

'Next time buddy, I will let you go, and you can do your worst.'

I called to say goodbye to Meg, deciding not to mention my exchange with Isla – no point in upsetting her further. I needed to talk to Zen and Aurora about this latest development. Washing Line Gate was far from over. We just needed to gather the troops and draw up the battle lines. More importantly though, I needed to offload to my bestie about how much Isla had rattled me, but that would have to wait. So, I took a deep breath, pasted on a smile, and put on a performance for Meg that was worthy of a BAFTA.

'The time's flying Meg. Most of my friends will be going before we know it. We've all had such a lovely time. I'm going to be sad to see them go.'

'They're just lovely folks, Ellie. It's been a pleasure to meet them even though Bert and I haven't really been much company

111

lately.' She sighed. 'Too much going on, but next time they're here, hopefully everything will have settled down and Bert will have his new hip. He's due to go in for his pre-op soon.'

'Yes, Zen and I are going to take you to the hospital, and when the time comes for his admission, we'll drop you in Alnwick so you can get settled at your sister's when Bert is in the hospital. Do you good to have a little break.'

'I just want him home as soon as possible.'

'Oh, he will be, don't you worry about that. He'll be on those legs quicker than a new-born foal knowing Bert. He won't stay away from his island a day too long.'

'And you and Zen don't mind coming to stay in the cottage?'

'No, of course not. Makes sense us being here to look after everything.'

And keep an eye on that poison poptart…

'Ellie.' Meg suddenly went all serious. 'I'm putting on a brave face, but I'm so worried. After seeing how suddenly Grace got ill and couldn't come home, I'm terrified the same thing will happen to Bert.'

I looked into her terrified eyes.

'Meg, he's going to be in the best possible hands, and you know he can't go on trying to cope with the pain he's in. Hip replacements are relatively straightforward these days. My grandad had his done, and he was back playing tennis in no time.'

'I know pet, don't mind me. Just feeling very maudlin.'

'Well, that's hardly surprising, considering what's been going on. One small step at a time Meg, and that will go for Bert too.'

'And where are you all going today for your outing?' Meg changed the subject.

'It's Toby's choice today, so we're off to Hadrian's Wall. Stan and I are swapping places. He's going in the camper with Zen to talk coffee, and I'm going in the minibus to get the lowdown from Sophie, otherwise known as Mata Hari. She and Jake were going to the castle for supper last night. I cannot wait to hear what went on. Jake wasn't that keen on going and only went because he thought Aidan might let a few financial nuggets slip. It turns out that Aidan went to school with this posh guy that Jake plays squash with called Sebastian the Snout. He's some big cheese in finance and Jake's always up for some financial gossip.'

'Sebastian the who? I can't keep up Ellie, but you'd better ring me the minute you get a chance and let me know what they're up to over there.'

'I will, although it may not be until in the morning, as it will be a late one with the tide times today.'

'Okay Ellie, now get a wriggle on lass, and you go and have a wonderful day with your friends.'

CHAPTER 20

Sophie, Tara and I sat in the back row of the minibus as we made our way across the vast Northumberland National Park towards Hadrian's Wall country in the far West of Northumberland. The day was bright. We'd had a good run of weather for April, and the scenery was spectacular, but I'm ashamed to admit that we didn't notice a great deal of the open rolling landscape due to listening to Sophie about her night in the witch's den. I'd already decided to continue the pretence that all was well. Today was Toby's special day, and it was important to him, so I wasn't going to ruin it by being all morose. Time for that later when I got Sophie on her own.

'So,' I said brightly, 'tell us the goss!'

'Interesting to say the least,' said Sophie. 'Firstly, it was crystal clear that she didn't want us there and that she thought we were way below her paygrade. She said that my outburst the day before had been totally unacceptable. God knows how, but I bit the bullet and apologised, even though I didn't mean it.'

'I hope you kept your fingers, toes and your nunny crossed.' Tara laughed.

'Anyway, once we got that out of the way, she defrosted... slightly. They started by taking us on a grand tour of the castle. What an amazing building, so full of history, and I loved that ship room where you held Aurora's wedding. She did say something interesting that you might not like, though. She said they were considering opening it up as a tearoom, that it made sense to capitalise on the castle. All stately homes and the like have gift shops and cafés these days, and that's where the income comes from.'

'No. That's not good news. I mean, I can't argue with her logic because it's probably the case, but from my understanding, James and Grace look at Lindisfarne as a whole, not just the castle, and don't do things that might affect existing businesses. A tea shop there would ruin Aurora's business, and not forgetting *Love Lindisfarne* too. And what did Aidan say?'

'He agreed Ellie. Said it made financial sense. Sorry, probably not what you wanted to hear. Anyway, we got back to their apartment after me asking to see your old gaff, but she said that was now the staff quarters'.

'Suppose it was when I was staying in it – best staff accommodation ever.'

'We met Cyril and Rosa, said staff, who were lovely,' continued Sophie, 'but she treats them like something on the bottom of your shoe. They served us canapes and drinks, and if it hadn't been for Aidan thanking them and telling them to go to their apartment, I think she would have had them at her beck and call all night.'

'She's gruesome,' said Tara, screwing up her face.

'Jake and Aidan started talking business, so I was left to listen to her drone on. Talk about me, me, me. She's relentless, and I had avoided drinking to keep on my toes, so you owe me big style 'cos I had to go through that sober. Anyway, she kept getting messages and she would say, "that was Barnaby checking that we are okay for Friday," or whatever, and Aidan just rolled his eyes, not looking at all impressed. The messages kept pinging, and she couldn't wait to reply.'

'Rude cow,' said Tara, passing us the Maltesers.

'Aidan then said something like, "we have guests, Isla," and she just ignored him, and us. Eventually she put the phone down and in that awful bloody fake posh voice of hers, explained that Barnaby was from a television company, and she was in negotiations with them. Aidan then did that unspoken thing, you know, *the* look that means shut the hell up, and she went quiet, at what was probably the most exciting bit.'

'No way. This morning, she was on about bringing some "important" people around the castle, including the yard. I wonder if she meant them. None of this sounds good really, does it?'

'Nope,' agreed Tara, shoving in a handful of Maltesers. 'My mind is boggling as to the possibilities of what kind of television show it could be, though. Bet it's some naff reality thing.'

'*The Only Way Is Isla*.' Sophie laughed.

'*Hate Island*,' I chipped in.

'*Divorced At First Sight*,' offered Tara.

'*Come Whine With Me*. She's good at that.' I laughed, feeling so much better in the company of my friends.

'Anyway, Ellie Nellie, what I can say categorically, is that all is not right between those two. They are not a couple in love in the traditional sense of the word. I think it may be some kind of marriage of convenience. I quite liked him. He seems like a nice guy and has some idea of life in the real world for such a posh bloke, but as for her, she's devoid of any likeable traits whatsoever. By the way, he's back off to London for a few days today, tying up loose ends.'

116

'He should have stayed here and tied up one massive loose end.' Tara laughed.

'Don't even joke, Tara. It's so tempting. I can see what Isla might get out of an arranged marriage, if that were the case, but Aidan?' I mused.

'Don't know babe, but I could see him getting more and more exasperated by her, and she was oblivious, totally wrapped up in herself. It was not the behaviour of a happy couple about to be married – like me and you Jakey Wakey,' she guffawed.

'Anything you say babes. But you're right about those two,' he shouted from the driver's seat, 'I'm putting a monkey on them never making it down the aisle.'

We stopped talking long enough to look out at the amazing scenery as we drove along what was known locally as the Military Road. It was ramrod straight, just how the Roman's liked it, and from either side of the road all you could see were acres and acres of glorious countryside, much of it wild, interspersed with agricultural land. The far-reaching views were a feast for the eyes, and whilst the actual Hadrian's Wall was far from a complete structure, there were still stretches that gave you an idea of just how spectacular it would have been.

We pulled into the car park at Vindolanda Roman Fort, where we joined forces with Zen and Stanislaw.

'Hadrian came to Britain in AD122,' explained Toby as he got out of the minibus. 'He began building the wall, not himself of course. Oh no, that was left to Legionnaires who were drafted in. You might be surprised to learn they weren't all from Italy, but from wider Europe, and even as far as North Africa. The Legionnaires hated it here. The cold really got to them. The wall ended up being some eighty odd miles long and was intended to keep the barbarians out, not the Scots as is commonly thought.'

'Very interesting,' said Stanislaw. 'I wonder if anyone came from Poland.'

'Guys, I promise I'm not going to bleat on today. I know I can get, err, over enthusiastic.' Toby smiled. 'So welcome to Vindolanda. There are nine forts here and you get a real sense of what life was like back then. There are also the excavations going on, which are particularly interesting. I'm going to let you all just go off and explore by yourselves though, even if it is just as far as the café, as I'm keen to go and view the dig.'

'I'm with you Toby,' said Zen, and the rest of the boys nodded. 'I want to hear as much as you can tell us, so we can do the whole site with you as our personal tour guide.'

'I'm coming too, darling.' Tara smiled. 'Baby Bee Dee will find it all thrilling, I'm sure.'

'There's a fabulous museum, if you two want to stay indoors. There's jewellery, and even shoes.' Toby smiled, looking at me and Sophie. 'Then let's meet up at the café for a coffee.'

Sophie took no persuading and I readily agreed. It would give me an opportunity to have some one-on-one time with her.

As we entered the foyer for our tickets, Toby spotted someone he clearly knew. She was a willowy flaxen blonde woman of about our age wearing shorts, a fleece and boots caked in mud. Her hair was held back from her face by a woollen head band and she didn't have a scrap of make up on. She looked radiant – the epitome of natural beauty.

'Anya!' exclaimed Toby, 'How great to see you.'

I hardly listened to the conversation as I was too busy watching her reaction to Zen. She politely nodded at each of us in turn. Did her eyes linger longer on Zen? More importantly, did his linger longer on her more than was necessary? I tried to pull myself together. This was all down to Isla filling my head with nonsense.

'Is Anders here too?' I heard Toby ask.

'Yes, he is. We just got engaged.' She smiled, waving her hand. 'Come and say hello. He's over at the dig.'

Sophie poked me in the ribs.

'That's some resting bitch face you've got going on there,' she hissed in my ear, 'and you don't even have one of those. What on earth's up?'

'Tell you later. Now let's go and have a quick spin around the museum and then the coffee is on me.'

We turned to go.

'Erm Ellie.' Zen smiled, coming towards me, and pulling me in for a hug before kissing me.

'Love you,' he whispered. 'Have a good time with Sophie.'

I felt ridiculous. If it had been Isla's intention to unsettle me, it had worked, and even thinking that way was disrespectful to Zen.

'Love you too,' I said kissing him back. 'Now go learn about rocks!'

CHAPTER 21

The museum was interesting. It was hard to believe that the Romans had made some of the objects on display. It was amazing how advanced a civilisation they were, considering it was almost two thousand years ago.

'Never in a million years would I have thought I would enjoy something like this,' said Sophie as we meandered, looking into the glass display cases.

'Nor me. I can see why Toby would get all excited to dig up something like that.' I pointed to an ornate metal hair pin.

'Anyway, time for coffee I reckon. We've been around the entire museum; Toby will be proud of us,' I said, high fiving her.

We made our way through the site.

'It's really remote here, isn't it?' said Sophie. 'And there was me thinking the island was out of the way. I hadn't realised just how big Northumberland is.'

'I thought exactly the same when I arrived, and according to Zen and Aurora, there are even more remote places than this.'

We walked down a bank to a café, which was in a glorious setting with a replica of a Roman temple next to it. A bank of trees was in full spring leaf and made a spectacular backdrop to the glade-like setting. Drinks and cake chosen, we sat at a quiet table in the corner. Sophie wasted no time.

'So come on, spill the coffee beans, what the heck is going on babe… or should I guess? Has it got something to do with Poison Pylon?'

'I don't really know where to start. I'll get the worries about what she's up to out of the way first.' I proceeded to tell Sophie about the washing line and Isla's comments about showing people around the yard, her lack of understanding that it was a working zone, and that the animals were priority.

'She has no concept about what Meg and Bert are going through at the moment,' said Sophie angrily. 'You need to talk to Aidan about that when he gets back. I mean, you can hardly bother James about a washing line, but I get it – it's not really about the line, is it? It's about her abuse of power.'

'And poor Meg isn't even sitting out in the yard with her cuppa anymore. Honestly Sophie, I could throttle Isla for that alone, before I even start on...'

'You've got that face on again. That's twice in a day so you'd better nip that in the bud before it becomes permanent.' She smiled.

'I can't help it when I think about her.'

'Babes, I get it. I think I've got an Isla face too.'

Sophie screwed up her pretty features into a scowl that would sour the milk in her cappuccino. I then told Sophie what Isla had said about Zen, at which point the scowl returned, even deeper, before transcending into anger that was written all over her face.

'Right Ellie. Let's get one thing straight. DO NOT take any notice of one word that comes out of that cow's mouth.'

'I know Sophie, but she hit a nerve. I suppose I'm still smarting over the whole Matt debacle and how I'd got him all wrong. We'd been together three years, and I still didn't see through him. I'm scared that could happen again.'

'Ellie, we've had this conversation. Firstly, most of us go through at least one Matt in our lives – they're out there everywhere – but the thing is, Zen is nothing like him. Not one tiny bit. Believe you me, he is not that kind of guy. Secondly, do you know how gorgeous you are? You are certainly not punching.'

'I detest that expression,' I interrupted. 'It's so demeaning.'

'It's a case of transference Ellie; she was actually talking about herself. If anyone is punching – sorry babe can't think of how else to say it – it's her with Aidan. And much as I like him, he will be the one to stray, if he hasn't already. He's in London now. What might he be up to? Aidan will always come into contact with gorgeous women. Men in his position are always at events full of models and celebrities who see him as an aristocratic catch, and Isla is fair game to relegate to the divorce courts – if they actually do get married that is.'

I listened to her wise words, and I knew she made a lot of sense. I had to stop acting like an idiot, before I ended up ruining what Zen and I had by doubting that it was real. I loved Zen. I knew that for certain, and I knew he loved me and for now, that was all that mattered.

'You're right Soph, as always – well nearly always! I'm going to miss you so much when you go back. Not many more days left now.'

'Well, let's not spoil it by allowing that awful woman to ruin it for us. She's not fit to lick the crumbs off this plate. Talking of... another coffee... and cake? It might be ages until the others get here. Toby only has about two thousand years to take them through to present day!'

The others eventually appeared having had a brilliant time at the dig where they had witnessed a child's leather shoe being found.

'It was amazing,' said Jake excitedly, 'so well made and almost looked like a tiny football boot.'

'Shoes were real status symbols back then,' said Toby.

'Still are babes!' Sophie laughed. 'Ask Jimmy Choo!'

'Who knew Roman history was so interesting?' said Tara. 'But maybe not as interesting as that chocolate cake,' she whispered to me and Sophie.

'I've been trying to tell you that for years darling.' Toby grinned. 'So, chaps, after we have coffee, we're going for a look around the visitor centre, and then a late lunch at the pub along the road. After that, well, that's between me and Zen, and you'll all see later.'

Our last stop for the day required a walk along a path with crags to our left and a spectacular open view for miles over to our right. It was late afternoon, and the sunshine of earlier had disappeared. The sky was filled with heavy grey clouds, and the landscape looked bleak and foreboding. We trooped along in single file behind Toby and Zen who took the lead.

'Where are we going?' shouted Sophie. 'There's absolutely diddly squat here.'

She was right. There appeared to be nothing that we could be aiming for, just masses of open space.

'Not far,' yelled Toby from the front.

'I hope not,' muttered Tara. 'I'm freezing and, quite frankly, have done my wifely quota of Roman stuff for the day.'

'It is very grey and windy,' said Stanislaw. 'Aleksy's hair is like mop.'

Toby and Zen came to a halt. Looking to the left, we were in a dip between two hills and in the middle was what appeared to be a square fence housing the stump of a tree.

'I know this place,' I said, remembering an image that hung on the wall at Aurora's cafe. The photograph Zen had taken of a magnificent lone tree with the Northern Lights dancing behind it. But now the tree was gone.

'It's Sycamore Gap, isn't it?' said Jake. 'I read about the tree being cut down in the night. I thought it was a practical joke at first.'

'It is Sycamore Gap,' confirmed Zen. 'And we all hoped it was some kind of internet prank. The tree being felled rocked not only us Geordies, but people from all over the world. I expect some might wonder why the fuss about "just a tree" but look at where it grew. It was totally exposed to the fierce winds and winters, and still it managed to grow and survive for around 150 years. It was one of the most iconic natural landmarks, not just in Northumberland, but in the whole of Britain, and symbolised so much. I personally still feel incredibly sad that it is no more.'

'Me too,' agreed Toby. 'A bit of our heritage was destroyed forever that night.'

We all stood quietly looking at where the tree had once majestically grown, greeting countless visitors over the years from across the world who came to walk Hadrian's Path and see the Roman wall. There was an air of sadness about the site and, as the wind whipped up and the ever-darkening battleship grey sky threatened rain, we silently made our way back to the vans reflecting on the loss of a Northumbrian icon.

CHAPTER 22

The next morning, Zen, Aurora and I sat in the flat discussing the plans to turn the Henrietta room of the castle into a café-cum-giftshop, Washing Line Gate and worries about what Isla was up to in general.

'I cannot believe that Aidan would agree to something like that,' fumed Aurora. 'He's been around Lindisfarne all his life; he's seen how James and Grace run the island, and to even think of doing something that would affect an established business is unforgiveable. For goodness' sake, me and Zen rent this entire building from the estate, so what is he proposing if the café goes under? How is that going to help the finances?'

'Probably re-let it as a beauty salon or something,' I said, wishing I could retrieve the words as soon as they popped out of my mouth.

'Not helpful, Ellie,' said Zen.

'No, sorry, you're right,' I apologised.

'My other concern,' continued Zen, 'is how they even think that turning such an important historical room into a café could be a good thing.'

'What about Imogen as well? I haven't told her yet. Another gift shop in the castle would affect her too. I know her niche is specialist because it's a craft hub, and Isla would probably just stock cheap tat, but for me this whole issue is about them turning the castle into a destination day out and keeping people there for as long as possible,' I mused.

'Some visitors may not even venture over to the village once they've been fed, watered and bought a castle fridge magnet to take home,' said Aurora miserably.

We all sat looking at each other forlornly.

'And what's all this about the washing line?' asked Aurora. 'Has the poison witch become too posh for such things?'

'I think there's more behind her asking for that to be removed,' I said.

I told Aurora what Sophie heard about the television company and Isla saying she was going to show people around the castle and yard.

'What the heck? Seriously, she's taking Meg's line away over my dead body.'

'Drastic, sis, but I'm with you!' Zen smiled.

'So, what do we do about all of this?' I asked.

'We could kidnap her, and I'll get Jack to dump her on Little Reef. No one ever goes there. She could live at one with nature if she survives,' said Aurora.

'Erm, we don't even know that this is all Isla's doing. Maybe it's Aidan too?' I added.

Zen strummed his fingers on his jeans. A sign I had come to learn that meant he was deep in thought.

'We need to talk to Aidan,' said Zen. 'Or I do. Alone. We go back a long way and I think, well, I hope, he'll listen to me. Does anyone know when he's coming back from London?'

'Sophie said he was going for a few days, so maybe by the weekend,' I answered.

'I'm not going to ring him,' said Zen. 'This needs to be face to face, so it will have to wait until he's back.'

'And what about in the meantime? She said that the washing line had to be down by Friday, which is the day Sophie thinks her very important people are coming.'

'Meg is going to go ballistic; she hangs her animal towels out on Fridays, weather permitting. And as for her and Bert seeing strangers poking about the yard, well that will just finish them off,' said Zen.

'They're going to be more sad than mad,' said Aurora. 'Yet another change to contend with. Listen, I've got a plan. We get Bert and Meg off the island somewhere on Friday. Any suggestions?'

'Meg mentioned that her and Bert had never been to Chillingham Castle. That's Tara's choice of day out. So, why don't we make that Friday and take them with us? They'd love that. Meanwhile, we tell Lady Muck that the washing line will be down on Friday by 10am. Her guests can't get here until then anyway because of the tide. We'll probably pass them going the other way.'

'Can you take time off to come over and be here on Friday morning to keep an eye on proceedings, Aurora?' asked Zen.

'I'll make sure I am. I'll tumble the washing while I'm there, and it will all be dry and folded by the time they come home, with the line back in place. Hopefully, they'll be none the wiser. And maybe I can earwig! Anyway, I really don't think we should leave the animals unattended with strangers prowling around.'

'This is just a temporary stopgap as none of us want Meg and Bert to get any more upset, and there's no need for them to find out about any of this for now. I'll negotiate more permanent arrangements with Aidan when he's back, and hopefully we can nip it in the bud,' said Zen.

'Sounds like a plan,' I said. So why did my gut tell me that this was never going to work and there was far worse to come?

***

It was much easier to persuade Meg and Bert to have a day out with us than I thought.

'How lovely, Ellie. Wasn't I just saying the other day that me and Bert had never been to Chillingham? It'll do him the world of good to have a day out. His pre-op is next Monday, so it might take his mind off things. He reads all that nonsense about the ghosts you know, and he's keen to see for himself if it's true.'

'And you say you've already arranged for Aurora to come over to see to things here?'

'We have it all sorted, Meg, so no excuses. We're taking you for fish and chips at that lovely restaurant in Bamburgh on the way back too.'

'Me and Bert would be happier at Seahouses pet. Fish, chips, tea, bread and butter. We don't do posh.'

'I'm not sure it's really posh.' I laughed. 'But okay, we'll go to Seahouses if that's where you would prefer.'

'And Stan and Alex are giving up their seats for us? Are they sure? Seems such a shame, as it's their holiday,' said Meg.

'Stan is absolutely terrified of ghosts,' I said, my fingers crossed behind my back.

'Eeh, is he pet? That strapping young man? Well, I never!'

When we had explained the situation to the others, Stan and Alex had immediately offered to stay behind with Aurora. They had loved their afternoon with the animals and had formed quite a bond with the menagerie, seeing it as an opportunity to help.

'We be security. We have done before when we worked the doors when we first came to London,' said Stan.

'They do not mess with us, these people from the television.' Aleksy smiled. 'We protect Aurora and animals.'

***

My gut instinct about worse to come had been right. On Thursday morning, Zen and I were having breakfast when he got a call from Bert. As he put the phone down, I could see that he was angry.

'What's happened now?' I asked, almost scared to find out.

'Well, no prizes for guessing,' he said. 'Isla. Again. She's just banged on the cottage door and told, not asked, Bert to make sure that the animals are all out of the yard by 11am as she is expecting a delivery, and that the gates will be left open when it's being delivered, whatever it is. Bert is fuming. He'd already let the chickens and turkeys out and the dogs were about to have a run after breakfast before their walk down to the paddocks.'

'She really doesn't get that the yard is just like a farmyard and not her personal space, does she?' I muttered.

When I had arrived on the island, I had learned that the studded arched gates into the yard remained closed at all times, due to animals being loose. No vehicles were allowed, except by prior arrangement, and we used the door set within the gates for entry.

'She must have known about the delivery long before now, and if she'd given him warning, Bert could have delayed letting the hens out. Now he's got to try and round them up and, quite frankly, they will not want to respond because it's not their time for bed. Ellie, I've got to get on over at the roastery and pack up a big order. Do you think you could pop across and make sure they are both okay?'

'Of course I can. I'll just stick a note on the shop to say I'll be back soon. I'm intrigued, anyway, to see what couldn't wait.'

Trying to get the girls back into their run was like a slapstick comedy. I hoped that the poison witch wasn't at that window filming us.

'This way Ellie,' shouted Bert. Then immediately he shouted, 'That way Ellie.'

I shooshed the chickens towards the coop, but two of them decided to make a run for it and ran off in different directions.

'That's Korma, that light one. She's a nightmare at the best of times.' I laughed as she eyeballed me in a chicken stand-off. Tikka, the dark red escapee, was squawking as if she was about to be murdered and was making a beeline for the five-bar gate. Her squawks set the dogs off barking – it was pandemonium.

'Bert, leave it to me. Your hip must be hurting. You go and try and get the turkeys. They'll hopefully respond to the idea of food. They're far too fat and lazy to run.'

132

Sage and Onion were standing in their usual position at the gate looking into the world beyond.

'Okay Ellie, pet. What time is it? How long have we got?'

I glanced at my exercise watch, noticing my heart rate. Blimey, chicken catching was good for a cardio workout.

'Ten minutes Bert.'

Bert managed to get the turkeys locked up, and the dogs settled back down, and I ran around the yard like, well, like a demented chicken, chasing Tikka and Korma who were also demented chickens! With seconds to spare, I managed to get them into the coop with the other three and locked the catch. It was at that point I heard a slow hand clap coming from the far end of the yard.

'Well done, Ellie, that's really cheered me up this morning. The expression on your face was priceless.'

'I could swing for her,' I muttered to Bert.

'Aye, you, and me both, lass, but don't rise. Just let's take the weight off on the bench and wait and see what's so important.'

'Is Meg in?'

'No. Thankfully she'd gone over to the Crafty Lindisfarners' coffee morning so doesn't know anything about this.'

'Good.'

We didn't have long to wait. Isla yelled for Cyril to come and open the gates, like it was way beneath her to open them herself. A large articulated truck from a garden design company was waiting to get in, but there was a problem – it was too high to fit under the arch.

'You said this was accessible missus,' moaned the driver. 'We're now going to have to carry everything in, and it's going to take much longer.'

'And that's my problem how?' sniped Isla. 'Just get on with it. Standing there complaining isn't going to hurry things up. Cyril, I suppose you can lend a hand, but first, find me a chair so I can sit here and give directions as to where everything is going, and bring me a coffee. From a pod, not a jar. Do you understand?'

Bert and I looked at each other shaking our heads.

'That might have been me if they had kept us on; so, in hindsight, I'm pleased they laid us off. That poor bloke. First chance I get, I'm taking him over to the *Crab* to meet the lads, and you lass, can try and encourage his missus to go to the café and find out what she likes to do. I don't want them thinking we are all like her.' He nodded towards Isla. 'This island welcomes all our newcomers, and those poor souls need a bit of kindness shown to them.'

'Like you welcomed me, Bert.' I smiled, thinking it wasn't that long ago since I was the newcomer, and I'd been bowled over by the way I was accepted into the community. And me a soft southerner, according to Maurice.

The chair and coffee arrived, and Isla sat barking her orders. The first item was carried into the yard. It was a huge fir tree shaped into a spiral.

'Put that there.' Isla pointed to one side of the stone stairs, and then another tree the same size was placed at the other side. Then, item by item, the entire back wall of the castle was suddenly transformed into a garden centre. There clearly had been no thought as to design – Chelsea Flower Show this was not. She may have just asked for a couple of every plant they had in the nursery; the lorry must have been absolutely packed. I couldn't imagine how much it must all have cost, and it really was a case of less would have been so much more. It looked awful, tacky, and totally out of place for an ancient castle. Bert's eyes were like saucers.

'Is she having a laugh?' He shook his head. 'I tell you now, firstly there's no sun in this yard other than up at the top next to the gate, and half of those plants she's got there will not survive without it. Secondly, the chickens are going to have a field day – what a place for a good scratch about. There'll be soil everywhere. And as for the dogs, well we've got three that like to cock their legs. Perfect pee station, if you ask me!'

'Well, what do you think?' said Isla, rising out of her throne and surveying the back of the castle. 'Much better. Brightened this god-awful dull space up don't you think?'

'Whatever you say, Isla.' I smiled sweetly.

'Aye missus,' nodded Bert, theatrically doffing his cap.

She was so self-absorbed; she didn't even notice our sarcasm.

'By tomorrow, the chickens will have started on those ornamental cabbages,' Bert whispered. 'And imagine if the catch on the goat's stable accidentally breaks... Nanny and Holly would go at the whole bally lot like it was an all you can eat buffet.'

'Bert. You are naughty!'

'Well, lass,' he said, tapping the side of his nose. 'Slowly, slowly, catchy monkey, but I'm telling you now, if she hurts my Meg, then there will be no slowly about it.'

It was just as well we hadn't told Bert about the washing line or the television company – it would be all out war. A thought suddenly dawned on me. This entire process would have to be repeated tomorrow to make sure the animals were safe when there were people milling around. Even though Stan and Aleksy would be fast on their feet, I'm not sure they were quite up to those wily chickens.

'Bert, you leave everything to Aurora and the boys tomorrow. Don't even let the chickens out. Have the morning off. We have an early start because we are all meeting at the holiday house for breakfast, including you and Meg,' I said, thinking on my feet. 'Tara's cooking.' I laughed. 'Just in case you thought it was going to be me.'

'Grand, lass. We'll take the day off. I'm really looking forward to our day out, and I know Meg is too.'

We met at 8.30am the following morning at the holiday house. Toby was on prep duty as Tara fried bacon at the aga.

'Thanks very much, Ellie!' Tara smiled. 'We had to beg and borrow all the breakfast ingredients, as we didn't have anything other than Cocoa Pops for Jake and Muesli for the rest of us. I'm still waiting for the stottie bread buns; Ethel has a load of them in her freezer and said she would drop them in.'

'It's just stottie, or stottie cake.' I laughed. 'But I get your meaning. Sorry for springing this on you, but we needed to get Bert and Meg away from the castle as early as possible. By the way, you didn't tell Ethel why we needed the breakfast stuff, did you? It will be all over the island if you did.'

At that, the kitchen door opened, and Ethel arrived with enough stotties to feed an army.

'I might as well stay for breakfast, if you're offering,' she cackled, sitting down at the table before anyone got the chance to answer.

'You're looking nice today, Ethel,' I said, taking in her bright blue going-out coat and capacious handbag.

'Well, I was just thinking that I wouldn't mind a trip out to Chillingham too. Been years since I was there, so I'm sure you've got room for a little one.' She grinned.

And that's how Ethel became the third wheel in Ravi the campervan, squashed between me and Zen. It reminded me of when Isla had done the same thing, but I would rather have Ethel any day of the week, even though she didn't stop talking for the entire journey. As we crossed the causeway, a fleet of shiny black people carriers passed us going in the opposite direction towards the village and castle.

'Is something going on we should know about? Those are from a television company, mark my words. I've seen plenty of them when they come to film on *our* island,' said Ethel defensively. 'Any chance of turning around and taking me back? Don't want to miss out. It might be Robson Green.'

'No chance, Ethel,' said Zen, laughing. 'Now have you got any sweets in that Mary Poppins handbag?'

She delved into the enormous bag and began taking out a range of items whilst scrabbling about looking for sweets. There was a hot water bottle, a hip flask containing who knows what—

'Medicinal,' she said, noticing me eyeballing it.

—her Elvis Presley sunglasses, a copy of a magazine called Gangland Gangstas, and a family pack of crisps.

'What's that?' I asked, pointing to what looked like a television remote control.

'That's a ghost detector,' she said, zapping it at me. 'Got it at the car boot sale. If that poor woman is still haunting the castle, then she won't get past Ethel.'

'What poor woman?' I enquired, immediately regretting asking.

'Lady Mary. Her husband Lord Grey of Wark, run off with her floozie of a sister. It's said that to this day, Mary still walks the corridors of Chillingham and can be heard by the rustling of her silk dress as she passes along the corridors on her vigil, praying for her husband's return. She must be bloody mad. If my husband – if I'd ever had one – run off with me sister, he would be the one doing the wailing after I'd finished with him. She's not the only ghost. Some say Chillingham is the most haunted castle in England, and I'm going to find them.'

I looked at Zen and could see he was struggling not to laugh.

'Sweet, please, Ethel,' he squeaked, as she eventually found a giant bag of Wine Gums, which might well have been lying in the bottom of her bag since Lady Mary was alive.

From the exterior, Chillingham Castle was not unattractive. Square and uniform in design, with a castellated roof and tall windows. However, the minute we walked into the drab matt-grey courtyard, it was if someone had trickled crushed ice down my back and I shivered.

'This place looks foreboding,' said Sophie. 'Hope it's warmer inside. I'm not sure I'm much of a ghost hunter.'

We spent a couple of hours going around the ancient building. It was fascinating, and when you learned a little of the history, you understood how it might be packed to the rafters with paranormal activity.

'Here, listen to this,' said Sophie. 'It is said that this really evil guy who was the worst torturer in England worked here and killed thousands of people within these very walls, and that his malevolent dark presence is thought to harm visitors – like us,' she gulped.

It didn't help that Sophie was telling us this as we stood in the torture chamber with a cornucopia of medieval torture devices surrounding us.

'I find this fascinating,' said Tara, with a gleam in her eye. It had been her choice to come to Chillingham because she absolutely loved programmes like *Most Haunted*. 'Look at that rack. Imagine being stretched on that.'

'You can pop me on and stretch me to five foot four inches, if you like.' Sophie laughed.

'You'd better watch your back, Toby mate. Upset Tara at your peril,' laughed Jake. 'She seems to have an unhealthy interest in the afterlife!'

'I don't like it down here; it's giving me the creeps,' said Meg. 'Is the tearoom open?'

Suddenly, the ghost detector burst into life and started to emit a high-pitched squeal which was drowned out by Ethel squealing even louder. I'm not sure which of us jumped the highest.

'Tea sounds like a very good idea,' I said, my heart racing. I linked my arm with Meg and nodded to Sophie. 'Let the Ghost Busters get on with it. They can catch us up later.'

After tea, Zen and I wandered off around the gardens together leaving the others to finish the inside of the castle. His phone pinged.

'It's from Aurora,' he said, reading out the message.

You will not believe how many pretentious arseholes are currently trampling around the yard like they own the place. Just as well me

and the boys are here. Too much to report by text so come to café for drinks when you get back, 6.30. Invite the others and will have council of war. Stanislaw says please bring him back a ghostly souvenir x

'More drama,' I said. 'I was so looking forward to us getting back to the flat for an early night. It's been so full on lately that I feel we haven't had much alone time.'

'I know exactly what you mean, Ellie,' said Zen, putting his arms around my waist and drawing me towards him. 'I love seeing our friends but add that to the stuff going on at the castle with Storm Isla blowing in and uprooting everything, then trying to fit in work around our days out, and I'm exhausted. I was going to work tonight when we get back, but I'll get Stan and Alex to help me catch up tomorrow.'

'Doing the extra hours to help Bert, working in *Love Lindisfarne*, and having the gang here, it's been so full on, and I'm exhausted too. I miss our me and you alone time.'

'Me too.' He smiled taking my hand in his. 'Are we good Ellie? You've seemed a little distracted lately, but I'm hoping that's just you trying to keep up with everything.'

'It is,' I said. 'We're great. And I can't wait to get you all to myself to show you how good we are.' I smiled. It was true, I had calmed down since Isla had filled my head with nonsense.

'You fancy staying at mine tonight?' I asked him. 'Or are you too tired?'

'I'm sure I can find the energy from somewhere.' He winked.

'I'll be moving into yours next week, if I ever find the time to pack. I can't wait to wake up next to you every day.'

'Even when I snore?' He laughed.

'Even when you snore!'

CHAPTER 24

After a pitstop at Seahouses for fish and chips, we made our way back to Lindisfarne. Zen and I dropped Meg and Bert off at the castle where everything looked exactly as we had left it that morning, thank goodness.

'Thank you. We've had such a lovely day. Done us the power of good to have some time away with you young ones. Oh, and not forgetting Ethel.' Bert laughed. 'Pity we didn't find any ghosts, mind, but every time that contraption beeped, she screamed like she was being tortured. It's no wonder the spooks decided to have the day off. Even ghosts would fear Ethel!'

***

We joined the others in the café. By the stony look on Aurora's face, things must have been a little fractious over at the castle. I watched Zen looking at his sister, then our eyes met, and he shook his head.

'I know that face, sis.' He half smiled. 'This isn't going to be good news.'

'Correct, bro,' said Aurora, a large glass of Merlot in front of her – and she never usually drank red wine. 'Listen up. As you know, whilst you lot were having fun ghost busting at Chillingham, me and my two new best friends here,' she smiled at Stan and Alex, 'were keeping toot on the proceedings over at the castle. I tell you what, if there was a choice of being banished to the oubliette at Chillingham or spend a day with Isla, I know which I'd choose.'

'That bad?' I said, giving her arm a reassuring squeeze.

'It was just as well we were here, and you had the foresight to keep the animals indoors. I did as instructed and removed the washing line, even though it cut to my craw, oh and on that topic, what the hell is all that greenery she's had installed? What an eyesore.'

'Then *she* came out,' joined in Stan. 'She look like she on shoot for magazine, and small woman running behind her carrying a toolbox and keep dabbing her shiny face with brush.'

'I'd like to dab her arse with a much bigger brush.' Soph laughed, knocking back her first glass of red.

'By the way, the gates had been left open and just after 10am this fleet of black people carriers arrived, and all these lovies piled out. The big cheese was called Barnaby. We three were sat on Meg's bench – the poisonous cow had the cheek to ask us to leave but…'

'I hold Aurora back.' Alex smiled, 'but I think fight like Alexis Colby and Krystal Carrington good for television, so maybe I should have let go.'

'We love Dynasty,' said Stanislaw.

'So, we stayed put. She took them into the castle first, but after a while they came back down into the yard and started poking about,' said Aurora.

'Then we get up and we go with them. We stop them opening doors to animals' houses. Princess not happy. Not happy at all,' said Stan shaking his head.

'Barnaby Big Bollocks says that he needs to see inside the stables and outhouses to assess how much space there is,' fumed Aurora, taking a big slug of wine.

I glanced at my gorgeous Zen. His usually perfect pale complexion had turned the colour of the Merlot in my glass. He was near combustion point.

'He what? What for?' Asked Zen.

'Well, here it is folks and don't shoot the messenger. From what we gather, this reality telly thing is about a television crew following that bloody giraffe with hair extensions about 24/7 as she settles into the castle, leading up to her wedding to the bloody aristocrat that is Aidan, and she gets whatever title goes with the job. I can think of a few titles myself, but none with which she'd be happy.' Aurora held her glass out for topping up.

'Lady Bamburgh, to be correct,' said Toby, who received a poke in the ribs from Tara for his help.

'Lady bleedin' Muck, more like!' Jake laughed.

'Zen, you and I both know what it's like when they film things,' said Aurora. 'Honestly guys, this island has had more starring roles than George Clooney, and it's chaotic. It's bloody trucks and people with lanyards and clipboards all over the sodding place. It's like a new village appears overnight.'

'That might not be too bad,' said Tara. 'Hopefully, the crew will be far enough away not to bother Meg and Bert, and they won't be filming in the yard, surely. It might be quite exciting.'

'Oh, it can be exciting,' said Zen. 'For all the people who want to go and watch it being filmed. Suppose this might be slightly different as it's reality based and not a drama.'

'Not a drama?' hooted Aurora. 'Everything that woman does is a drama – and where she's concerned, reality doesn't enter into it. Believe you me, this will turn into a circus, and not one that you two can juggle at.' She smiled at Stan and Alex.

'More wine anyone?' asked Jake. 'Guys, try to stay positive. If it doesn't affect Meg and Bert directly, think of the benefits it might bring to Lindisfarne.'

'And they are?' asked Aurora caustically.

'Financial. More tourists means more income,' replied Jake.

'Yes, potentially, but that witch is already planning on keeping visitors in the castle like prisoners until they have to catch the tide to go home. That won't really benefit the village.'

'Not all about money, babes.' Sophie smiled at Jake.

Zen's fingers were frantically strumming on his leg.

'How long is it until the wedding?' he eventually asked.

'Erm, about a month,' I replied.

'Well, maybe we can manage to get through that without any issues, and then they'll be gone,' said Zen, who hadn't watched one single reality show in his life.

'Hello,' said Stan, 'we are up to series thirteen of *The Real Housewives of Beverly Hills*.'

'You what? You mean people keep watching these things?' said Zen, an incredulous expression on his face.

'Yes, like us, we do, and if there is a pantomime dame...' said Alex.

'You mean pantomime villain, Alex!' Tara laughed.

'Yes, one of those. Then people like it even more – can go on years.'

'Well hopefully those two will not be in the castle for years, but what a mess. You got a bottle of hooch stashed, Aura? I need a proper drink.' Zen smiled as Aurora went to the kitchen.

'We need to talk to Aidan as soon as he gets back,' I chipped in. 'You, me and Aurora.' I looked at Zen.

'Okay, tomorrow. If he's back, we get him on his own and see what he's got to say.'

'Agreed,' replied Aurora, who had come back in the room carrying a bottle of the famous fisherman's brew.

It looked like a night of passion with my gorgeous boyfriend might be on hold if he started on the hooch so, in the best tradition of 'if you can't beat 'em, join 'em', I held out my glass as Aurora opened the ancient looking bottle. This situation was more than worthy of a mild hangover.

∗

I woke up the next morning with my head banging like a brass band was warming up inside it. Nacho must have crept up to the top of the bed in the night and was sandwiched on the pillows between me and Zen, who was still out for the count. We were in Zen's attic, having clearly not had the ability to walk the few metres down the street to my flat. We were both fully clothed except for shoes. I couldn't even remember getting up the stairs. As I began to regain consciousness, I recalled the night before, how we had all hit the hooch, apart from Tara, who I think had gone back to the holiday house as soon as the bottle was opened. I remembered us moving the tables in the café and creating a makeshift dance floor and... was I imagining it, or did Maurice appear like the island's version of *Dial a Drink* to deliver another bottle and then stay to enjoy the party? It was all very hazy. I grabbed my phone and there was the evidence. Loads of photos of us, drunk as skunks, but it looked like we were having a fabulous time!

Nacho climbed on top of Zen's head and began to lick him awake.

'Morning,' I croaked. 'Not a good one if you're feeling anything like me. I'm broken.'

'Me too,' he rasped, his voice sounding like he had smoked heavily all his life.

We peered at each other, like two Chillingham Castle ghosts, and both burst out laughing.

'Ellie, you look like Alice Cooper on a bad day.'

'And you look like Captain Jack Sparrow after a bender.'

'That stuff needs to carry a health warning, and I think I only had two.'

'And the rest,' he croaked.

An image of Maurice and the boys dancing to Kylie popped into my head.

'Make it stop,' I laughed.

Zen tentatively swung one leg out of the bed.

'I'll get us some coffee and paracetamol, and then we're just going to have to grin and bear this. Another busy day in paradise ahead. Today we need to tackle Aidan.'

'And tonight?'

'Well, that will be paradise of a very different kind, and that's a promise, Alice!' He said as he swayed off towards the kitchen.

CHAPTER 25

When Zen was almost back in the land of the living, he phoned Aidan, who had returned to the island the previous night. Arrangements were made to meet him in the craft room at the back of *Love Lindisfarne* so I could keep an eye on the shop at the same time. Aurora, however, was in bed with one heck of a hangover and couldn't even make it into work.

I'm dying. I will never drink red wine or that ... even saying the word makes me feel sick! Relying on you two to put Aidan right, sorry, good luck and keep me posted. I might just live xx

When Aidan appeared at the shop, he wasn't alone.

'Who's this?' I asked, looking at the small dog by his side.

'This is yet another of Papa's ideas to turn me into a responsible citizen. Apparently, she's been returned to the sanctuary three times and Pa decided if I can cope with her, I can cope with anything.'

'Do you even like dogs Aidan?' I asked, wondering on the advisability of the placement.

'Yes, Ellie, I do. As you know we've always had a mish mash of canines running around at Bamburgh, and I always wanted dogs of my own... eventually, but perhaps a couple of Labradors, not this erm... she's a Patterdale I do believe and not exactly a looker, is she?' He smiled.

The small wiry terrier looked up at me with almond brown eyes that held the milky bluish tinge of age. She was black, flecked with the grey of advancing years, her muzzle sporting a white beard, her jaw overshot. She was a chunky girl, for sure, who looked like she hadn't had much exercise.

'She's gorgeous.' I smiled, getting down to her level and waiting to see if she would come to me. It didn't take long; she virtually sprang onto my lap.

'How old is she? What's she called?'

'One question at a time Ellie.' Zen laughed.

'She's around nine, we think. No one really knows for sure. She was found in Shoreditch and brought into *Dogs are for Life* but none of her placements have worked out.'

'I like Patterdales a lot,' said Zen. 'They're feisty, with minds of their own, but can be challenging if they aren't in the right environment.'

'You're not wrong there, Chambers. As to her name, Ellie, she was called Duchess up until last night, which I thought was highly fitting considering, well, you know...' He laughed. 'However, Isla has renamed her Swift after Taylor Swift.'

'It's a long time since that dog was anywhere near swift,' said Zen, looking at the rotund animal, whose little legs looked like they might buckle keeping her upright. Duchess Swift seemed to have picked up the scent of Nacho, who was over at the castle with the other dogs, and she sniffed around the floor before dropping down with a contented bump onto the rug.

'She looks like a Duchess to me, the Dowager Duchess of Lindisfarne. It's hardly appropriate to rename a nine-year-old dog, although Swift is quite a nice name – just not for her.'

'That's as involved as Isla is going to get. She doesn't like dogs and doesn't want Duchess Swift here at all – and made that abundantly clear last night.'

'I bet she might have tolerated her if she fit in a handbag and looked cute on Insta,' I said, glowering.

Thankfully, Aidan ignored me and continued.

'Papa will be less impressed if we, I mean, I, don't give Duchess the attention she deserves. I imagine that's part of what Isla is unhappy about. The more attention I give to the dog, the less Isla gets, and she's not at all happy about it,' said Aidan, a deadpan expression on his face. 'I can imagine what you two are thinking. That I shouldn't be taking on a dog right now, and I would agree with you. The timing isn't great, but I'll try my best. I'll take her across to meet Bert and Meg. They might semi adopt her into life with the others and be there for her when I can't be.'

Zen and I both looked at each other despairingly.

'That's not looking after her, Aidan, it's passing the buck. Anyway, why has she been returned three times? Do you know?' I asked.

Just as the words came out of my mouth, the Dowager Duchess let out a spectacular trump for such a little dog.

'Oh my God, open the window!' I gagged. This was almost worse than the hooch hangover. 'Do you think that's why she keeps being returned?'

The only bright side, as we all sat trying to ignore the pungent aroma wafting from the Dowager Duchess, was thinking how Isla would cope with a flatulent Patterdale terrier... not well I imagined.

'Christ,' said Aidan, 'what have I landed myself with? Hopefully, it's only because Rosa and Cyril gave her some Thai food last night.'

'Aidan!' Zen and I said in unison.

'Anyway, I can see that you didn't get me here to talk about rescuing old Patterdale terriers, and you sounded pretty serious on the phone, Zen. So, hit me with it. What's Isla done now?'

Aidan clearly had the mettle of his wife-to-be. I let Zen talk. He put all our worries and concerns over eloquently, but held back on discussing the television show, focusing on the cruel way Meg and Bert had been removed from the role they loved, and how things were beginning to change around them so quickly, to the point that they didn't feel part of the castle anymore.

'Guys, we had this conversation, and I did say that both Pa and I were in absolute agreement that Meg and Bert were an integral part of castle life – and that standing them down from their role was beneficial to them in the circumstances. We hope they can just enjoy time with the animals and relax more until my aunt and uncle get back.'

When Aidan put it like that it sounded so reasonable, but the reality was starting to look a lot different.

'By the way, I had an update on Grace earlier. She's almost fit to fly so they are off to California as soon as they can. Grace is still extremely poorly. Her speech, coordination and mobility have been badly affected, so we are keeping everything crossed that this rehab clinic can help her progress. James is coming up to stay for the night to gather some things soon. I'm sure he will be making time to see Meg and Bert.'

'That's good to hear,' I said, 'but I'm going to be straight with you Aidan. What isn't good is the attitude of your fiancé towards them, Meg in particular. Isla seems to think she is in control of what happens in the yard, and, quite frankly, it shouldn't have anything to do with her.' I mentioned the washing line, leaving open the gates and the animals having to be kept locked up.

I saw a look of frustration pass across Aidan's face. I got the feeling he wanted to agree with me but held back.

'So, you'll tell Isla to stop hassling them?' I persisted.

'Okay, leave that with me, and tell Meg and Bert they are to continue as they have always done. For now, at least.'

'And what do you mean by "for now at least"?' asked Zen angrily.

'Zen, nothing lasts for ever and change is inevitable. Even when James and Grace come home, things will probably have to be different. I do not see this as a permanent arrangement for me. It's certainly not what I signed up for, and I want my aunt and uncle back in their home too.'

'I get that,' said Zen. 'Whilst we are on the subject of change, what's all this about opening a café and gift shop in the castle?'

At the mention of this, Aidan's demeanour changed. He bristled in front of our eyes and suddenly became the Aidan I imagined that he was when battling in the boardroom.

'Ah, Jake and Sophie been filling you in, have they? No secret, but yes, I have been looking at ways of increasing revenue into the castle. What I choose to do there is for me and me alone to decide, and Pa too I suppose. I will not be railroaded Zen. You run your own business, and I'm sure that you constantly think of ways to try and expand and increase turnover. Pa put me in charge to widen my experience of running an estate, and if I feel that making certain changes will benefit the estate as a whole, then where's the crime in that? I've got to prove myself and even though you don't rate Isla, she does come up with some good business ideas.'

And some very dodgy ones like turning the castle into Game of Thrones...

'And please, if you are thinking of running to James about any of this, do remember he's got far more important things to worry about at the moment. This might turn out to be a positive step for us all. It could mean a lot more business coming your way. We would need coffee, for example.'

'At the expense of taking business away from my sister? I've got family loyalties too Aidan. You need to at least consider the estate as a whole.'

'Look,' he said, sounding exasperated, 'I need to do a full business plan which will naturally include all our portfolio across the island. If it concludes that turning the castle into a destination hub offering a wider visitor experience will generate more income for the estate overall, then I'm not going to abandon the idea, nor do I need to discuss it with you. Clear?'

'Crystal,' muttered Zen, looking mutinous.

'Now then, anything else? Because this dog needs some exercise.'

'Yes, there is something else. What's all this about some television company coming to film at the castle?' I asked bluntly, aware that this could be the last Jenga block to topple the tower – but it needed saying.

'And again, what has that got to do with you both?' he said frostily.

'Nothing at all. But it's got plenty to do with Meg and Bert,' I said.

'Look guys, I'll be honest, I'm not involved in that, it's Isla's baby. I haven't even talked to her yet about what happened when they arrived.'

'Well, I'll tell you what happened, shall I? They left the gates open, the animals had to be locked up all day, and your intended was incredibly rude to Aurora and our friends. The programme makers assumed they had the right to go wherever the hell they liked.' I took a deep breath. 'Just in case there's a little bit of you that's actually interested.' I glowered at him. 'We took Bert and Meg out for the day to spare them. That's called kindness Aidan, looking after your loved ones. They are blissfully unaware of all of this at present, because this is exactly the kind of situation that would upset them, and they too have got a lot going on at the moment.'

Aidan appeared to thaw a little.

'Well, I apologise if that was the case. I'll talk to Isla, but once again, I have to say that this could turn out to be massively lucrative for the estate.'

And that greedy cow, I bet...

I saw an expression flit over Aidan's face, and I couldn't quite work out what it meant, but we had touched a nerve, for sure.

'So,' continued Aidan, 'a decision on agreeing a deal with the television company will be made bearing income very much in mind, and if that offends you, I'm sorry, but this is business. I will keep you informed about anything that affects Meg and Bert. Okay?'

'There's far more to life than money, Aidan,' said Zen.

'We have opposing views Zen. I applaud you for sticking to your principles, but you are lucky. You have the benefit of being the captain of your own ship and can make your own choices, whereas I'm only about third mate.'

Aidan stood up to go.

'Now if you'll excuse me, I'll get back to the castle. It sounds like I've got a lot of catching up to do. Chambers, you and I go back a long way, and Ellie, I still think you are the most fabulous elf ever, so please let's try and remember that, eh? I don't want this to ruin our friendship. Look at it from my point of view. I've been given a job to do that I didn't even want, but now I'm here, I need to do it the way I see fit and bring the estate into the 21st Century. If James wants to shove it back in the dark ages later, that's up to him.'

And at that, he clipped Duchess on her lead and strode out of the door.

CHAPTER 26

As the shop bell tinkled marking Aidan's departure, Zen and I sat in silence, reflecting on the exchanges that had just taken place.

'Oh my God.' I eventually found the power of speech. 'That was heavy going and not the kind of experience you want to go through with the remnants of a hangover bouncing around your skull. I feel like I need another drink now.'

'You and me both, Ellie. Can you put the closed sign on the door, and we can go and get a drink upstairs in the flat? Non-alcoholic though. I'm not touching a drop today.'

He drew me towards him and wrapped his arms around me, folding me into a big bear hug. I held him tight, basking in his warmth, breathing in his espresso and pine nut aroma. I kissed him. He tasted of spearmint toothpaste and as he kissed me back, I could almost feel my hangover disappearing like an evaporating mist. We went up to my flat and I made us some tea. Zen didn't even complain, so I guessed he was still thinking about the encounter with Aidan and hadn't even noticed it wasn't coffee.

'I'm so proud of you standing up to Aidan like that. He's a bit formidable when he gets going isn't he? It's all those years of privilege, I suppose, but the way you spoke up for Bert and Meg was wonderful,' said Zen.

'Yep, he went a bit full on Alan Sugar, didn't he? And he's scary when he's in the board room. Pity we couldn't just say "you're fired" to Aidan.'

'True.' Zen laughed. 'Do you think he was okay Ellie? I got the feeling he was troubled about something.'

'Yes, me too, can't quite put my finger on it, but he seemed like he had the weight of the world on his shoulders. He certainly didn't seem to be someone excited about his forthcoming wedding. Did you notice, he didn't mention that once? That's odd, isn't it? Or maybe that's just how the elite deal with things like that, all cold and detached,' I replied.

'He seemed utterly focused on generating income, didn't he? Seems odd to me that he would want to do that as by his own admission he doesn't want to be here long, but who knows what pressures he's under from the family. I actually do feel sorry for him because it hasn't ever been easy for him being the second son, and maybe he just feels he has to prove himself when he has the chance.'

'Did you notice the shadows under his eyes? He looks shattered apart from anything else, or maybe he's just been partying too hard when he's been in London. Who knows? But question is, where do we go from here? I feel awful keeping things from Meg and Bert, even though we are doing it with the best of intentions,' I said.

'Well, he did say Meg and Bert should just continue as normal for now, so I don't see any value in saying anything for the moment. Bert's got his pre-op next week, and his admission a few days later, so let's leave well alone for now. I think Aidan will be true to his word and tell Isla to stop hassling them about the yard.'

'Yes, but will she listen?'

'He's going to come back to us about the television malarkey, so let's just wait and see what he has to say on that front when he finds out more. I'm a little less worried about the café and gift shop. At least he's doing a business plan, and something like that might take ages, so I think we can put it on the back burner. I hope that will alleviate the worry for Aurora and Imogen... for now at least.'

'You're right, good plan. But what about the Dowager Duchess? That little dog has had enough going on in her life without entering the witch's den. I'm annoyed at Lord B for even thinking that it was okay to allow her to go there.'

'Ellie, Lord B probably doesn't know the half. In his view, the dog is going to get a permanent home with his son and new daughter-in-law. Remember, he will have only met the charming Isla and be totally ignorant of the fact that his son is marrying Cruella de Vil. He probably thinks Duchess will be integrated with our other dogs and have the best life.'

'I imagine that is what will happen eventually, but then that's letting Aidan off the hook. He needs to prove himself as a responsible dog owner, but I'm really concerned about Isla where Duchess is concerned. Let's just keep an eye on the situation. I don't think we can take her in with the other dogs just yet anyway. Let's get Bert out of hospital and better first.'

'Absolutely,' said Zen, putting his mug down on the floor. He then took mine out of my hands and put it beside his, before sliding his arm around my shoulders. 'Ellie,' he trailed his fingers down my arm, and my skin started to tingle with desire. 'Shall we go and take our minds off everything and cure our hangovers at the same time? I know a miracle cure.' He began nibbling at my neck and massaging my back with his other hand. Hangover, what hangover? I grabbed the bottom of his tee shirt and began to pull it over his head...

It was nearly teatime before we surfaced, having fallen into a deep sleep after a very pleasurable way to get rid of a hangover.

'Is that the time?' said Zen, falling out of bed. 'Stan and Alex have put in nearly a full day in the roastery covering for me, and they're meant to be on holiday.'

'Chill out. From what I know of those two, they will have been in seventh heaven looking after the place and experimenting with all your different types of beans.'

'That's as maybe, but I've still got to go,' he said leaning over the bed, pulling me towards him and kissing me passionately, before trying to retrieve his clothes which were scattered from the living room to the bedroom.

'Are you sure you've got to go?' I said suggestively, throwing back the duvet. 'We might just need to make sure we've got rid of all that angst. I think I can still feel some, right here.' I pointed towards my heart.

He quickly sent a text, threw his phone down and got back into bed with a huge smile on his face.

'Can't have that can we? Let me see if I can kiss it better...'

CHAPTER 27

The last day for four of the inner-circle — my lovely, lovely friends — came around all too soon. We had all arranged to meet at the café for lunch to decide what we were going to do for the rest of the day.

'I can't believe we're going home tomorrow,' said Sophie. 'It's flown by and I'm not ready to leave you yet, Ellie Nellie.'

'Come here,' I said, pulling her in for a hug. 'I'm not ready to leave you either. It's been so good to have you here. Speaking online is okay but there's no substitute for the real thing, is there?'

'None, Ellie. You know I don't mind telling you that I thought I was going to be bored out of my tree up here. I knew it would be nice to look at, but then what? I'm a convert though. I have had one of the best holidays ever, including that time we went to Magaluf. Can you remember…'

'Stop! I don't want to be reminded. I'm so pleased you've enjoyed it, Sophie. I knew it was a little out of your comfort zone, you being a city chick, but you have really fitted in. Look at you in your jumper and jeans, and you look as gorgeous as you would in a designer dress.'

'Ellie, I love it. I love the beautiful scenery, the castles, but most of all, I like the people. Oh, except the Poison Pylon, but everyone else is just the best. I'm really going to miss Granny Ethel, as well you know. I'm being serious. She is one of the most fabulous women I've ever met and I'm going to keep in touch with her. You'll watch out for her too, won't you?'

'Of course. We all love Ethel. Could you live somewhere like this, Sophie?'

'I'll be honest, probably not. Not yet anyway. Maybe when we're older. Plus, the fact is that Jake is London born and bred, and it was difficult enough moving him from Bethnal Green to Chelsea. I know he's had a great time up here, especially with the boys. It's done him the power of good getting away from the pressure cooker that's the City of London. And as for me, Mr Chakravarti's corns await on Monday – it's straight back to the glitz and glamour!'

None of us had any real inclination to go off the island. We just wanted to spend our last day together, so had a long lazy lunch before returning to the holiday house and playing board games for the rest of the afternoon.

'Shall we all get wrapped up and go down to the beach for a barbeque tonight?' suggested Zen. 'Last supper and all of that?'

'Can't think of anything better,' said Jake. 'Need a hand getting stuff together? I never was that good at Dominoes.'

***

Like a line of sherpas weighed down by gear, we all followed Zen across the dunes to a beach chosen by him.

'Zen, there are much nicer beaches on Lindisfarne than this, like ones with actual sand,' I said, surveying the predominantly rocky beach interspersed with the odd patch of damp yellow sand. The view was special though. We were looking over to Pilgrims' Way, the long, straight line of marker poles connecting mainland to island. How many bare feet had crossed that expanse of seabed over the years, I wondered.

'Have faith Ellie. Trust me.'

It wasn't exactly a warm evening, but the boys had brought a few camping chairs and plenty of blankets, so Soph, and Tara and I sat huddled together, letting them do their Bear Grylls' thing.

'I'm with Tara tonight, not drinking,' I said. 'I can't bear the idea of another hangover, although me and Zen found a rather, erm, enjoyable way to cure it.'

'Ooh, tell me more, Ellie.' Tara smiled. 'Let me experience a sex life vicariously through you. Although, it's not all over for us yet.' She winked.

'Just let's say I've found my perfect match.' I blushed.

'You're happy, Ellie? We all love Zen,' said Tara, huddling into her blanket.

'I am happy. Very.'

'Good. And you're over the slight hitch of last week?' asked Sophie, drinking a cup of tea from a flask, having protested she was never drinking again either.

'Hitch?' Tara raised an eyebrow, not knowing what we were talking about.

'Oh, sorry Tara, you were off with the boys at the dig when we talked about it. I had a little meltdown, stupidly listening to the poison witch that is Isla. I let her get to me and it triggered my trust issues which I thought I'd managed to bury away.'

'Ellie, you have met a wonderful man, and are now living in the most perfect place I think I've ever been to. Enjoy it. You deserve it after Matt, not to mention all those wasted years in Randy flipping Parrot. I've decided I'm not going back. My days of working in public relations in the centre of London are done. I'm going to put my notice in at the right time. I need to look into it, but I've made my mind up.'

'I've never looked back, Tara, and you won't either,' I said, handing her a plate of crackers and dips the boys had somehow acquired.

'Coming here to Lindisfarne has really made both Toby and I think about our future. You know I already said that we were wondering if London was the best place to bring up a child; well after being here and experiencing a much less hectic pace of life, it's kind of confirmed that we want Bee Dee to grow up appreciating nature. We want the big garden, a dog... maybe a pony or even an alpaca.'

'That's sort of wonderful,' said Sophie, a tinge of sadness to her voice.

'Sort of wonderful?' Tara raised her eyebrow.

'I am so pleased for you both, and baby Bee Dee,' replied Sophie, 'but I feel I'm being abandoned. I'm just happy that the boys have opened the Peckham branch of *Island of Beans*, so they can't leave me... yet. Anyway, don't mind me. Where are you thinking of going?'

'We haven't quite got that far, so we may not be abandoning you for a little while yet. There's maybe a bit of a pull to go back to the old Emerald Isle. The Butler and Dunne clans would like to see that happen, especially now they are going to be grandparents. Probably not the best location for Toby's work, although him being freelance, he could travel, I suppose. It's a "watch this space".'

Just before 8pm it became apparent why Zen had brought us to this particular beach. Over to the west, the sun was dropping into bed for the night. The sky had turned to burnt orange which cast a hue over the sea, reflecting the light in golden lines across the calm water. The evening was eerily still and quiet, with only the faint sound of birds as they returned to their homes until dawn. There was all but a gentle breeze, and we were mesmerised, watching nature do what it did best, as it turned day into night, the sun sinking into the horizon like a giant glowing fireball.

None of us said anything, all lost in our own thoughts. What a way to end what had been a wonderful two weeks with some of the people I cared most about in all the world. As usual, island life had been far from drama free, but with the inner circle all being there supporting us, it hadn't been half as difficult to get through. I was going to miss them all – especially Sophie – enormously. I looked around the group staring silently across the bay at the setting sun, immersed in the view. I imagined Tara and Toby were maybe thinking about the arrival of baby Bee Dee. Sophie and Jake about their wedding plans. Stan and Alex would possibly be thinking about world coffee domination with Zen. And as for Zen, I looked at him standing on the shoreline, his long dark curls blowing in the gentle breeze and a faraway expression on his pale face, which almost glowed under the radiance of the sunset. What was he thinking about, I wondered. I know what I was thinking about. Him.

The beautiful silence was suddenly shattered as mobiles started going off.

'Ethel,' said Sophie, looking at her phone.

'Bert,' said Zen.

'Meg,' I said.

'Ellie lass, where are you all? Just get yourselves over to the fishing club NOW!'

Ten minutes later we were packed up and making our way across the island, to what turned out to be a farewell party for the gang organised by our adoptive grandparents.

'Just remember, guys,' I said, 'no drinking the hooch or else you will not be going home tomorrow. And don't be persuaded by Maurice, no matter what he tells you.'

'Jake, you drive, so you drink then you cannot drive and we get to stay,' smiled Stan.

'Don't tempt me mate, but the wheels of commerce keep turning. I need to get back on that floor to kick some ass, and you need to get back to your own branch of *Island of Beans,* to put into practice everything you have learned on this trip.'

'And Mr Chakravarti would kill me if I didn't go back and sort out his smelly feet.' Sophie laughed. 'So, no, Ellie Nellie. No hooch tonight.'

***

'Surprise! Except it's not a surprise anymore,' shouted Ethel, as we pushed our way into the tiny Fishing Club.

'Trust you lot to disappear at the crucial moment,' laughed Meg.

The hut was full of islanders who had come to say a fond farewell to the gang. Those who couldn't fit inside had spilled utside into the cool night air. They were a hardy lot, these Lindisfarne fishermen. Maurice appeared with a tray of glasses and a bottle of the famous brew.

'Drinks all round?' He enquired.

'Not tonight, Maurice,' said Aleksy. 'We go home and need to keep our brains about us.'

'Come on lads, it's your last night,' he wheedled.

But the resolve held firm and we all stuck to soft drinks much to the disgust of him and Ethel.

'This is so cool,' said Stanislaw, looking around the small hut with its range of fishing paraphernalia randomly dotted about the space. 'I think it is the best fishing club I have ever been to.'

'I think it's probably the only one mate,' said Jake, 'but I doubt we'll find better anywhere.'

The lack of alcohol didn't spoil the party. It was just so lovely to see the way our friends had been accepted into the fold.

'To our London friends.' Bert raised a glass. 'Come back and visit us soon, and when you do, make sure you bring some more of that curry!'

CHAPTER 28

As we waved the minibus off, I felt a lump form in my throat.

'I'm going to miss them so much,' I said to Zen, clutching his hand.

'Toby and Tara will be back later; they've only gone to collect the hire car, so we'll still have their company for two more weeks.'

'True,' I said, brightening up.

'Anyway,' said Zen, 'I really must try to catch up at work. All that time off has disrupted my schedule.'

He wrapped himself around me, his dark curls tickling my arm. As I breathed in the familiar scent of freshly ground coffee, I immediately felt calmer.

'We've had a busy, not to mention stressful, couple of weeks, Ellie. Next week looks just as hectic, what with Bert and Meg going to the mainland to get him ready for his op, and us moving into the cottage and taking full charge, so I'm off to the coal face, or should that be coffee face.' He laughed.

Today was my moving in with Zen day. Imogen had returned to the island, as lambing at her girlfriend Harriet's farm was just about over. She had been both happy and sad when I told her I was moving in with Zen, but I was still going to work a few hours a week in *Love Lindisfarne,* so we would see each other often. Easter was almost upon us and always heralded the official start of the holiday season, with the whole island gearing up to welcome the influx of tourists, so Imogen had to be back at the helm of her shop.

'See you later – in *our* flat,' said Zen. 'Let's have a nice meal, just us. I'll cook, then you can choose a film on Netflix, and we can chill…'

I punched him gently on the arm.

'I know exactly what you mean,' I said, smiling, knowing that even if I chose the latest blockbuster, we wouldn't get beyond the first ten minutes!

***

Meg was feeding the chickens when I arrived at the yard. There was no sign of anyone from the castle and the washing was gaily blowing away in its rightful place.

'They get off alright, pet?'

'They did. Oh Meg, I'm really going to miss them, especially Sophie.'

'I know lass, they're such a lovely bunch, but you'll still have Tara and Toby. I do like that young man. He is so knowledgeable about the castle; I think he knows more than us, and Bert and me came here with the Vikings!'

'He's a walking Google when it comes to the history of Northumberland. He's starting on his volunteer dig over at Bamburgh on Monday,' I said, 'so I will be spending a lot of time with Tara, and baby Bee Dee of course, so that's nice, and we can keep in touch with Sophie online. Anyway, we bumped into Aidan yesterday,' I said casually.

'He's back?'

'Yes, came back Friday night apparently. And he didn't come alone. Have you noticed anything?'

'Ellie, you're making no sense. Who was he with?'

'A Duchess no less.'

'A Duchess? Please tell me he's got another woman already. That would make my day if it meant getting rid of that streak of...' Meg gesticulated towards the back door of the castle.

'No, she's way too old for Aidan. She's called Duchess, and Lord B, in his infinite wisdom, seemed to think it was a good idea that Aidan earned his doggy stripes and took care of her. She's an old Patterdale, overshot and overweight.'

'He what?' said Meg incredulously. 'Seriously? He mustn't be thinking straight worrying about Grace.'

I told Meg what I knew about the Dowager Duchess and how Cyril and Rosa had fed her Thai food. Meg was apoplectic.

'Not their fault Meg. They probably haven't got a clue about dogs and were trying their best, but Aidan would have been given his new owner pack like I got with Nacho. It's his responsibility to make sure Duchess is cared for.'

'I'm going over there right now.' Meg bristled.

'No Meg. Please don't. Let me keep an eye on things. I promise I'll talk to the housekeepers and make sure they know how to feed her properly at the very least. Aidan seemed to think Duchess would automatically join our dogs, but I said no.'

'Ellie, why did you say that? We never turn any animal in need away.'

'I know that, but Lord B has given Duchess to Aidan for a reason. Don't forget, Bert is going for his pre-op next week, and you're both going to stay over at your sisters. Now isn't a good time to bring in a new dog, until Bert is on the mend. You know how he likes to manage the integrations for himself.'

'You're right pet, but I'll worry about her now.'

'You leave the Dowager Duchess to me. Zen and I will be around anyway whilst you are away, but just let me know if you hear anything before then, or if anything concerns you.'

'Okay, I will. You promise me, Ellie – if you think that poor little dog isn't being cared for, just take her, will you?' said Meg.

'I promise, but I'm sure once they get a routine established, she'll be fine.'

'And what about madam, is she okay with having a dog?'

'Truthfully? No, apparently not, but she hasn't got much choice.'

'By the way Ellie, we got a text from James. He's coming home on Monday for the night to collect some things, so we will be able to see him before he goes off to America.'

'That's good. Toby had a text from him too. James said he could give Tobes half an hour whilst he's here. They'd met before at seminars or some academic thingies and made arrangements to get together when Toby was up here on holiday. But then, of course, Grace took ill so Toby thought the meeting wouldn't happen. How nice is it that James has found the time, considering he didn't have to, and he'll be so busy whilst he's here?'

'He's a nice man is James. Old school as you young ones say. Pity his nephew isn't a chip off the old block, eh!'

'I'm moving in with Zen later today,' I said, changing the subject.

'Congratulations, my pet. I hope that you are both very happy together. I haven't seen our Zen look so relaxed in a long time, and that's all down to you. He was incredibly sad when he first got back from Brazil. I don't know all the details about what happened. One minute he was due to get married and the next he was back to the island, and we were all so worried about him,' she said, handing me the bowl of eggs as she closed the coop door. I stood rivetted, hoping she was going to say more.

'But we now have our old Zen back, and I couldn't be happier that he's with you. I never met Bethania – saw some photos of her and there's no doubting she is an incredibly beautiful young woman – but it obviously wasn't meant to be.'

I was dying to ask Meg more about Bethania, and see if she still had the photos, but I managed to stop myself. I was better off not knowing, especially if she was so beautiful. Zen had told me as much as I needed to know, and Bethania was now ancient history, on the other side of the world.

'Bert and I decided the flight to Brazil was far too long,' continued Meg, 'and we didn't want to leave the animals. Just as well considering what happened. We'd have got there one day and come back the next. Now don't be telling Zen, but I'm pleased the way things turned out. Otherwise, we might not have got to keep you here.'

Meg set off across the yard towards the cottage.

'Come with me, I've got a housewarming gift for you.'

'A housewarming gift? We don't need anything.'

I followed her into the kitchen as she went to the freezer, pulling out a casserole dish.

'Here,' she said, 'homemade veggie lasagne for tonight. Just heat it up. I'm sure even you two can manage that.'

'Thank you so much. Zen said he would cook, but do you know what? I think this is much safer. And by the way, I'm secretly pleased the way things turned out too.' I smiled, giving her a hug. 'But that's just between me and you – right?'

'Absolutely lass,' she replied, putting a finger to her lips. 'Now go and enjoy your first night together in your new home.'

CHAPTER 29

On Monday, I was working in *Love Lindisfarne* so Imogen could concentrate on a stock check. Hand crafted bunnies, chickens and eggs in soft pastel shades, and bright spring colours, had been arriving for weeks. Knitted, crocheted, felted and all equally gorgeous. At about 11.30am, the shop bell tinkled – it was Linda who was the leading light of the Crafty Lindisfarners Craft Group and also ran the *Crab* with husband Ian.

'Morning, Ellie. There's a few of us coming to help Imogen transform the shop, but we don't come empty handed!' She smiled, holding out a Tupperware box full of gooey chocolate brownies. 'Has anyone told you about the Fete we hold in the pub garden on Easter Monday? And then a few days later, as Easter is so late this year, it's Maypole Saturday on the Village Green – you really can't miss that.' She winked.

'In my diary.' I smiled, thinking how much Tara would enjoy the activities too.

Soon, Linda was joined by Dora, the butcher's wife, carrying a plate of homemade sausage rolls, and Muriel, from the guest house, with warm cheese scones and a tub of butter. Bringing up the rear was Ethel, with two bottles of liquid that resembled blue loo disinfectant.

'Where's Meg?' asked Ethel, delving into her bag, and producing paper cups. 'She not here yet?'

'They're seeing James,' I said. 'Hopefully she won't be long.'

I had felt on edge all morning knowing that Meg and Bert were meeting with James. I just prayed that he didn't mention anything

175

that we had so far omitted to tell them, due to us not wanting to worry them until Bert was fixed. The bell tinkled and in came Meg. I looked at her face intently. She was smiling, which was a good sign, and I felt an inward sense of relief that hopefully all was good.

The little shop was buzzing as the Crafty Lindisfarners set about transforming it into an Easter Eggstravaganza. When the bell tinkled again, I looked up from sorting through a box of the most gorgeous, felted eggs to see Tara.

'I've been abandoned.' She laughed. 'Toby has gone to the castle to meet James. There was no scandal on *This Morning*, so here I am. Room for one and a half more?'

The Crafty Lindisfarners fussed around her like she was the only person on the island to have ever been pregnant, but from what I gathered she was the first to be 'with child' on Lindisfarne for many years, and if there was one thing the Crafty Lindisfarners loved, it was babies. We sat in the craft room at the back of the shop, having lunch. It seemed that everyone was desperate to hear what Meg had to say about her catch up with James – nobody more so than me.

'So, pet,' said Ethel, looking like she had heart trouble, her lips blue with whatever was in those bottles she had brought. No one else took her up on the offer of a drink, which was maybe not a good thing as Ethel would probably sink the lot. 'What did James have to say?'

'The upshot is that Grace needs intensive rehabilitation, but James is hopeful that she will make a good recovery – eventually. As you all know, they're off to that clinic in California soon. I hoped they would be back home in a few months, but James said he's decided to take a year out. They'll be staying on in America even when Grace comes out of the clinic, so they can spent more time with the family.'

'A year?' I gasped. 'Are you okay with that Meg?'

'I have to be, pet. I can't say I relish the idea of having Aidan and her-who-shall-not- be-named as neighbours, but it's done now. They're already in, and there's nothing much we can do to change things.'

'Did you ask him if he had been party to you being chucked on the scrap heap?' asked Ethel bluntly.

'He said that he felt it was a good opportunity for Bert and me to take a rest at the same time as him and Grace. He doesn't see it as being put out to grass, more like an extended holiday until they get back, and he's probably right.'

'And what about Aidan and her? What did he say about them?' asked Dora, on to her fourth sausage roll.

'That's where it all got kind of interesting. James has the best interests of the Lindisfarne estate at heart, and he felt that keeping its management in the family was the most appropriate way forward. He said he was sure that his nephew would do a good job and he had told Lord B that, unless the Vikings invade, he didn't want to be bothered by the day-to-day running issues.'

'Well, if the shit hits the fan,' said Tara, 'all we need to do is find some Vikings.'

'He and Grace have been exemplary custodians of the estate for over thirty years, with you two along their side every step of the way. I, for one, think you all deserve a break to recharge the batteries,' said Muriel. 'But Meg, pet, don't let the new brooms sweep too clean.'

'Like we can do anything to stop them. And anyway, this has given me and Bert a bit of a wake-up call. We aren't getting any younger and maybe it's time that we retired.' She sighed.

'Time waits for no man.'

'Aye, pet, you're right. None of us here are spring chickens, except for those three,' said Dora, pointing to me, Imogen and Tara.

'Hoy, cheeky, I'm only fifty-four,' said Linda. 'Plenty of work left in me yet!'

'You enjoy it while you can, pet,' said Meg. 'In the blink of an eye, you'll be as old as the rest of us. Anyway, James said it wasn't fair to involve himself in the way Aidan chooses to run things and that if he wants to introduce some new ideas then, as long as they fit in with his ethos of the Lindisfarne Estate, he is fine with that.'

'It's a "watch this space" then isn't it?' I said. The Crafty Lindisfarners didn't know the half of it. My gut was still telling me that none of this felt right, and that James wouldn't be halfway to America before changes began to take place.

'Ethel, I'll have some of that blue stuff,' I said, holding out a paper cup.

By the time the shop had been transformed, Ethel and I were cackling away in the corner like a couple of blue lipped crones. Someone had to fill in Sophie's place and keep Granny Ethel company. I clicked a selfie to send to our mutual bestie. Tara was emotional because of all the promises of baby clothes and blankets from the group of warm-hearted strangers she had met for the first time. And as for Meg, well, she was as stoic as ever and happy in the company of her friends. The Lindisfarne Estate could implode, but I doubt even that could take away from the camaraderie between the fabulous group of islanders that I had come to know and love.

CHAPTER 30

'And you're all good to go?' I asked Bert, as he got back in the car after his pre-op.

'I'm tickety-boo, Ellie lass, passed with flying colours. Said my blood pressure was better than men half my age.'

'Don't exaggerate Bert.' Meg smiled. 'But it's smashing to think that in a few days you might have your new hip and be raring to go.'

'Meg, I haven't been raring to go for about twenty years, pet. Don't be expecting miracles.' He winked.

When we pulled up at Meg's sisters in Alnwick, I hugged them both tightly.

'Sorry we can't come in for a cuppa. Got to catch the tide otherwise your pride and joy here,' Zen patted the small 4 x 4, 'might end up waterlogged.'

'Don't be worrying about anything at home,' I said. 'We've got our stuff all ready and will be moving into the cottage as soon as we get back. Meg, just try and relax. I bet Bert might be out the day after his operation.'

'I hope so, Ellie. Now have you...'

'Meg! Everything will be fine. Go and put your feet up, the pair of you. Enjoy a couple of days relaxing with your sister and brother-in-law before Bert goes in. You sure you don't want us to come back and take you to the hospital?'

'No, our Olive and Ernie are going to take us. Let Zen concentrate on work for a few days. He's had a lot of time away from the posh shed lately.'

'Roastery!' Zen laughed. 'Love you both.'

'Me too.' I smiled.

I dropped Zen off at the roastery and made my way to the cottage. I was crossing the yard with our bags as the back door to the castle creaked open. Isla made her way down the steps and came towards me.

'You!' she shouted.

I stopped and looked around me.

'Who are you talking to?' I asked.

'You.'

'Ah, just I can't see anyone here whose name you don't know.'

'Ellie, then,' she said, sounding exasperated. 'Listen, I haven't got much time. Busy, busy, busy. Are the old couple going to be in later? Aidan needs to come and see them.'

'What about?'

'Nothing to do with you.'

I glowered at her.

'Actually no, they won't be in, but me and Zen will. We're staying for a few days, so it's us or no one – take your pick.'

'I'll tell Aidan. Got to rush. Got a meeting online with my wedding planner.'

'Before you go, how's Duchess?'

'Who?'

'Erm, this big, four legs, a tail. The dog.'

'Oh, that mangy old thing,' she said bitterly. 'It ate one of my Gucci slippers, limited edition, and one slipper is no good to anyone, is it? And, that creature stinks, so I said to Aidan it's me or the dog.'

I know which one I would have picked...

'So where is she?' I asked, starting to feel uneasy.

'It's still there, locked in the kitchen – for now. I've told Aidan in no uncertain terms, anymore and it's gone. It can go and live with, er, the staff.' She faltered like she couldn't remember the names of her housekeepers. 'Aidan can claim paternal rights and go and visit it, because for some God unknown reason, he's taken a shine to the flea infested mongrel.'

'She's a Patterdale Terrier, not a mongrel,' I said defensively.

'I don't care if it's won bloody Crufts. It's the ugliest dog I've ever seen.'

'And do Cyril and Rosa know anything about dogs?'

'Quite frankly, I neither know nor care.'

And at that she slammed the door.

I marched to the cottage and threw in the bags, wondering whether I should just go and rescue Duchess right now, however, before I could decide, my phone pinged.

Aidan.

Ellie, as promised I have news on the TV show. Can you and Zen meet tonight to discuss?

That suggested he was indeed keeping to his word, and he wasn't going to see Bert and Meg before he had talked to us, which Isla had implied.

Yes, we are staying in the cottage as Bert gone for his pre-op and staying on mainland until time for his operation. BRING THE DOWAGER DUCHESS.

He replied immediately.

I suppose by that you mean the dog and not my future intended?

I do.

I was tempted to put the dog was far more welcome but resisted.

Ok, will do. See you around seven.

Problem solved regarding Duchess. We would hopefully get the opportunity to give Aidan a crash course in responsible dog ownership and make sure the gorgeous old girl was cared for as she should be, not locked up in the kitchen or handed over like a parcel.

'Honey I'm home,' shouted Zen, as he strolled into the kitchen, a strong aroma of rich coffee immediately permeating throughout the small cottage. It smelled heavenly.

'You've been roasting today, haven't you?' I said, loving the way he smelled after a day in the roastery as always.

'I have. Been trying out some new Guatemalan beans. Super strong yet silky smooth and very, very sexy...' He laughed, giving me a hug and a kiss. 'What's for tea? I'm starving.'

'And I would know the answer to that question because?' I replied. 'WE need to do some shopping at some point, but lucky for us, there are plenty of eggs, and Meg has left us some bits in the fridge, so we're not going to starve. Tonight, we can have mushroom omelette, tomorrow tomato omelette, the next day cheese omelette... or we can go all out and have a full-blown combo for tonight, then hope for the best for the next few days. Anyway, get a wriggle on, Aidan is coming at seven.'

'Aidan? What for?' he asked suspiciously, biting into an apple.

'Got some news about the television show thing, apparently.'

'Suppose I'd better go and have a shower.'

'Have you got to? I rather like you smelling like a quadruple espresso,' I said, cracking eggs into a bowl and beginning to whisk furiously.

Aidan and Duchess appeared just after 7pm.

I had clipped Nacho onto his lead and held him so that we could introduce the dogs gradually, the way Bert had shown me. As Duchess came into the cottage, the two dogs looked at each other, tails tentatively wagging, and I would have sworn that Nacho suddenly had a big heart and arrow appear over his head. I knew that look; it was like the one I adopted when I first saw Zen.

'It would seem that we are going to be in-laws,' said Aidan, looking at the two dogs, who were gazing adoringly at each other.

'Hmm, if only humans got along so well,' I said, 'life would be so much easier.'

We settled down at the table.

'Before I get on to the matter at hand, how is Bert?' asked Aidan.

'Good,' I replied. 'His pre-op went well, and he's having surgery in a couple of days.'

'Great news, please pass on my regards.'

'Will do,' said Zen, 'and thanks for asking Aidan.'

'You might want to refrain from thanking me yet, Zen, as I doubt you are going to like what you are about to hear.'

I could feel my heart pick up pace, as if the finish line of a marathon had come into sight.

'I just want you both to know that this is business, pure and simple. There is no hidden agenda. It just makes good financial sense.'

'Aidan, will you just stop being so vague. What makes sense?' I interjected.

'The television production company have made us an offer that we really can't afford to turn down—'

Another case of money going to money, or so my gran used to say...

'—they want to start in a couple of weeks,' he said cautiously. They'll be following Isla about and filming her up until the wedding in four weeks – not so much me, thank God.'

'Ah well, I suppose it will be okay. If that suits you over in the castle, and you can get things sorted by then, good luck to you. I hope you aren't having to close, though, considering it's just re-opened. I can't see how it can affect Meg and Bert, so I'm sure they won't have a problem with it, will they, Zen?'

I looked at him, waiting for a nod of agreement, but a red mist had descended over his eyes. I had never seen Zen as angry, not even when he had rescued me on the causeway.

'Ellie, of course they're going to have a problem,' he snapped, then quickly apologised. 'We islanders have been around crews filming all kinds of shows, and even movies, over the years. We know exactly what it entails and quite frankly most of it causes disruption of one kind or another. Aidan knows this all too well; they've done lots of stuff at Bamburgh over the years.'

'Oh, right,' I said, beginning to realise that I had maybe been a little premature, if not naïve, in my response to Aidan.

'What size of production company are we talking here, Aidan? Are we going full on film unit, or more travelogue type with a minimal crew?' asked Zen.

'Err, well that's just it,' said Aidan. 'It's full crew. This is a big production, part funded by an American network,' he said proudly. 'They love all the British aristocratic hullabaloo over there, and to throw in a castle, well that's like the icing on the wedding cake for them. This could be huge, and Isla, as you can imagine, is extremely excited by the whole thing. It's the stepping stone into television she's always wanted.'

'Aidan, I'm not bothered if the Vikings and St Cuthbert are teaming up to fund it. I'm more concerned just where you are proposing the media circus that comes along with it is going to be located...' snarled Zen.

And the penny began to drop...

CHAPTER 31

Aidan bristled. I could see that Zen had touched a raw nerve.

'Okay Zen. Cards on table time. Yes, there will be a lot of Motorhomes and other vehicles housing all manner of things. They will be situated here in the yard. It makes perfect sense that everything will be contained near to the main place of filming.'

It was a wonder that my jaw didn't break as it fell rapidly towards the top of the table. Zen seemed to have suddenly taken a vow of silence, but I could almost see the cogs of his brain whirring around as he began to assess the whole situation. The deathly hush in the room was a little unnerving, so when Duchess decided to let out a big raspberry, breaking the stoney silence, it was a welcome relief, albeit a very smelly one.

'You need to sort Duchess's diet out,' I muttered, feeling on much safer ground discussing the dietary habits of an old dog, rather than attempt to tackle the bombshell which had just dropped and had already begun to break my heart.

'Not now, Ellie,' said Zen.

'Erm no, sorry. Just a little bit stressed and not thinking clearly. So, let's get this straight,' I said, returning to the topic in hand. 'What you are saying, Aidan, is that the yard, the animals' yard, Meg and Bert's yard, is to be turned into a caravan site for media workers?'

'Yes, I suppose that just about sums it up,' replied Aidan.

'Ellie,' said Zen, 'here's the reality check. What will happen is that at a given time, all these vehicles will roll up, and the ones that can fit under the arch – don't forget that minor issue, Aidan, unless you intend to knock it down, of course – will take over the entire space. It will soon be transformed into a small media village, with people bustling about looking important, cables strewn everywhere, lights erected, areas cordoned off housing all manner of things needed to run the operation – oh and not to mention the portaloos.'

'And catering,' said Aidan, 'and from what I'm told, they do a mean bacon sarnie.'

Zen and I looked at each other in despair.

'Oh, that's okay then,' said Zen sarcastically. 'Bacon sandwiches all round. That's some incentive to put up with all the upheaval. What planet are you on?'

'We, that is, the media company, will of course compensate Meg and Bert for their, err, inconvenience,' Aidan ploughed on.

'Inconvenience?' I echoed. 'From what I'm understanding, they are virtually going to be trapped in their own cottage. If not, they'll run the risk of tripping over some cable, or will be perceived to be in the way as they are going about their business. Their rightful business, I may add.'

'Well, maybe they might consider taking a little holiday when it's happening?'

'For a month? What you are failing to grasp is that Bert will be recuperating. He may have only been home for a week when all this kicks off. They will not want to go on holiday. They will want to enjoy the peace and quiet in their own home. I can't believe you have the

189

audacity to sit here and even think that this is acceptable in any way, shape or form and present it like a *fait accompli*.'

'I'm sorry, Ellie, but it is a *fait accompli*, I'm afraid. Look, I'll be honest. I can't say that it's something I'm eager to participate in. This is Isla's project. She is the one signing the contract. I'm just a bit part – the posh knob who turns up every now and again to be filmed quaffing port, or whatever they want me to do. I am sorry about the timing. If there was anything I could do to change it, I would, but the wedding is already set, and we can't change that.'

'You could just put your foot down and refuse to do this,' said Zen bluntly.

'If only it were that simple. I can't, Zen. It's far too big a deal.'

'I take it you have discussed this with James. What does he have to say about it?' I asked.

'Yes, of course. We've already spoken to him. Whilst he wasn't exactly thrilled by the prospect, even he could see the long term financial benefits the show could bring to the Lindisfarne Estate.'

My heart sank. I thought if anyone could have stopped this from happening, it would be James, but it appeared that he had given it his blessing.

'This island has done okay up until now; its history sees to that. I don't know why you need to do this, aside from lining your pockets and giving Isla her fifteen minutes of fame. And how do we know this is going to be a tasteful representation of Lindisfarne? This all might backfire if it turns out to be some tacky reality show,' growled Zen.

'It's not. I promise you that. It will be really rather regal. They are ploughing a lot of investment into it. A lot.'

Yep, Queen Isla reigns. Until she's beheaded for treason, with any luck...

'Plus, the fact that my life would be over if I put the block on this. Isla would never forgive me.'

'And Bert and Meg's life will be over too when they hear about this,' I said drily.

'A bit dramatic, Ellie. Let's get real. No one is getting murdered.'

That could be arranged...

'And you never know, they might enjoy the experience.'

'It would appear that even after a few months, Ellie knows Meg and Bert a whole lot better than you do. They won't enjoy it – let's get that clear.'

'All I'm saying is that they might. You never know. And,' he went on, 'there may be some crowd scenes the locals could get involved in. I'm sure some of them would get right behind it.'

'I wouldn't bet on it, Aidan. Not when they hear how Meg and Bert have been treated. If I were you, I'd warn the company to keep filming well away from any locals otherwise they may not get the shots they want,' said Zen.

'Is that a threat?'

'No, of course not. Just a realistic assessment of the situation,' replied Zen angrily. 'Anyway, shall we move on to the elephant in the room? The big daddy of all elephants, or should that be

hickens, horses, goats... which, so far, you seem to have forgotten
ɔ mention.'

I had no idea what Zen meant, then a lightning bolt struck –
ne of those eureka moments that once you think something, you
annot unthink it. Not just pennies, but the entire currency of
urope started raining down on my head. The animals – what on
arth was going to happen to them while all of this was going on?

CHAPTER 32

As the door closed on Aidan, Zen and I sat lost in our own thoughts.

'Grab your coat, Ellie. Let's get the dogs and go down to our bench. I just need to get some fresh air, clear my head, and think.'

'Good idea. I could do with some divine intervention.'

We sat huddled together, hand in hand, on what we now referred to as 'our bench.' Zen had always come here if he had anything to think about, and I could understand why, as it was such a beautiful place for quiet contemplation. It looked out across the bay, beyond Greater Reef with its red and white striped lighthouse and whitewashed cottage, to the expanse of North Sea, lit by hundreds of twinkling stars on this clear, spring night. The only noise we could hear was the ebb and flow of the tide, the faint chatter of birds bedding down for the night and the occasional bark from the dogs, as they ran around the pebbled beach chasing each other.

'Look at them enjoying themselves. They're like a little family,' I said eventually, breaking the silence. 'I can't bear the idea of splitting them up, even for a short while. It just seems so unfair.' And at that, the tears I'd been bottling up since listening to Aidan began to flow.

Zen wrapped his arms around me and a stray tear fell down his cheek too, which I gently wiped away. Aidan had told us that the production company would need full use of the yard during the time they were filming, and that they would be, in effect, renting it lock, stock and barrel. That meant it would need to be completely animal free. Something to do with insurance, or so Aidan said.

'I don't think I've ever been so angry. Not even when I caught...' he faltered, but I knew he meant when he had found his fiancée Bethania in bed with one of his best friends. 'It took all my resolve not to punch Aidan, and seriously, I don't do violence, but I wanted to flatten him.'

'Me too,' I sniffed. 'But and I can hardly believe I'm saying this, I seriously don't think it's Aidan we should be blaming for all of it. He seemed genuinely remorseful, if not just a little bit naïve about how difficult it would be to arrange things in relation to the animals, and not to mention what it's going to mean to Meg and Bert.'

'Ellie, you seem to be defending Aidan. I know you said that nothing had gone on with you and him over Christmas, but...'

I could see the look in Zen's eyes. I recognised it immediately. It was the flickering seed of doubt which I had experienced myself only very recently.

'Hey, as I told you at the time, nothing happened between us other than a bit of Christmas flirtation.'

What I hadn't told Zen was that in a moment of utter madness, I had come very close to sleeping with Aidan.

'I got on well with him and we had fun over Christmas, but that was it. I was only interested in you – and still am. This is stressing us both out, but we need to keep strong, together. I'm not defending Aidan. I wish he would stop this nonsense. But we don't know what is driving him.'

'Sorry, Ellie.' He held me even tighter. 'I shouldn't have even thought that, never mind said it. This is all getting to me. I do love

194

you, and still have lots of those kisses,' he pointed to the star filled sky, 'to claim.'

'And I will be claiming them. I know this is horrible, but all I'm saying is that you know as well as me, that Aidan, whilst a bit of a dick at times, is not really the instigator. There's something going on with those two that we aren't party to.'

'I agree, and maybe it will all come out in the wash.'

'Just not be hung on the washing line. Boom boom!' I laughed, trying to lighten the mood.

Zen managed a brief smile which made my insides flip, and I held on to him, pushing a stray curl away from his contemplative face.

'We'll sort this together.' I kissed him on the cheek.

'We will. Moving the animals temporarily isn't great but is achievable with some thought behind it. What has upset me the most is what all this means to two of the most important people in my world. And for what? So that vacuous, thoughtless, excuse of a woman gets her face on the telly.'

'Not just the telly. Honestly, if this show takes off, Isla will be everywhere you look. If she breaks a fingernail, some trash mag will pay her for the story.'

'Then I just won't look. You can understand Ma and Pa wanting to live the life they do over there.' He gesticulated to the little island. 'Most people think they're mad for choosing such a cut off existence. Me? I'm not always so sure.'

'Before we think about Meg and Bert, shall we just go through the animals and work out a plan, of sorts?' I said. 'It's business as usual for the donkeys and alpacas. They're in their paddocks and will happily live down there. The horses can go into their summer paddock; hopefully, the weather will be kind. I do feel for Stout, though. The old girl loves her stable. Hannibal will protest, but he's bred for the weather in the Shetlands.'

'All sounds good in theory, but we will need to put some thought into how we store the food and things we need to care for them. We'll need some kind of shed on site, if we can't use the yard,' said Zen.

'True. Never thought about that. Then there's the goats. They can stay in a paddock, but we're going to have to sort out a milking area for Nanny. And what about Meg's girls?' I said, meaning the chickens. 'They need somewhere safe they can roam about and be tucked up at night. We haven't got enough space to create anywhere new for them.'

'We'll have to find them a temporary home for sure, and for Sage and Onion. Don't suppose many people will want to take on two old turkeys. There's nothing we can do about the cats. I'm just going to have to be firm with Aidan and tell him that you cannot rehome three part-feral cats. They will have to be left to do their own thing. However, I suspect they may not even venture into the yard with all the kerfuffle, so we'll have to think about how we can feed them.'

'Oh, I do hope Lulu makes herself known.' I smiled, thinking about the feisty little madam, who looked like butter wouldn't melt yet could scratch you before you even knew she was there.

'And that brings us to the dogs – our happy band of misfits,' said Zen, looking at the three of them, plus Nacho, bouncing around the beach. 'Even though I know Meg and Bert will say they can all stay with them, there's not enough space in the cottage for three dogs, especially when Bert will be recuperating.'

'Poor Robson and Tri. They've already been moved out of their home in the castle as Grace isn't there to look after them, and now they will need to go elsewhere. Can we take them?' I asked.

'In our tiny attic up three flights of stairs? Hmm... Robson might be okay, but we will have to find Tri somewhere more suited to his three legs.'

'My head hurts,' I said. 'I'm sure we will find somewhere nice for Tri and the girls.'

'And I'm confident we can sort out the rest in the paddocks, although it is going to mean a lot of preparation, starting, like, tomorrow.'

'Now to the biggie. When and how are we going to tell Meg and Bert about all of this?' I asked.

'As soon as we know Bert has come through his operation and is ready to come home, we'll tell them. Not a squeak before then. I don't want his blood pressure to rise through stress, and I know this will really get Bert fired up,' said Zen.

'It's just as well they're off the island for the moment, out of Isla's way, because whilst I kind of trust Aidan to keep quiet, I'm not so sure about her.'

'Not a word to anyone, Ellie. We owe it to Bert and Meg to tell them first. We've got a week or so to get organised, so we just carry on until then, ordering in what we are going to need and getting things ready. If Maurice or any of the others start asking questions, we are just putting a few temporary measures in place to help Bert with his recuperation.'

'Absolutely,' I said, standing up to go. 'Look up, Zen. See that?' I said, pointing to the candyfloss pink moon in the navy-blue night sky. It will be there tomorrow, and the night after, and the night after that. It's a constant, just like our love for Meg and Bert, and we will get them through this, whatever it takes. Now, let's get that kiss ally down a little, shall we?'

CHAPTER 33

After a sleepless night worrying about what we needed to do, and how we were going to do it, I sat at Meg's bench in the yard with my early morning coffee. Zen had also been up half the night, and, as soon as morning had broken, he had taken the dogs for a run along the beach before he went to work. I was waiting for Maurice to come and help me get the chores done. The back door to the castle creaked open and a fraught Isla appeared, pulling Duchess down the steps, screeching at the little terrier more loudly than a pair of seagulls fighting over a discarded ice cream. Duchess looked terrified. Before I could get to them, Isla had dragged the dog to the door in the gate, opened it and shoved her out, slamming it shut behind her. All the while, she was yelling expletives about how much she hated the dog, how she never wanted to see her again, and that she hoped Duchess would fall off a cliff.

'What the... what did you do that for?' I yelled angrily, far more concerned about Duchess than the poison witch. I was still reeling from the news of last night and she was the last person I wanted to see. I couldn't get any sense out of her as she stood screaming blue murder, tears running down her face. If we were in a soap opera, at this point I would have slapped her hard across the cheek, which was very, very tempting. Aidan, followed by Cyril and Rosa, came running down the stairs.

'Aidan, what the hell is going on? She's thrown Duchess out.'

'She's what?' Aidan looked like he was going to combust. 'Good God, Isla, have you got anything between those hair extensions of yours?' He fumed. 'What did you do that for? Do you know how much that cost? Oh, yes, of course you do, considering you made sure it was the most expensive ring the jewellers had made this year, and almost bloody bankrupted me in the process.'

'Ring? What's this got to do with a ring?' I asked, torn between hearing the end of the story and going to look for Duchess.

'Dog ate ring,' said Rosa.

'She what?'

'Dog ate ring,' confirmed Cyril. 'Miss Isla say she left on coffee table.'

'And my highly intelligent fiancée has just scared the dog half to death. God knows where it might deposit said ring as it's running around terrified, probably shitting itself in fear.'

On hearing this, Isla immediately stopped crying.

'I never thought of that,' she whined.

'You never think, Isla, that's the problem,' said Aidan angrily.

'Far be it for me to interfere...'

'When has that ever stopped you before, Smellie Ellie?' said Isla bitterly.

'That's one I haven't heard since primary school. At least there was no danger of you being called Smiler Isla.' I glowered at her. 'I'm concerned that the ring will damage Duchess internally. It's hardly small, is it? Be like swallowing a giant pebble.'

'Oh my God, you're right, Ellie. We've got to find her and get her to the vets,' said Aidan.

'I'll call Zen. He's out with our dogs and he'll put a shout out on the village group chat. And Isla, just to be clear, we'll be doing this for Duchess and not you or your ostentatious ring. You got that, you poisonous bloody cow? I'll never forgive you for treating Duchess like that.'

This was all for Duchess. It was hard to comprehend that we were doing something to inadvertently help the woman who was systematically destroying life at the castle, but the poor little dog wasn't responsible for that. Cyril and Rosa went off to search.

'Right, where's her lead?' I asked.

'In the kitchen, Ellie. I'm just going to speak to the vets. Isla, you go and get the lead.'

But Isla just stood there like a statue, staring wistfully at the empty space on her hand where her ring had once been.

'I'll go and get it then, shall I?' I muttered.
I ran up the stairs into the kitchen of their apartment and looked around for the lead and some treats. I spotted the chewed Gucci slipper in the corner of the room. What was that catching the light, half hidden in the toe of the slipper? Thank God. It was the ring. Duchess hadn't swallowed it, so wasn't going to need surgery. I pocketed the heavy diamond, grabbed the lead, and went off to join the search. There really wasn't any need to mention finding the ring yet. A little run around the island inspecting any poo she might find, may just do Princess Isla the world of good.

There were people all over the island yelling for Duchess. She was nowhere to be found, and after an hour, I began to get really worried.

'I've been all around the island on the quad. No sign anywhere. She might have fallen into the sea,' said Maurice bluntly. 'She wouldn't be the first.'

'Please don't say that, Maurice. She might have just gone to ground. She was terrified, poor little thing.'

'Ellie, darling, it's not looking good. We put a message out to check outbuildings and sheds too. Maybe someone has picked her up and taken her away off the island,' mused Linda.

'Well, they're in for a big windfall,' chuckled Maurice. 'Imagine when that sparkler comes oot the old poop shoot.'

'Maurice!' exclaimed Linda. 'I've got to go and get ready to open. Tell everyone the coffee will be on. I hope you find her soon.'

After another hour, we piled into the *Crab* to regroup and decide what to do next. On the dot of opening time, the door opened and in came Ethel, with a happy looking Duchess trotting contentedly by her side on a lead made from a silk scarf.

'Ethel, you found her!'

'Found who?'

'Duchess. The dog.'

'Eeh pet, she found me. Is she missing? I was just taking something to the bin and when I got back in the house, this little monkey was curled up on my settee like she owned the place.'

'Have you not seen the village messages?'

'Pet, I'm not like you youngsters, surgically attached to my phone. I've been watching *Homes under the Hammer*. I like a bargain.'

'It's Aidan's dog. She went missing.'

'Is it? Then how the bloody hell did she get from the castle to my house on her own? Mustn't be doing a very good job of looking after her. She's a proper little pet. What you say she's called?'

'Duchess.'

'Have I got to give her back?'

'Yes, you bloody have,' said Isla marching through the door. 'She's mine and she's called Taylor Swift, not bloody Duchess. Now give her to me.'

'Actually, Isla,' said Aidan, 'she's mine and I'll be deciding where the best place is for her – and it won't be anywhere near you, once we get the ring back.'

I'd forgotten all about the ring. I patted my pocket to make sure it was still there.

'We're so grateful. Aren't we Isla?' he said, turning around to look at his fiancée.

But Isla had stormed off back to the castle.

'So, can I keep Duchess? I've always wanted a dog, and she and me seem very well suited. Two hairy old dolls living out their twilight years together.'

'We need to get her to the vets first,' said Aidan.

'Why?' asked Ethel. 'What's wrong with her?'

'She's swallowed yon lassie's ring,' said Maurice, 'and it's the size of a golf ball by all accounts.'

'Err, not quite, Maurice. Let me speak to the vets, Aidan. I'll check what they say. It's been a while now. Maybe it's too late to give her medication to make her sick. They may just say let nature take its course and she looks fine,' I said, knowing full well that the little dog was not in any danger.

'If you're sure, Ellie, I'll leave it to you. Shall we all just sit down, have a coffee and a chat?' said Aidan. 'See if we can decide what's best for Duchess. Mind, Ethel, she has somewhat of an erm, flatulence problem. I'll just put that out there.'

'Well pet, so do I. Better out than in, as me da used to say. Me and Duchess can just blame it on each other. I tell you what. If you let me keep her, I'll bring her poos over to the castle for you to inspect – how's that?'

'I think Isla should do that all by herself. Don't you Aidan?' I smirked.

'Sounds like a plan to me!'

CHAPTER 34

That afternoon, I slumped in Bert's armchair exhausted, with Flo on my feet, and Nacho curled up on my lap. I was just contemplating a little snooze, when my mobile rang.

'Sophie,' I said, grinning at the screen. 'I can't tell you how pleased I am to see you.' I saw she was wearing her navy-blue work scrubs and at once began to feel uneasy.

'How come you are ringing from work? You never call from there.'

'Don't panic, Ellie Nellie. Someone's bunions were clearly not as bad as they thought, so I had a last-minute cancellation. I have news. BIG news,' she said excitedly, 'and I knew you would want to hear it.'

I wondered what it could be. She was too happy for it to be anything bad, thankfully. I'd had enough of that to last a lifetime.

'I'm intrigued. Are Stan and Alex okay?'

'Yes, they're fine. *Island of Beans* has been doing so well since they came home from Lindisfarne full of ideas.'

'So, what is it, tell me...'

'Well, babes, Jake was playing squash with Sebastian the Snout last night. Remember? He's the posh guy Aidan went to school with. Anyway, they went for a drink afterwards, as Jake and him enjoy talking hedge funds and all that guff. Listen to this – it transpires that Prince Bunk Up has been dabbling a little bit too enthusiastically on the stock market recently and has made some horrendous bloopers. He's in a bit of financial difficulty by all accounts.'

'Down to his last million you mean?'

'I don't know, but he's in a bit of a sticky situation, according to Sebastian – been borrowing from the company to cover the debt, and it's all got a tad hairy.'

'Oh my God! Does Lord B know about this?'

'Nope, apparently not.'

'Sebastian was sworn to secrecy but told Jake because he thought he might be able to offer some advice to help dig Aidan out of the hole. Jake and Seb go back a way and he knows he can trust him to keep quiet, which he will, apart from telling me.' She guffawed. 'But I know you can keep this to yourself. Well, maybe share with Zen, but no one else, babes.'

'No, promise,' I said, still in shock.

'Soph, I was going to call you later tonight anyway. I'm not supposed to say anything about this, but you don't count, and I needed to talk to my bestie. I haven't spoken to Tara about it – only because she's on the island, and I don't want to put her in a difficult position. Besides which, we really need to tell Meg and Bert first.' I told Sophie all about the television company's take over, and what that meant for us all at Courtyard Cottage.

'Poor Meg and Bert. As if they need this on top of everything else,' said Sophie.

'He's after the money, isn't he? All kind of makes sense now,' I said.

206

'Sounds like that. It could be his way of paying back the money before he's rumbled, I suppose.'

'What about Isla? I wonder if she knows about this. Maybe that's the reason he's marrying her. She knows his secret and is bribing him, threatening to out him,' I speculated.

'I don't know. Seb didn't say anything about her so I'm not sure. I will see if I can find out anything else. I suppose it's possible, the money grabbing cow that she is. Are you really going to be able to sort all the animals?'

'We have to. Zen's already working out how to manage it all. Trouble is, we don't want to ask anyone to take in the poultry or Tri yet, because the minute we do, the cat is out of the bag. Pardon the dreadful pun.'

'My poor chicks,' said Soph. 'I love those hens nearly as much as Meg does.'

'Yes, Meg will miss the routine with her girls. Anyway thanks, Soph, was good to get that off my chest. Before we go, what's that thing behind you, on the shelf?'

'That was my leaving present from Granny Ethel. Apparently, it's the only thing she ever made at the Crafty Lindisfarners before she hung up her knitting needles. That is meant to be your lighthouse on Greater Reef but it looks more like, well, a phallic symbol!'

'She only goes for the chat!' I laughed.

'You can see why. Anyway, Jake banned it from the apartment, so I keep it here and it's a great talking point with the clients.'

'I bet!'

'We have got Zen's beautiful canvas of the castle and the Northern Lights on the wall, though. It looks amazing.'

'I'll tell him. By the way, you have a rival for Granny Ethel's affections. Sorry but she's replaced you already.'

'What? Who with?'

'Ethel is now the proud carer of an old Patterdale Terrier called Duchess. It's a long story… basically the dog ate the Poison Pylon's engagement ring…'

Sophie's eyes widened like two full moons.

'Oh my God, I need to hear this, but I have to go,' she said, checking the time. 'Call me tonight, promise?'

'Ethel and Duchess are smitten with each other, and after a lifetime of being passed from pillar to post, Duchess has found her happy ever after, but I promise I'll ring you at home tonight and tell you the whole story.'

'Aw, that is so lovely. Right best go. Athlete's foot awaits… my favourite afternoon cheesy delight! Laters.'

***

I then called Meg, desperate to find out how Bert's operation had gone.

'It went well – him and his new bionic hip are in recovery. He's already asking when he can come home,' said Meg, sounding relieved.

'Aw, that is such good news, Meg. Have you managed to get through to Zen? He was acting all mysterious before. Said he had an important meeting to go to.'

'Ooh, maybe he's gone to buy you a present? Or more likely, he's probably off trying to sell more coffee.' Meg laughed. 'No, I couldn't get through, so please tell him as soon as you can. I've spoken to Aurora, though, and she tells me all seems quiet at the castle.'

'Erm, yes, it is. Nothing much to report...'

The calm before the storm...

'That's good to hear, pet. If madam isn't sticking her beak in the yard anymore, then it will be safe to sit outside, and Bert can at least see what's going on in the world. He's not going to be able to get up and down that bank to the paddocks for a while, so at least he can watch what's going on and shout his orders.'

'So, when do you think you might get home?' I asked, trying to keep my voice steady.

'Depends on how he goes when they do their rounds later. Might be as early as tomorrow, but don't worry because I've arranged for our Olive and Ernie to pick us up. I've decided to have an extra couple of nights with them on the mainland so we're nearer to the hospital – just to be on the safe side – before we come back to Lindisfarne. Can't wait to get home, Ellie. Even a few days away from the island and the animals is too many. I hope you can maybe pick us up from Alnwick on Monday morning? That would be good because it would mean I would be able to pop over to the Easter Fete. I've not missed one of those in years. I'll get Bert all nice and comfy and sorted with what he needs, and him and Flo can relax in peace in the cottage. Then I can catch up with everyone and fill them in on the news.'

'Erm, yes, sounds like a plan.' I said, perhaps a little over enthusiastically. 'As soon as we know, we'll be there to pick you up and bring you home.' Whilst I was looking forward to seeing them both, it meant breaking the news to them was imminent. I felt sick to the pit of my stomach.

CHAPTER 35

'Are you okay, Ellie?' asked Tara when we met for coffee on Easter Saturday. You seem a little subdued.'

'Oh, just, you know, it's been so busy lately. I feel like I'm running to catch up with myself. Bert's coming home on Monday. We're picking them up from Meg's sisters at 11am.'

'That's really good news. He came through the operation well?'

'Yes, he did. We Facetimed yesterday when Meg was visiting him, and he looks good.'

'You'll be pleased to get back to your attic. You didn't have time to put your toothbrush in the mug and claim your rights in the wardrobe before you had to move back out again.'

'Yep, hardly the romantic start we'd hoped for when we decided to live together, but seriously, I don't mind. Bert and Meg have been so kind to me. And how is it going over at the dig?' I asked, changing the subject.

'Toby is living his best life, coming back covered in mud every night. They haven't found anything of any great interest yet, but he lives in hope. I'm loving staying on the island, Ellie. Only one more week and we have to go back to London. I can't bear the thought.'

'I feel like I've hardly seen you this week with us being over at the cottage.'

'Well, you'll be back in the village soon. I feel like I've developed a lovely little routine. I pop in the shop and see Imogen, I've started going to Crafty Lindisfarners, and me and Bee Dee like our afternoon stroll around the island with coffee in Aurora's café – I'm almost a ocal. I'm trying to persuade Toby to see if we can keep the house on onger, but it's probably already let.'

'I would love that, Tara. Believe you me, I want to keep you here or as long as possible.'

'Are you sure you are all right, Ellie? You seem very pensive.'

I really wanted to tell Tara what was on my mind, but I had promised that Meg and Bert would be the first to hear the news, so I kept quiet.

'Don't worry,' I said, squeezing her hand. It's just me not wanting to let go. You know how I tend to cling on to things.' I laughed. 'Anyway, are you looking forward to one of the highlights of the Lindisfarne social calendar?'

'The Easter Fete? Toby isn't at the dig so the four of us can hopefully catch up and spend some time together. Will I need to get dressed up?'

'I've not been to one, Tara, but believe you me, most things on the island seem very casual affairs, and if there's not a barrel of hooch involved, then my name isn't Ellie. There's a bit of a fly in the ointment, though. It will depend on what time we get Bert settled back into the cottage.'

'You're picking them up at 11am, you said. That should give you loads of time.'

'Oh well, you know Bert. He will be wanting chapter and verse on everything that's happened, which might take more time, but we'll be over as quickly as we can. Right, best get back. If Toby's at the dig tomorrow and you fancy a walk across, it would be lovely to see you.'

'I might just do that. I'll give my little friend Amelia a knock at the post office, and maybe we can do an alpaca walk, if that's okay.'

'Absolutely – she and they will love that.'

***

'So, you're back from your mystery outing?' I said to Zen, peering around the room for a bouquet or any sign of a gift. There wasn't one.

'Cup of tea?' he asked.

He never offered me tea.

'So, is it a state secret or are you going to tell me where you've been?'

'I've been to see Lord B.'

'Please don't tell me you dropped Aidan in it. Sophie told me that in confidence,'

'What do you take me for, Ellie? As much as I would like to drop Aidan somewhere, I'm not that person.'

'Sorry I shouldn't have even thought that.'

'It's okay. I'm sorry too. We're both under pressure,' he said, squeezing my hand.

'I went to try and see if I could get Lord B to see reason and stop this madness before we have to tell Meg and Bert.'

'That looks like it's going to be on Monday.' I told him the arrangements I had made with Meg. 'Anyway, what did Lord B say? I can tell from your demeanour that it wasn't good news.'

'No, it was not. I like Lord B, always found him to be reasonable, but on this one, he was unmoveable. Said it was good for Aidan to show initiative, that it was only for a few weeks, and he really didn't see the inconvenience to Meg and Bert, even though I told him about Bert's op and how he would be recuperating. He offered to take all the dogs if that would help. I declined his kind offer of course.'

'Would he like five chickens and two turkeys instead? Oh, and maybe an old shire horse who likes being in a cosy stable?' I said bitterly.

'So that's it, Ellie. We've got nowhere else to turn. We are stuck with this. Sorry for snapping. I'm just so stressed, and you telling me that all this madness might be a result of Aidan being bloody irresponsible, gambling on the stock market, has just tipped me over the edge.'

'I'm sorry, too. I suppose it's hardly any wonder we're both tetchy. I met Tara earlier, and she kept asking me if I was okay. I'm finding it hard to relax and it must be showing,' I said, giving him a brief hug. 'I'll make the tea, shall I? At least I would if I could get to the Aga.' I clambered over all four dogs who were taking up a lot of floor space in the small cottage.

'Just felt right to bring them in. Nacho hardly counts. He's not much bigger than a cat.'

'I know there's no way they could all be in here with Bert and his new bionic hip, that's for sure. He'd be bound to trip over one of them. On the menu tonight is either plain omelette, boiled eggs, fried eggs, poached eggs, or, if you really want to go all experimental, some weird thing called coddled eggs. We never did do that shopping.'

'Can we just ditch tea for now?' said Zen, climbing over the dogs and taking the bowl of eggs out of my hands. 'This is our first week officially living together, and it's not the honeymoon period we might have hoped for. We're under stress, not in our own home, sleeping in those bunk beds which must have come out of a doll's house – I was probably eight the last time my legs fit in. I just want to hold you. I miss being in bed with you and spooning, and we're going to be here days yet. My poor back. I'll be crippled by Monday.'

'Having your smelly feet dangling in my face is no joy either. Meg did say we could have their room.'

'No way, Ellie. That would just be wrong on so many counts.'

'Just saying. I agree with you,' I said, as I pulled him towards me, wrapping my arms around him and running my fingers through his unruly dark curls, then letting my hands work their way down his spine.

'How about a massage?' I smiled. 'You feel very tense...'

'Sounds good to me,' he murmured. 'You feel tense too,' he said, his hands beginning to massage my back. As he began to undo the buttons on my shirt, I buried my face in his curls, breathing in the heady aroma of coffee, and all thoughts of eggs and bickering were instantly forgotten.

't's just so good to be home,' said Meg as we went into the cottage. ᴇn was helping Bert across the cobbled yard on his crutches.

'Bloody new-fangled things,' grumbled Bert as he came through ᴛe door. 'It'll take me a while to master the art, and those cobbles ᴏn't help. I'll probably fall down and break the other blooming hip.'

'Don't even joke about it, Bert,' said Meg.

'Right, who's for a cuppa?' I asked, trying to keep my hands ᴄcupied even though they were shaking. I was so anxious about ᴇlling them the news.

'Good idea, Ellie. Bert, before we get you all comfy in your ᴦmchair, can you manage sitting at the table and we can, err, tell ᴏu everything that's being going on?' said Zen.

'Aye, lad, I can manage that and then bugger the chair. I've been ᴦapped indoors for days, so please help me outside on the bench ᴨd let the dogs out. I can't wait to see the old reprobates. Eeh, I've ᴨissed all the brood, even Hannibal.' He laughed. 'Maybe you can ᴦing them all to see me if I can't get to them?'

'I'm sure that can be arranged.' Zen smiled.

'I was going to ask if you could get the table and chairs out of the ᴏuthouse and put them next to the gate so that Bert can see down ᴏwards the paddocks, once he has got the hang of using the ᴦutches on the cobbles and can get that far,' said Meg.

Zen looked at his feet, and thankfully, Meg just carried on ᴠithout noticing his lack of a reply.

'And thanks for the flowers, Ellie,' she said, pointing to the vase of pretty daffodils and hyacinths I'd put on the table.

'You're so welcome. And I've taken a casserole out of the freezer so you can heat that up for tea.'

'I hope that you and Zen helped yourselves when we were away so you didn't have to cook?'

'We just couldn't stop eating the lovely fresh eggs,' I lied. 'It being Easter and all of that.'

I put the big brown teapot and a plate of biscuits down on the table next to Meg.

'Your job to pour, Meg.'

'So, down to business,' said Bert, clearly keen to get outside. 'What's to report? All looks ship shape here.'

'I've got to tell you both something, and I know it's going to be difficult for you. I wish with all my heart I could have made it go away, but I cant.'

'Zen, you're scaring me,' said Meg. 'Make what go away? Oh, good God, are you ill?'

'No, nothing like that. Everyone's fine.'

I could see Zen was close to tears. It was time I stepped up to the plate and got through something difficult without dissolving into a warm puddle for once.

'Meg, Bert... the thing is... Isla is going to be making a television show about her getting prepared for the wedding,' I began.

'Is that all? Good luck to the stroppy madam, but what's that got o do with us?'

'Well, the thing is, it's a big production. There's going to be a lot of vehicles and all the things they need to make the show, and they have… well, they've hired the yard to put everything in so that it's all in one place.'

I could see Bert's eyes clouding over.

'Like when they filmed that drama thing and took over the entire village car park, you mean?' He said, looking directly at Zen.

'Yes.'

'Bloody three ringed circus that was. It was chaotic,' muttered Bert.

'And noisy,' said Meg. 'Winnie Bell, who lived next to it at the time, was demented by the whole thing. Said generators were whirring around day and night. And you say they are going to put all those caravans and trucks in *our* yard?'

'Well, they can't,' said Bert. 'I'm not having it and James would never allow that. I'll call him now.'

'Bert, James has actually said it can go ahead. He hopes it will mean more income for the estate in the long term, and no doubt they'll be paid well by the television company.'

'And how long will this be for?' whispered Meg.

'About four weeks, leading up to the wedding,' I replied.

'And from when?'

'Erm… this Thursday,' I stuttered.

'Thursday? As in three days' time?' gasped Meg.

'Yes. We didn't want to tell you until Bert came through his operation. Believe me, I have tried to stop it. I even went to see Lord B, but no joy. I'm so very sorry. The timing stinks,' said Zen, sadness etched over his face.

'It would stink whenever it was,' said Bert, his cheeks flushed with anger.

'I can't believe it,' said Meg. 'So, *our* yard will not be ours for the next four weeks? It's been bad enough both Grace and Bert being poorly, then getting put on the scrap heap, and Lady Muck,' Meg gesticulated towards the castle, 'and her nitpicking and turning the place into Kew Gardens, but this. I can't believe it.'

A tear rolled down Meg's face. She looked absolutely crushed.

'It's going to be really noisy, isn't it? And we're banned from sitting around the front of the castle. We are going to be trapped indoors. I don't think I can take any more. This isn't feeling like home, and after all the years we've been here,' she sobbed.

'I'm so sorry, Meg.' I could hardly bear to look at the pain on her face and Bert looked like he was going to explode.

'And will someone please tell me what the bloody hell is going to happen to the yard animals during this time?'

There was a silence as I looked at Zen. Neither of us wanted to answer the question.

'We move everyone down to the paddocks,' said Zen, morphing into practical mode. 'It will only require some minor work, and a new storage shed, which I can organise. We'll do all the feeds and mucking out by entering from the gate at the bottom, so we won't need to go through the yard.'

'And my girls?' said Meg. 'They can't run around *their* yard. And what about Sage and Onion too?'

'We're going to find them temporary accommodation, Meg, don't worry. I'm sure we will find them somewhere on the island.'

'I am telling you now, where my girls go, I go. I am not staying in this cottage without them.' shouted Meg.

'Meggie lass, the young 'uns have done everything they can. Don't take it out on them.'

'I'm sorry,' she whispered, before breaking down in tears again. By the time I wrapped my arms around her, I could hardly see through my own tears, which were cascading down my face like a waterfall in full flow.

'Listen, this has been such a shock for you. Coming out of hospital, then facing this, but we felt we had to tell you before anyone else did,' said Zen.

'Well, at least the dogs can all stay together with us,' said Bert.

'You have to be kidding, Bert. How the heck can you manage on those crutches with three or four dogs running around in this small cottage? That's never going to work,' said Meg.

'Flo can stay here with you as normal. We'll take Robson to the attic. Him and Nacho love each other. And we'll find Tri a temporary home. I'm thinking Maurice might take him. He lives in a bungalow so it would be ideal,' said Zen.

'Ideal. None of this is ideal,' snapped Bert. 'Can you imagine Grace letting this happen if she were here?'

'Not in a million years,' I said, 'but, unfortunately, she's not in charge at the moment.'

'I'm ringing James. I hear what you said lad, but I need to hear it myself from the horse's mouth.'

'I understand, Bert. I think you and Meg just need a little time to absorb all of this. It's been a huge shock. Ellie and I will leave you to it, give you time to talk.'

'I don't suppose you want to come to the Easter Fete now, Meg?'

'No, I'm not leaving Bert after hearing this,' she sniffed.

'Do you want us to stay too?'

'No, Ellie, you two go. You've carried this around with you for days. I can see how stressed you both are, so go and have the afternoon with your friends,' said Meg, trying to raise a smile.

'We'll be back at teatime to close down for the night, and we can maybe have another chat then and see how you're feeling. And as soon as you give us your permission, we'll be able to find those temporary homes,' said Zen. 'We're going to take Robson and Tri to the Fete with us. We'll leave Flo with you; she'll be so excited to see you both. Can I do anything else to help before we go?'

Bert wiped his eyes before grabbing Zen's hand and shaking it.

'You've done all you can for us, the pair of you. I really appreciate it. *We* really appreciate it. Now go and have some time away from all of this nonsense, and we'll see you both later.'

We met Toby and Tara at the Fete. I'd been looking forward to it for ages, but now all I wanted to do was go back to the attic and bury myself away.

'This is just gorgeous,' said Tara, looking around the pub garden which had been transformed into an Easter wonderland with bunny bunting and pots of spring flowers.

A small marquee had been erected in case of bad weather, but the afternoon was bright, and most people were sitting in the garden at tables, watching the kids run around excitedly looking for hidden Easter eggs. The Crafty Lindisfarners had decorated the inside the marquee with pastel-coloured tablecloths and jars of daffodils. There was a trestle table to the side with all kinds of afternoon tea treats, and a big tea urn. Another trestle table had been placed at the top of the tent. It had a beautiful Easter flower display in the middle, and a big sign proclaiming 'reserved.'

'Wonder who that's for?' asked Tara, nodding at the VIP table.

My heart immediately sank, although in fairness, it didn't have far left to plummet.

'Let's go sit outside and grab a drink,' said Zen, clutching my hand.

The boys went off to the bar, and Tara removed her sunglasses, staring at my face.

'You've been crying and don't deny it. I can tell, you're all blotchy.'

'Thanks Tara. Say it how it is. You're turning into Sophie.' I tried to smile.

'Sorry, Ellie, but please, talk to me. It's not you and Zen, is it? I have to say, he doesn't look very happy either. Have you had a row?'

'No, nothing like that,' and I began to tell her the whole sorry story.

The boys came back with the drinks, and Zen joined in on telling the tale. Toby and Tara sat listening intently, not saying a word.

'The bastards,' said Tara eventually.

'What Tara said,' muttered Toby, who never ever swore. 'Zen, count me in to help with whatever needs doing. I'm good at building things. Well, if making Billy bookcases from Ikea counts, but seriously, I'll abandon the dig to help.'

'Ellie, you know you can rely on me too. I want to be here for you. I'm not the right shape to do much, but I can offer a shoulder anytime you want to offload,' said Tara, squeezing my hand.

'It's great that you are both here, and thanks, we'll take you up on that,' said Zen.

'Right, let's just try and enjoy the afternoon, shall we? It's the kids' fancy dress next – best chicken costume.' Tara smiled.

'There's Amelia looking gorge...' I tailed off, staring beyond my delightful little bestie to four people making their way to the marquee.

The VIPs had arrived. Aidan and Isla with her parents, Gordon and Elspeth, made their way into the marquee and took their places at the top table.

'Oh my God, look at those hats!' said Tara giggling. 'Where do they think they are, a royal garden party?'

Isla was wearing a yellow dress covered in feathers with a huge matching hat sporting tiny chickens on the rim.

'Bloody hell! It's Big Bird!' Tara squeaked, hardly able to talk for laughing.

Elspeth, sour faced mother of the bride to be, was wearing a blue suit that looked as if it had last seen the light of day in the House of Commons circa 1985, topped off with a bin lid hat covered in pastel-coloured mini eggs.

'Wonder if you can eat those if you get peckish.' Tara giggled, clutching her baby bump, and crossing her legs. 'I think I'm going to pee myself laughing.'

'What on earth was Linda thinking inviting those?' I gasped.

'Linda doesn't know the half… yet…,' said Zen. 'James and Grace always do the honours presenting the prizes, so I assume that it's passed to those two now they are King and Queen of Lindisfarne.'

'Well, I hope they bloody enjoy it because they won't be invited to much more after tomorrow.'

'I wish Sophie was here,' said Tara, 'because right about now, she would be shoving that hat right where the sun don't shine. Princess there would be shitting feathers for days.'

'Don't give me ideas, Tara. You lot better keep her away from me because I can't be responsible for my actions. I'm just nipping to the loo to splash some water on my face and calm down a bit.'

'Do you want me to come with you?' asked Tara.

'No, I'm fine. Won't be long.'

As I came out of the toilet, Aidan was lurking in the corridor looking as shifty as a politician under oath.

'Ellie, Isla and I saw Bert and Meg earlier,' he whispered.

'So, you know we've told them?'

'Oh yes. They made that quite clear.'

'I hope you haven't upset them even more. Bert only got home today.'

Aidan's normally bright blue eyes looked as flat as a navy school blazer. He looked pale and drawn. A man under pressure.

'Listen, I can't talk now, but please, Ellie,' he said, looking over his shoulder to make sure no one was in earshot. 'Will you meet up with me? I really feel I need to talk to you.'

'Me as in just me, or me as in me and Zen?'

'Just you. PLEASE Ellie – and keep this between us.'

'You might be okay lying to your other half, but I'm not.'

'Please, Ellie. 8.30pm tonight when it's dusk, at the Lime Kilns. No one will be about by then.' And at that he hurried back to lord it up in the VIP area.

'Better?' asked Tara, as I sat down.

'Hmm, sort of,' I murmured noncommittedly.

I needed to think about meeting up with Aidan. It was a decision that couldn't be rushed.

Watching Lord and Lady Muck and their courtesans present the prizes was excruciating. Isla hammed it up like she was giving out Oscars, gushing and cooing at the kids yet blank behind the eyes and totally detached. As soon as the prize giving was over, they left. Job done. Box ticked.

'James and Grace would have stayed until the end,' said Zen, on to his fourth pint and looking a little glassy eyed.

'Zen, don't forget we've got to go and close up at the yard later.'

'I'll make this my last.' He smiled.

'Why don't I go with Ellie? I want to help, and anyway, I thought you were considering joining in with the band later,' said Toby.

'Good plan, Tobes. A few bars of 'Fog on the Tyne' and I'll be transported to a parallel universe. Now who's for another drink?'

***

When Toby and I got back from sorting the animals, Zen had finished his set and was in the corner winding down with the guys from the band.

'Was he okay on stage, Tara?'

'They were great. Didn't know many of the songs, but I liked what I heard. Probably did Zen good to let his hair down. Did you see Bert and Meg?'

'Yes, apparently, they tore strips out of Aidan and Isla, and for once, they didn't respond. Well, by that I mean her. She kept her mouth shut which must have killed her. Probably didn't want to risk Meg stamping on her stupid hat.'

It was gone eight by the time I managed to steer Zen up the stairs to the attic. He was very merry.

'Elleee, I love yoooo. You are my missing link... I mean missing half... I mean, I am missing my link without you. I love you more than coffee... even my favourite Columbian with the hints of blackberry.' He grinned. That was possibly the biggest compliment I could ever have received from Zen.

'You just have a lie down on the settee,' I said, pulling off his boots and putting a cushion under his head. He was flat out within minutes as I covered him with a throw.

I glanced at the clock. Twenty past eight. I had time to go and meet Aidan. I didn't have to lie about it as Zen would never know, or now – until I told him afterwards. I wasn't at all sure whether I should go, but curiosity was always going to get the better of any guilt I was feeling. I grabbed my coat, kissed my gorgeous sleeping boyfriend on his windswept curls, patted Nacho who was snuggled up in a tiny ball beside him, and quietly slipped out of the door.

CHAPTER 38

I hurried across to Castle Point towards the ancient Lime Kilns. A sea fret had rolled in, and there wasn't a star to be seen in the sky. The kilns at that time of night were quite foreboding. They were housed in a big stone building to the east of the castle and were once used to produce quicklime. I ran down the steps feeling quite spooked out. The lower kilns had arched entrances and could have been concealing ghosts, smugglers, serial killers... I shone my torch and heard Aidan whisper, 'Ellie, in here.'

I joined him in the cold, damp arch, tucked away from the eyes of the island.

'I could think of better places to meet,' I said, staring at him in the gloom.

'I did think of the rescue box,' he said, 'but knowing our luck we'd get trapped in there. Anyway, thanks for coming, Ellie. I hope I haven't put you in a difficult position with Zen.'

'No, you haven't,' I replied. 'Aidan, I wouldn't have come, but I saw how dreadful you looked earlier...'

'You don't know the half, Ellie. Right, here goes...' He took a deep breath. 'Firstly, I am truly sorry for all the crap that has been happening at the castle. I know it's breaking the old couple's hearts and I understand.'

'So why do it?' I rasped.

'Please can I just try and say what I need to?' He took his Puffa jacket off, spread it on the ground and sat down, leaving space for me. I joined him, keeping as much of a distance as I could.

229

'I'm in a lot of financial trouble. A lot. I've been so stupid and listened to some very bad advice and everything has just caught up with me,' he said, running his agitated hands through his hair.

I kept silent. I wasn't going to say I knew about the stock market and put Jake in the firing line.

'I tried to put it right but couldn't. And that's where Isla comes in.'

'Isla?' I raised an eyebrow.

'Yes, and Ellie, what I'm about to say makes me sound like the absolute shit that I am. I am not proud of myself, but desperate men do desperate things.'

'Oh My God, what on earth...'

'Do you promise me that you can keep what I'm about to say to yourself? Please, Ellie. I really need to offload otherwise I'm going to burst. I've got no right to ask you, but you have a kind heart, and I'm praying you will listen without too much judgement; although, it's no more than I deserve. I know that when I've told you the story you may never want to speak to me again, but at least you might understand things better.'

'Aidan, I can't make a promise about something when I don't know what you are going to tell me. All I can say is that I will listen and go from there.'

'Okay, Ellie, I get that. Isla followed me back to London after Christmas. We had that week together on Lindisfarne, hardly out of bed. I have to say, the sex was fantastic. Call me shallow, but that's what kept me there because, even after a few days, I began to get why no one liked her. Anyway, we parted on okay terms, no promises, no plans to keep in touch. Until she showed up at the London house with a suitcase and a sob story about how much she missed me. Stupidly, I said she could stay for a few days.'

'Mistake number one,' I murmured.

Aidan shuffled, trying to get more comfortable.

'By that point, I was well and truly in debt and frantically seeking ways to raise capital. Maybe I wasn't thinking straight. Anyway, then it dawned on me...' he tailed off, looking out into the murky night. 'My thirtieth birthday is soon.'

'Yes, you said.'

'I get to access a trust fund when I reach thirty.'

'Lucky you,' I said sarcastically.

'The fund was established years ago. It's archaic and the old grey guardians of the trust never got around to changing the terms. The way it is currently set up is that, basically,' he faltered, 'if I'm married, I get double.'

My brain was whirring around like a wind turbine. I was beginning to see what was going on here.

'So,' I chipped in, 'you decided to get married, and who better to do that with, than Isla?'

'Just about sums it up.'

'Does she know about the trust fund?'

'No, not a thing. But Ellie, she's not marrying me for the right reasons either. Isla doesn't love me anymore than I love her. She only loves herself.'

'Two wrongs don't make a right, Aidan. You're as bad as each other. So, you marry her, then what?'

'We get married, the fund gets released on my birthday, the proceeds of which, along with the money from the television show, will hopefully mean I can cover my debts.'

'What? Even with the trust fund you still need that extra income?'

'I do, Ellie. I owe a lot of money. Plus, there's the fact that the show is keeping Isla off my back as she's so focused on herself and becoming the next big thing. I can't bear it, but even though it's being done for the wrong reasons, Lindisfarne Estate will hopefully benefit. They're getting a huge payment for the use of the castle and yard. There's been a royalty clause put in place meaning the estate will benefit financially from the show if it takes off massively, like it might, so income could trickle in for years to come...' He stopped mid-sentence. 'Shhh, can you hear footsteps?'

Aidan jumped up and went to the front of the arch shining his torch.

'No one there. Must have been wildlife of some sort. Ellie,' he continued, 'we don't know how long it's going to take Grace to get back home. Her treatment is costing a fortune, so this is one way of keeping the estate solvent if James has to step back a little when they get back to the island.'

I tried to digest the information, but it was difficult with a numb bum, so I stood up and began pacing around the tiny arch.

'Christ, Aidan. What a mess.'

'It is, but my main focus is paying back what I owe, as I don't want to let…'

I knew he was about to say let his father down but he stopped. The truth was that the Bamburgh Estate was also going to suffer if he didn't sort this mess out. He then began to cry. The Right Honourable Aidan Ettrick Bamburgh, with a backbone of steel, sobbing like a baby. I immediately crouched down and folded him into my arms.

'Aidan, you've been stupid, but at least you're trying to put things right. Tell me though, if you go ahead and marry Isla, won't she be entitled to half of everything if you get divorced?'

'Ellie, I do listen to you, and one of the best bits of advice you gave to me was about getting a prenup, and I have. She'll get very little. Although, by then, she won't be bothered because if this show works out, she'll be raking it in.'

'If she fell in a cow pat, she'd come up with buried treasure,' I muttered.

'And just to make matters even worse,' he picked up from where he left off, 'there was the ring debacle. We still haven't got it back, and because we just moved to the castle, I haven't had time to swap the insurance details so it's not covered. I need to do that show now more than ever.'

I felt my face flush. I'd had my few days of fun with Ethel depositing little bags of poo on the castle steps.

'Err, Aidan, almost forgot.' I took the ring out of my pocket. 'We found it.'

The relief on his face was tangible.

'Thank God. Which end did it come out of?'

'Best not ask, Aidan, but it's been well cleaned so one less thing to worry about. Do you even like Isla?'

'God no, not in any way, shape or form. When I first saw her, I thought she was beautiful. Now I only see her for what she is. That adage about beauty only being skin deep is so true in her case. I believe in love, you know. Okay, so I'm a walking cliché – the man about town – but deep down I want to meet the right one. She's out there somewhere. Do you love Chambers?' He smiled.

'Yes, I do. Absolutely. Although I have to say that all of this stress is not conducive to two people in the early stages of their relationship getting off to the best of starts.'

'I'm sorry, Ellie. He's a good man. Wish I could be more like him.'

'We'll be okay. So, what next?'

'Much as it pains me, Ellie, I have to carry on along this path I've started on. We do the show, we get married, and then the shit really hits the fan, but at least I'll have cleared my debts, and...' he stopped mid-sentence, 'I know it's not of any great consequence, but I have managed to get an increase on the payment to Meg and

Bert for their inconvenience. I know it counts for nothing to them, but it's something.'

Aidan stood up and looked at his watch. 'I'd better go otherwis she'll be sending a search party out for me. Isla would put a tracker on me if she could.'

I didn't doubt that for a moment.

He stood in the archway, zipping up his coat. The moon had jus peeped through the clouds and was reflecting on his desperately sad face. Aidan Bamburgh was a broken man.

CHAPTER 39

When I got to the cottage the next morning, Ethel and Maurice were already there and clearly had been brought up to speed on the developments.

'What the hell is this all about, Ellie?' demanded Ethel as I walked through the door. 'I'm going to go and give that witch a piece of my mind. And as for Aidan, well that's the last time I'll take a drink off him.'

I couldn't help a wry smile. Hell would freeze over before Ethel would turn down a freebie, but she meant well.

'I'm taking yon Tri,' said Maurice. 'Me and Nora will look after him like our own. He can come to the oyster farm with me. He'll enjoy that.'

'And I'm taking the chickens,' said Ethel. 'Sorry, but I haven't got enough space for the turkeys.'

I could see Meg's bottom lip quiver.

'Don't worry, Meg. I'm sure they'll find them a home over at the farm,' I said, trying to reassure her.

'Howay, Meg pet, you can come and see the girls any time and they'll be grand with me. Mind, someone will have to come and sort out the run and my old hen house. Hasn't been used for years.'

'That won't be a problem,' I said, thinking about the list of jobs that needed to be done within the next couple of days.

'I feel bloody useless,' said Bert, propped up in his armchair, a look of abject misery on his face.

The door opened and in came Linda, Dora and Muriel from the Crafty Lindisfarners. Isla probably had a point about everyone on the island knowing the gate code.

'We were coming anyway to welcome you home, Bert,' said Linda, 'but we've just heard the news.'

'How on earth… Ethel, have you…' said Meg.

'Yes, I have. I put it on the village chat. Everyone needs to know what they,' she gestured towards the castle, 'are doing to our friends.'

'Get the kettle on, Ellie pet,' said Dora. 'Let's have a cuppa. I've brought Bert's favourite sausage and black pudding rolls, baked fresh this morning.'

The council of war took their places around the kitchen table. If words could shrivel people, Isla would be the size of a Borrower.

'And as for that Aidan,' said Linda, 'I always thought better of him than this. And to think how we looked after him at Christmas.'

I hadn't stopped thinking about Aidan. The image of him standing in the arch, broken, was imprinted on my brain. Zen had been up early to take deliveries across to the mainland, so I hadn't had the chance to tell him about my rendezvous, but I would as soon as the opportunity presented itself.

'We don't really know what's going on behind closed doors,' I said, struggling to think of what to say.

'Listen pet, they don't need the money. All this is about is her getting her face on the telly, and at our expense,' growled Bert.

I nodded. In my heart of hearts, I couldn't really defend Aidan. He was trying to do right, but only after doing quite a few wrongs. After listening to Aidan last night, I did get that the future income may be beneficial to James and Grace, but that didn't make the current situation any better.

'Well, maybe the treatment in California is costing an arm and a leg and...'

'Do you know something we don't?' barked Meg, cutting me off.

'No, just saying. Anyway, let's just work out what we need to do to get things organised. We can think of what to do to those two later.'

'With great pleasure,' cackled Ethel, shoving in a sausage roll. 'Do you think we can borrow that torture rack from Chillingham Castle?'

***

Later that afternoon, I was back at the attic finally sorting my clothes into the wardrobe. I heard Zen running up the stairs, and he came into the bedroom; his face was like thunder.

'Hey, what's wrong? Am I taking up too much space?' I said, laughing.

He didn't crack a smile.

'Ellie were you down at the Lime Kilns last night?' he asked bluntly.

I didn't know where to look. He had caught me totally off guard. There was only one way to deal with this and that was with total honesty.

'Yes. I was.'

'Who with?'

'Aidan.'

'So, he was right.'

'Who was right?'

'Jack. He took Duchess out for a walk beside the kilns last night and thought he heard you and Aidan talking; although he couldn't hear what you were saying, for which I'm eternally grateful. Top tip Ellie, voices carry when it's a still night. Just for future reference if you're planning anymore secret assignations.'

'Aidan asked to meet me. I wasn't sure whether I should go, but I'll be honest, he looked so miserable yesterday that curiosity got the better of me. You were fast asleep when I went and when I got back, and you were away early this morning. I was going to tell you the minute you got in. And it wasn't a secret assignation in the way you clearly think it was.'

'What am I supposed to think Ellie? My girlfriend meeting not only another man, but the man responsible for causing all the problems we're currently facing and one who she had already had some sort of fling with.'

'Fling? Are we back to this again? I've told you; Aidan and I had a bit of harmless flirtation over Christmas when I kissed him. But that was all, nothing more.'

Zen sunk down on to the bed, his head in his hands.

'Ellie, just tell me what you were doing there, because my head just about screwed. I've spent most of the afternoon ordering ncing and sheds and God knows what to sort the animals out. e've only got a couple of days, don't forget, and I've had it up to ere with bloody Aidan.'

'I'll tell you, but I'm not happy about you immediately jumping conclusions about why I was there. Listen, I know you've got trust sues – so have I – but honestly, Zen, we need to sort this out.'

I was almost talking to myself as, only a matter of days ago, I ad stupidly imagined him making goo-goo eyes at some Swedish rchaeologist he'd never even met before. I was just as bad as him, uth be told. He immediately lifted his head and looked into my yes.

'Ellie. I'm tired and grumpy and sometimes my imagination gets e better of me.'

I sat down on the bed next to him and told him the full sorry tory.

'And he cried? Aidan?'

'Yes, he did. Sobbed his heart out, and I'll just put it out there, I ugged him. He's not coping well, Zen, and whilst I'm not defending vhat he's done, he's paying the price by marrying Isla.'

'And has he got to marry her and do the television show?'

'Yes, according to him, in order to clear the debts and not let it ffect the Bamburgh Estate and face the wrath of his father, he has.'

'I don't really know what to say,' he replied.

'Well, I'll tell you what else he said, shall I? He said he was glad that me and you loved each other, that you are a good man, and he wishes he was more like you.'

Zen's pale cheeks flushed pink as embarrassment crept over him.

'Maybe I'm not as good a man as he thinks. Maybe I'm more like him than I'd like to admit. The way I've just behaved wasn't so good, was it? I'm sorry – so very sorry – but you can imagine how I felt when Jack told me. I just didn't know what to think.'

'I can imagine. It must have looked very suspicious, I suppose. Has Jack told Aurora? I don't want her thinking ill of me.'

'No, he hasn't, and he won't.'

'Well, I will. I'll talk to Jack and Aurora without breaking Aidan's confidences. I've got nothing to hide.'

He reached out for my hand and gave it a brief squeeze.

'Sorry again, Ellie. I'm going for a walk with Nacho. I need to clear my head. I'll collect Duchess and take her too.'

I knew he would probably be going to our bench to sort his thoughts out.

'Okay, sounds like a good idea. Take your time. We can talk more later when we've both calmed down. Now, am I to continue putting my clothes in the wardrobe?'

'I really hope so.' He managed to muster a tiny smile as he headed for the door.

CHAPTER 40

Between me working in the shop, Zen in the roastery and us both spending every other waking moment either over at the castle or sorting out the places we were moving some of the animals to, Zen and I never really got to finish our conversation about our trust issues, but we seemed good, other than the fact we were both just about falling asleep on our feet. I was in the horses' stable, collecting their gear to move down to the storage shed that Zen and Toby had just finished building down in the paddocks.

'I'm sorry you have to go and live down there permanently for a few weeks, old girl,' I said, stroking Stout's velvety soft nose and giving her some carrot. 'You've got a nice shelter and Han is still going to be with you.'

Stout whinnied and nuzzled me.

'What's that you say? You would like to do what to the witch responsible for all of this?' I laughed.

'She's far too sweet an old girl for that kind of thing,' said Zen.

I jumped. 'Oh, you gave me a fright!'

'Ellie, can you remember when you first came and you were giving Han a talking to in this very stable, wearing that big yellow coat and your Viking hat?'

'I can.'

'I thought you looked gorgeous then and you're more gorgeous now, even in Bert's old boiler suit. I do love you, you know. As soon as we get this sorted, let's do something just for us.'

'Sounds good to me. I love you too, and I thought you looked so sexy in your beanie and scarf that day. I'd give you a hug, but you're covered in sawdust, and I don't want to get Bert's designer boiler suit dirty! Anyway, where're we at with things? I'm nearly done here, and the horses are ready to be moved down.'

'Toby is just sweeping out the storage shed and then we can start moving all the gear. The goats and Jenny are now in their new home with their shelter and milking bench all sorted, so once we get these two down, we've just about cracked it.'

'And how are the long-term residents down there taking the changes?'

'The alpacas seemed happy enough to meet their new neighbours over the fence, and it's business as usual for Wonky and Wilma ignoring everyone but each other. Maurice is coming over with the tractor to take the feed down, and a few of the lads from the village are coming across to lend a hand. Toby and I are going to Ethel's later to sort out the hen house. Have we heard about the turkeys?'

'Oh yes, meant to say – there's a trailer coming from the farm, they're going to take them for now.'

'Great. We'll move the chickens in the morning straight from the coop, lock up all the doors, and that's that. By this time tomorrow, this yard will be full of trucks and *very important people*,' he said, his voice dripping with sarcasm.

'I know, it's so sad, isn't it? Meg has asked us for tea tonight. I think we need to be with them as much as possible over the next few days, but I'll tell her you might be a little late if you have to go over to Ethel's.'

'Okay,' he said, grabbing me and purposely covering me in sawdust. 'Gotcha! Right, see you at the cottage later.'

***

The day we had all been dreading had arrived. Zen and Toby had been and taken the chickens over to Ethel's early that morning, and that was it – the yard was clear of any trace of animals ever having been there. The weather was grey and miserable which matched our moods.

By the time I walked back from the paddocks to the cottage the long way around, (as the five-bar gate was now sporting a shiny new padlock) the place was packed. Five dogs, and what seemed like half of the villagers, appeared to be there to support Meg and Bert, and maybe to gather the gossip when the television company started rolling in.

'Cup of tea, Ellie?' Aurora smiled. 'Help yourself to something to eat. We've got quite a party going on here.'

'Just mind those dogs, Ellie,' shouted Bert from his chair, his crutches propped up next to him. 'You don't want to end up with a pair of these by tripping over them.'

'Where's Meg?' I asked.

'In the bedroom,' said Bert, 'putting her lippy on in case she gets a starring role.'

I went and tapped gently on their bedroom door.

'Meg, it's me. Can I come in?'

'Yes, pet,' she said, her voice thick with emotion.

Meg was sitting on the edge of the bed clutching a tissue. I sat next to her and neither of us spoke for a few moments.

'I'm all over the place. I hated the idea of my girls leaving. Oh, Ellie, I know they're only hens, but to me they are my girls. All five of them have their own little quirky ways, and I'm sure they know me, especially Tikka. She was such a funny little bird.'

'*Is* Meg,' I said. 'She still *is*, not *was*. And yes, I do understand. We form such bonds with our animals, and even though I've not been around that long, I love each and every one of them. They're all still with us and will be back. I'm sure about that.'

'I wish I shared your positivity, because I don't think they'll ever be back. Maybe now all the outbuildings are empty, Madam will turn them into shops or something.'

I gulped. I had never even thought of anything like that happening, but now Meg had said it, maybe it wasn't as far-fetched as what it might have first sounded.

'Anyway,' she said, wringing the tissue into a ball, 'some of these tears are happy ones. Bert and I are blessed with good friends, all here to support us through what they know for us is unbearable. Mind, half of the nosey so and sos will only be here to see what's going on.'

'Meg, that's not true. They're here for you and Bert. Now let's go and see them before Ethel finds your stash of cooking sherry!'

The tide went out at 11am, and by 11.15am, the first of the vehicles started to roll into the yard. At that point, everyone inside the cottage went and stood outside to watch the proceedings. A chair was brought out for Bert, and we all stared as motorhomes and trucks were manoeuvred into the yard. A man wearing a black tee-shirt bearing the name of the production company, who I assumed to be the location manager, was frantically running around barking orders into a walkie talkie. Isla made her grand entrance down the castle steps and we heard her telling, not asking, the man to ensure that the wardrobe and makeup vans were parked as close as possible to the castle. Heaven forbid she should have to walk the length of the yard.

'What's she wearing today?' whispered Tara. 'I mean it looks like it cost a packet and it's rather gorgeous, but a Versace trouser suit for parking caravans, really?'

'Oh, no – incoming...' Toby grinned as Isla picked her way across the cobbles in vertiginous silver heels.

'Her falling over would really be the warm-up to the main event!' Aurora laughed.

'What are you lot gawping at? This is now a private space and you are no longer welcome.'

'We're visiting Meg and Bert,' said Maurice. 'Nowt you can do about that.'

'I think you'll find that after today, Dex, Rex or whatever he's called,' she said, pointing towards the man in black, 'will be responsible for the yard and who gains entry, and it won't be any of you.'

Dex or Rex joined us. 'Sorry guys, I'm going to have to ask you to move. Health and Safety and all of that. Don't want anyone getting injured.'

'We bloody live here,' said Bert, frustratedly bashing his crutch on the ground.

'I'll be coming to see you and your wife later this afternoon so we can establish protocol,' said Dex or Rex, 'but for now, if I can ask you all to move indoors and take the dogs away. No animals allowed in this yard.'

'Now there's irony for you,' muttered Zen.

'Come on guys,' said Aurora. 'Let's head back to the village. Bert, why don't you and Meg come to the café? We can take you in the car.'

'No, pet. I'm staying here and seeing what this lot are up to. Me and Meg will see you all later. Thanks so much for coming over, and for walking Flo, Toby. She'll have a nice snooze now. She'll miss her friends, make no mistake about that.'

'We'll be back later to do the lockdown, and we'll bring Robson and Nacho to see you when we're done,' said Zen.

'If they let you in,' grumbled Bert.

'They'll let us in, don't you worry about that. You call us earlier if you need us. Promise?'

Meg nodded looking as if she had the weight of the world on her shoulders. She looked almost too crushed to speak, and I wasn't the only one near to tears as we waved them goodbye.

CHAPTER 41

It was just gone six when we finished our first full shift at the paddocks. I carefully carried the jug of goat's milk as we walked round the long way, up the curved hill to the gates of the castle. Zen inputted the code into the pad and it wasn't recognised.

'They've changed the code,' he said angrily, pressing the buzzer and keeping his finger on it.

'Yes, name,' barked a voice at the other end.

'Zen and Ellie here to see Bert and Meg.'

'Just a moment. I'll see if your names are on the list.'

'Are you kidding me?' shouted Zen impatiently at no one in particular.

'Calm down, they're just doing a job they've been given to do. It's not their fault.'

'Is that Zen Chambers and Ellie Montague?' asked the voice.

'I don't think there are many Zens about,' he replied sarcastically. 'So that must be me.'

The door set in the big arched gates opened.

'Oh my God!' I gasped, gazing around the yard which had been completely taken over by vehicles of one sort or another.

There were a couple of motorhomes immediately outside the back of the castle, one declaring 'Make Up' on the door, the other 'Wardrobe.' Well, at least the poison witch would be happy. There were a few more motorhomes and some trailers up at the top of the yard. In the middle, next to the goats' outbuilding, was a catering truck with a few tables and chairs next to it, the smell of bacon already permeating the air. What was immediately noticeable was the hum of generators. None of it felt real.

'Told you,' said Zen, shaking his head. 'This place will be on the go from early morning until late evening.'

A young woman in a fleece and baseball cap approached us.

'Can I help you?' she asked, hardly taking her eyes off Zen. 'Oh, sorry you *must* be in the show,' she drooled. 'Are you the husband?'

'No, I am bloody not, thank God,' he said, stomping off towards the cottage.

'Don't mind him. You must work with his type all the time. These A listers, eh? Nightmare!' I said, watching her face flush.

We went around a walkway which had been laid to the cottage. As Zen pushed open the door, Robson and Nacho rushed in to see Flo. What greeted us was the sight of two suitcases near the door, and Meg and Bert sitting on the settee with their coats on. Flo was on her lead ready to go out.

'So, they deigned to permit you entry then?' grumbled Bert.

'Just,' I said. 'But never mind that, what's going on? Why are the suitcases there?'

'I'm not staying a minute longer,' said Meg, getting up and heading for the door.

'Whoa, hang on a minute Meg. Please sit down and tell us what's wrong,' said Zen.

Bert shook his head. 'That fellow, me lad, Rex or whatever he's called…'

'Him with the walkie talkie superglued to his hand,' sneered Meg.

'Well, he came over earlier and gave us the buggery bollocks about what we cannot do. There wasn't much about what we can do. So, in a nutshell, it means we are virtual prisoners in the cottage. We can walk around the designated walkways to the gate, or the catering van, but that's it. Apparently, it's in case we sue them for cowping our creels—' said Bert.

'What does that mean?' I whispered to Zen.

'Fall over,' he whispered back.

'—but that's poppycock, they just want to keep us out the way,' said Meg. 'He said we can have anything we like from the catering van – like I'd want to use that greasy spoon anyway.'

'Hey, I think they usually have really good foo…' began Zen, but stopped, obviously realising that would not be what Meg wanted to hear.

'We had to give them the names of regular visitors, so we gave them yours, and they said anyone else would have to be by prior arrangement.'

'I could live with that, sort of,' sniffed Meg, 'but I cannot bear the noise. I can't even hear the seabirds anymore. I used to love walking to the five-bar gate and hearing the sounds coming in from the sea, and from all the wildlife on the islands. This doesn't feel like home and it's not going to work for Bert and his rehab either, so

250

we're going to stay with Ethel. I'm not coming back until this lot have gone – every last bally one of them. Can you take us over in the car please, now?'

'Yes, of course, if you're absolutely sure. Are you sure Bert?' I asked.

'If Meg says she wants to go, we go, lass. And she's right, I do need to be able to get out for walks so that will be easier in the village. I can pop to the café and the pub and Flo can run around in the garden. Better all round,' he said, sounding like he was trying to convince himself.

'We'd both rather be here in our home, but I suppose everything comes to an end,' she said morosely.

'Forty odd year, man and boy,' said Bert, 'and it's come to this.'

We locked the door of the cottage and walked around the designated path to the gate. Bert and Meg looked straight ahead, not turning back once. I drove them over to Ethel's as Zen walked back with the dogs, and not a word was uttered on the short journey. They were both absolutely bereft.

***

'So, Meg and Bert, they move out of their cottage because of this television show?' asked Stan as we all met online for our inner circle catch up.

'That's about the size of it,' I said. 'On the upside, they're settled in Ethel's and at least Meg gets to look after her girls, although I know they miss the cottage terribly.'

'It's a disgrace that they've had to do that though, and after ...rt just got out of hospital. That bloody woman needs to be taught ...esson. I hope the show is an almighty flop,' said Sophie.

There were nods of agreement all round.

'Any luck with finding a job yet, Ellie?' asked Stan.

'Haven't had time to even look,' I said. 'I'm going to do a few ...ifts in the café and I'm sure Zen can keep me in the style to which ...e become accustomed until I find something.' I laughed.

'That won't exactly tax him,' joked Sophie. 'You've taken casual ... the extreme since you got on that island.'

'Once we get Meg and Bert back home, and Bert's back on his ...et properly, I'll be able to commit to more hours. Probably just as ...ell I've got the time to devote to the animals right now.'

'Anyway,' said Tara, 'it's time we had some fun, so we're all ...oing to Maypole Saturday and we're going to let our hair down and ...rget all about what's happening at the castle.'

'And Bert and Meg are coming too, so we're going to make sure ...ey enjoy themselves,' said Zen.

'I wish we were there,' said Aleksy. 'I like letting my hair out.'

'I wish you were all here too.' I smiled.

'It's usually a fun afternoon,' said Zen. 'Starts off with the kids ...oing the dance around the pole, and then later, it tends to ...isintegrate into chaos with a few hairy fishermen drunk on hooch, ...rutting their stuff.'

'I'm not quite over the nativity yet.' I smiled, thinking about how that had degenerated into chaos.

'But you're right, Tara, we all need a break, and everyone will be there. I hope Lord and Lady Muck decide not to make an appearance though.'

Tara laughed. 'I hope not, but if they do, maybe we could use her as the pole!'

CHAPTER 42

It was my turn to go and sort the morning chores over at the paddocks. Zen had gone off early to catch up on his work before our afternoon at Maypole Saturday.

I set off towards the castle, Nacho and Robson happily running ahead past the upturned fishing huts. The island was serenely quiet, and, as I was under no time pressure, I decided to go down to our bench and watch the day come to life. I sat and looked out to sea, a tangerine glow fading on the horizon, the castle perched on the hill to my left. Ahead, in the bay, was Greater Reef, with a cacophony of sounds coming from the nesting birds. We were just at the beginning of the mating season and my favourite inhabitants, the clumsy, comical Puffins had arrived with the hope of making some baby pufflings. I'd been lucky enough to visit the small island the week before with Zen which had been amazing, and when he had told me about the baby pufflings and showed me photos of the tiny balls of the fluffiest down, my stomach constricted into a knot – they must have been one of the cutest things I'd ever seen. The downside of the visit was that divebombing to protect nests by the other bird residents was beginning to pick up and it had scared me rigid. I spent the visit walking round holding a tea tray over my head.

From the bench, there were no clues as to what was going on in the yard. I could only see the front elevation of the castle which looked as magnificent as always, bathed in the pearlescent early morning light. I adored the view, and whilst I was still so angry about what had happened recently, I had to hold on to the fact that in four short weeks, during which time thousands of new birds and mammals would make their way into the world in this glorious location, the crew and cameras would hopefully be gone. Bert and Meg would return to their cottage, our charges to their outbuildings, and we would all get the peace and tranquillity synonymous with our stunning island back.

When I got to the paddocks, I couldn't see anything of what was happening in the yard from there either, but I could hear and smell evidence that the production company had sprung into life for the day. Trying to ignore it, I got on with the task in hand, spent some quality time with the brood, who all seemed quite happy in their surroundings, and made my way back across the island to get ready for Maypole Saturday, which I was really looking forward to.

As usual, the islanders had worked hard to organise the event, a highlight in the Lindisfarne social calendar. A maypole had been erected on the village green. It towered like a ship's mast and was bound in yellow and red ribbons to celebrate the Northumberland flag. Tables and chairs spilled out of the village hall, where the temporary bar had been set up, and as usual, there was enough home baked food to feed an army. There was the addition of a converted caravan selling hot food, the aromas from which would give the catering van in the castle yard a run for its money. A small area for the band had been kept clear. I was beginning to learn that it was always the same few musicians who kept us entertained at all the island events, with Zen joining in when he felt like it, but it seemed they had quite a lengthy repertoire.

'This is so cute,' said Tara, taking her seat at a trestle table where we could all sit together. 'How many of these have you been to, Meg?' she asked, as Meg flapped around getting Bert comfortable.

'More than I care to recall, pet. The set up hasn't changed that much over the years to tell the truth, maybe the band playing through electricity and being able to get a pizza from a caravan, but otherwise...'

'You pleased you came, Meg?' I asked, knowing that right up to the last minute she had said she didn't want to come.

Meg and Bert had been staying with Ethel for a few days, and whilst it was working out well in many ways – Meg had her girls, they got to see all the dogs, and Bert was managing so much better on his crutches making it as far as the *Crab* – they naturally missed their home and were desperate to return.

'I am pleased we came, Ellie. I'm a daft bat, aren't I? So, this afternoon can we all just have a good old island knees-up? Not you mind, Bert pet. You'll do yourself an injury on those crutches.'

'We can indeed,' I replied, feeling the most relaxed I had in days.

'I'll drink to that,' said Ethel. 'I wish me grand bairn was here though. She would have loved this.'

'She would, Ethel. Let's Facetime Sophie later,' I said.

Watching the kids dancing around the pole in a haphazard fashion was such a tonic. Their little faces were furrowed in concentration as Miss Brown, their teacher, hissed instructions at them before they got totally tied up in a knot. When they had finished, Amelia skipped over, her big brother William following her.

'Did I do well?' She grinned at everyone on the table.

'Amazing,' I said. 'You'll be on *Strictly* soon.'

'He,' she said pointing to Tara's bump, 'will be doing this when he's big enough.'

'He will?'

'Yes, all the children on the island do, but he will have to learn to walk first I suppose.'

'I suppose,' said Tara, laughing.

'She's really sure it will be a boy, isn't she? And that he is going to be living on the island,' Tara whispered in my ear. 'Is she like the Wednesday Addams of Lindisfarne or some junior soothsayer? She's convinced me I'm having a boy.'

'You and William go and see Pip,' said Aurora. 'She's looking after the café this afternoon. Tell her I said you could both choose an ice cream.'

And they were off like a rocket.

The band made their way to the corner for the first set of the day.

'You joining in today, rock star?'

'You know what, I'm feeling mellow today,' said my handsome boyfriend, 'so I think I will.' He went and joined the others on stage – if a patch of grass could be referred to as that. I looked at him as he tuned up his guitar, before tucking his wayward hair behind his ears to keep it out of his eyes. My stomach did its customary flip. I was in lust. Zen in a vintage band tee shirt and tight black jeans was every inch the rock god of Lindisfarne, and the best bit was, I'd be going home with him later. The band started with a Beatles medley d soon people were dancing around the grass and singing along the well-known songs.

'This is such good fun,' said Toby. 'We've had a wonderful time the island, haven't we Tara? Even though I found nothing more citing than a few common coins at the dig.'

'We have,' she agreed. 'I seriously don't want to leave. So much that we've got BIG news, Ellie.'

I saw a look of pure excitement pass between her and Toby.

'Toby and I have booked the holiday house for another month.'

'Woo hoo! That's great. I'm surprised it was available though.'

'Well, that's the really exciting bit,' said Toby.

'Ooh do go on,' I replied, agog with interest.

'Muriel hadn't taken any more bookings because she is nsidering selling the house. She feels it's too much for her to look ter these days, so we have been talking to her about buying it.'

'You what? Tara you dark horse,' I screeched, throwing my arms ound her, big bump, and all.

'Calm down, Ellie Nellie. It's not a given. There's a way to go, but uriel is agreeable in principal. We need to sort out our house in ndon, not to mention my job and all of that, but we are both osolutely serious that we want to live on the island.'

'Well, if this comes off it means that Amelia was right. Maybe e can predict the future after all.'

'Eeh pet, that's fabulous news,' said Meg. 'Just think, a new baby on the island. Now that is something that we will celebrate when the time comes.'

'Too right,' I said. 'Tara, Toby and not forgetting baby Bee Dee, you have all made my day and I hope that everything falls into place, so here's to new beginnings.' I raised my glass of Prosecco.

'New beginnings,' said Ethel. 'I'll drink to that.'

'I hope it all works out for you,' said Bert. 'And that you have as happy a time on the island as me and my Meg. I can't wish you any more than that.'

The band were halfway through 'Ticket To Ride' when Aidan, Isla and a group of people I assumed to be her posse from the television show, appeared.

'Here we go… trouble ahead,' muttered Aurora.

'Bert and I have had a word with as many people as we could and made it clear that we don't want any trouble. Today is all about us having fun as an island. Just let them get on with it. They'll be bored soon enough – won't be posh enough for the likes of them.'

When the islanders had found out that Meg and Bert had left their cottage because of events at the castle, feelings had run high. They were island stalwarts and very popular amongst the small community, who protected their own.

'Well, I hope they choose to go before the hooch comes out, that's all I can say,' said Bert. 'Some of the fishermen will take no prisoners with the likes of that London lot.'

'Might be fun!' Tara laughed.

But my attention was focussed on the band, because there right in front of them in what might pass as the VIP area, swaying about in time to the music, was the girl with the baseball cap we had met at the castle gate, and she was absolutely rivetted on Zen.

'Zen's got a groupie!' howled Tara. 'And I see the Poison Pylon has gone for designer rock chick today. Have you seen the bling on those jeans?'

'Pity they need a damn good darn around the knees,' tutted Meg.

'Hope they're not filming today – especially later – we would look like a right bunch of hicks from the sticks!' Aurora laughed.

'That's because we are,' hiccupped Ethel.

'Can't see any evidence of them doing that, and I'm sure that somewhere along the line I was told they were starting on Monday,' I said.

The band carried on playing popular rock songs, and more and more people were up dancing. The castle posse kept a respectable distance and seemed to be enjoying the afternoon. All was going well until Zen ruined 'Mr Blue Sky' with a completely bum note which was totally out of character for him. He immediately stopped playing, dropping his guitar on its strap where it hung on his hip, his eyes totally fixed on the rear of the village green. He looked like he had seen a ghost. It seemed like everyone then turned to look to see what had captured his attention.

And there she was...

CHAPTER 43

'Oh my God,' said Aurora. 'It's Bethania.'

Even though I had never seen her before, I knew who it was the minute I laid eyes on her. Everything suddenly seemed to be moving in slow motion. Zen remained like a statue on the makeshift stage as the band played on without him, but no one was taking any notice, all preferring to look at the beautiful stranger who had arrived at the party.

Bethania was stunning. She put the *voom* into *va va voom*. Her outfit, a white Bardot top and tight skinny jeans, emphasised her voluptuous curves. She was wearing simple silver jewellery and what looked like little make up, except for a pop of pillar box red lipstick on her generous mouth. Huge sunglasses perched on top of a mass of dark tumbling hair and a pair of sparkly red sliders finished off her ensemble. Bethania was as hot as hell and very, very sexy.

'What do we do now?' hissed Meg to Aurora

'I think I need to go and try and move Zen off that stage before he turns to stone,' replied Aurora.

'Now there's a bonny lass and no mistaking,' said Maurice, his eyeballs almost hanging out of their sockets like a pair of golf balls on springs.

'Who is that gorgeous creature?' asked Tara.

'Zen's ex from Brazil,' I said in a whisper.

'No way. Now I wish they had the cameras here today. Have you seen Lady Muck's face? It's priceless. She looks as jealous as hell.

ot to mention her future intended. He can't keep his eyes off the woman. We'd be able to wrap his tongue around that maypole, it's anging out so much.'

'I can understand why,' I said, feeling more than a little auseous. What on earth was she doing here?

Aurora rushed over towards Zen and beckoned him off the nakeshift stage, where she took the guitar from him and carefully aid it down on a nearby table before pulling him towards the door of the village hall. Bethania stayed still, smiling, her hands on her ips, watching the proceedings. Aidan, assuming his Lord of the Manor role, no doubt, began to get up from his chair, but was quickly yanked back by Isla whose scowling face would have turned he tide. Then one of the other guys from their party, who I had gleaned was Barnaby, the producer of the show, was off like Usain Bolt towards the beautiful Bethania. Aidan broke free and the pair of them made a beeline for Beth like they were in an Olympic sprint, ending in a photo finish. It would have all been so comical had it not been so blooming tragic.

Aidan and Barnaby were talking with Beth who was miming someone playing a guitar and pointing towards the now empty stage area. She then followed them back to their table where Barnaby handed her a glass and Aidan filled it with Champagne.

'They didn't buy that in the village hall,' said Ethel, copping the bottle. 'Look, they've got a crate of the stuff under their table.'

Isla had her hand, sporting the ostentatious ring, spread flat out on the table, where it caught the light and dazzled enough to blind. There was zero chance of Bethania not seeing it, which would have been Isla's exact intention. I just wanted Zen to come out of the hall, give me a hug and tell me everything was going to be okay. However, when Aurora eventually emerged followed by Zen, he strode straight past our table towards Bethania, not even glancing at me.

I could feel my eyes burning with hot tears that were about to break the floodgates, and Meg grabbed my hand under the table.

'Ellie lass, he's probably in shock. He hasn't seen her in... what must it be... well, at least three years since he walked out on the eve of the wedding. I don't think they've spoken since.'

Aurora sat back down looking ashen faced.

'He's in a right state. Was the last thing he ever expected to happen, and he's not too sure how to deal with it. He's going to talk to her and find out why she's here. He didn't even want to do that, Ellie; he was just going to go and do his usual and hide away, but that wouldn't have worked, so I've persuaded him to face this head on. Ellie, try not to worry. He'll never go back to her, if that thought has crossed your mind.'

Crossed my mind? Only about a hundred times since she appeared.

I watched Zen approach the castle posse's table, from where all eyes had transferred from Bethania to him. She stood up, put her hands on his shoulders and kissed him on both cheeks. Zen was rigid. He didn't return the gesture, but my heart still felt like it had been pierced with a skewer. Seeing them together was brutal. What a beautiful couple they made, sharing that *Je Ne Sais Quoi* thing that very few people possess; they both had it in spades.

As they walked away from the green towards the village, I heard Barnaby shout after them, 'I need to sign both of you up ASAP. DM me and let's talk.'

Neither of them turned, and they carried on walking away from the party... and me, and I felt as if my world was about to end.

'What do you want to do, chick?' asked Tara. 'Do you want to come back to the holiday house or wait here until Zen comes back?'

'Ellie, stay here. He'll be back and there's no point in sitting and stewing. Don't forget, I know my brother and he will do what's right. I promise.'

Easy for her to say. What was right for Zen might not be what was right for me.

'Where were they going, Aurora?' I asked, terrified she was going to say that they were going back to *our* attic, or anywhere else where they were totally alone for that matter. My mind had begun to work overtime.

'They've gone to the *Crab*. It will be quiet in there as everyone is over here this afternoon. Give them a chance to talk.'

That made me feel moderately better, but not much.

'I'll stay here,' I said. 'Might as well try and enjoy the afternoon,' knowing full well that was impossible, but better here than brooding alone.

'Good lass,' said Meg. 'Our Zen loves you, Ellie. All of us can see that, and don't forget what she put him through. He's not going to forget that in a hurry.'

'But she's so beautiful,' I sighed, 'and maybe she's changed for the better.'

'And you're beautiful too, lass. Zen has changed for the better too and that's all thanks to you,' said Bert.

I glanced around the table at my group of lovely friends, all of them having my back and trying to make me feel better.

'Come and dance with me, Ellie. Nora won't mind. She's got two left feet and by Christ if she stands on your toes you know about it,' chuckled Maurice.

'Not sure I'm quite up for dancing, Maurice, but Meg here hasn't got a partner until the Bionic Man gets better, so go on, Meg, strut your stuff.'

'You know what, pet, I think I just might,' said Meg, linking arms with Maurice and heading for the dance area. The band struck up with 'Show Me The Way To Amarillo.' Thank God it wasn't 'The Girl From Ipanema.'

'Ellie let's go and sit over there and have a talk,' said Aurora moving towards an empty table away from the crowd.

'Good idea. We'll be here when you get back.' Tara smiled.

'I think we've all had a bit of a shock,' said Aurora when we settled at the table.

'A bit? A massive one more like. I feel like I've had thousands of volts through my system.'

'No one's had a bigger shock than my brother. I want you to know that he had absolutely no idea that she was going to turn up like this. He thought that chapter of his life was well and truly closed, which it is. She's re-opened it temporarily, but believe you me, he will shut it down again.'

'How can you be so sure about that?'

'Because I know my brother,' she said simply.

'Tell me about her, Aurora. I've never asked before because I felt it wasn't my place, but now she's turned up, she's made it my business. What is she like, other than the fact that she is drop dead gorgeous?'

'Okay Ellie, I'll tell you. I imagine you want me to say she is a bitch like Isla, but hand on heart I can't. She is highly likeable, vivacious, and very funny. That said, is she my brother's type? No, not at all, but you can see why he was captivated, and he was – hook, line, and sinker. I've only met her twice though; he never brought her home to the island.'

266

'So, this is the first time she's been here?' I asked.

'Yes. I can't imagine the idea of coming to a tiny island in cold northern England was very appealing to her.'

'It was appealing to me, although in fairness, I didn't know it was an island.'

'And thereby lies why you are my brother's type and she isn't.' Aurora smiled. 'Both families met up in Barcelona to celebrate their engagement, and the next time we met was very briefly when we went over for the wedding. Considering I was only there a day before he caught her in bed with Lee, his band mate, we never had a lengthy friendship. She's very confident and self-assured, and why wouldn't she be looking like that? And she knows what she wants. Trouble was, she and my brother were far from being on the same page. Bethania just wasn't ready for marriage or settling down. Truth be told, not sure Zen was either, not to her anyway, but they both carried on regardless, unable to stop the runaway train as she had insisted on a huge wedding. I've told you already what he was like when he came home – absolutely shattered by her admissions of sleeping around, and then, of course, him seeing her with Lee.'

'And what if she's grown up in the last three years and is ready to settle down now?'

'I hope that's the case, but I can tell you now,' said Aurora grabbing my hand, 'she will not be settling down with my brother.'

I was hearing the words but I wasn't sure they were registering. The what ifs were mounting by the minute. We were so engrossed in conversation we didn't see Aidan approach. He coughed gently to let us know he was there.

'Sorry for interrupting, but we're just about to go. Listen, none of my business, but if er, Bethania is stuck for somewhere to stay, there's an empty motorhome in the yard, top of the range and no charge.'

'I'll be sure to let her know,' replied Aurora caustically.

'Anyway, thought you might appreciate this, Ellie,' he said, placing a bottle of very expensive Champagne down on the table.

'What's that for? To celebrate me losing my boyfriend?'

'Ellie,' gasped Aurora. 'That's not true. Don't listen to her, Aidan, she's talking nonsense. Of course she hasn't lost her boyfriend, and thanks, we'll take the Champagne and celebrate the fact that we've now only got three and a half weeks until Meg and Bert get their life back.'

Aidan's cheeks flushed before he turned and went back to his table.

'Cheeky bastard,' said Aurora. 'I think I'll insist Beth goes and stays over there. Now that would put the cat amongst the pigeons. Right Ellie, let's get back to our friends, get this bottle open, and watch the fishermen make right arses of themselves dancing around that pole semi-naked – every year they get into a huge tangle, and all end up on the ground on top of one another. It's like a giant game of drunken Twister in waders. I'm so pleased Jack is out on the boat today!'

We returned to the table. Zen had been gone for a little over an hour and I was feeling more stressed by the minute. The party was going on around me, the fishermen were doing their thing and the entire audience were rocking about laughing – except me.

'I'm going back to the attic,' I said to Tara. 'I just want to see Nacho and Robson and have some time to myself to make sense of this.'

'Are you sure, Ellie? I can come with you.'

'No, you stay and see that lot at their drunken finest. I'm just going to slip off quietly. Will you tell the others for me? They're too wrapped up in the performance to notice me go.'

'Of course. Call me anytime, do you hear?'

'Yes, I do,' I said, kissing her on the cheek. 'And Tara, talk about swinging from high to low today. Your news about coming here was just the best. I'm so pleased and keeping my fingers crossed it all goes through without a hitch.' But as I walked away towards Main Street, I did wonder whether I would still be on the island when Tara and Toby moved in permanently.

There's nothing like small furry friends to cheer you up. As I walked into the attic, Nacho leapt up as if he was on springs, and Robson headbutted me with his funny little Roman nose. Whilst the idea of snuggling up with them on the sofa and feeling sorry for myself was very appealing, their bright eyes and waggy tails were enough to remind me that they took priority and needed a walk after being cooped up in the flat for a couple of hours.

'I hear you both,' I said, mustering up a smile. 'Come on, let's go down to *our* bench,' the word our almost stuck in my throat, 'and you two can have a run and use up some of that energy.'

The dogs happily ran along the beach as I sat and drank in the view which was like a balm for the soul. The white tipped waves were rolling closer to the shore, a sure signal that the tide was

ming in, and the lack of tourists was testament to that fact. They
ould be hurrying back over to the mainland or face being captive
til the causeway re-opened.

The pale lemon afternoon sun danced on the ink blue sea. The
y was alive with terns who were mewing, circling around the bay
d the small island. I spotted Zen's dad, Mike, as he, and some of
e seasonal volunteers who were now staying on Greater Reef for
eeding season, walked the perimeter of the tiny island checking
e cliffs. I wondered what he and Simone would make of Bethania
rning up like this. Maybe Aurora had already told them. I was lost
a jumble of thoughts and didn't hear Zen approach, but Nacho
d Robson did as they both rushed towards him, their tails in
nger of wagging off and blowing right over to Greater Reef.

He slid onto the bench and looked straight out to sea. Neither
us spoke until I couldn't stand the tension any longer.

'So, what's *she* doing here? I blurted out.

CHAPTER 45

I turned to face him, noticing how drawn he looked. His fingers we
strumming on his leg and he was struggling to find the words to ta
to me.

'Truth, Ellie? I'm not too sure, but what she's telling me is that
she was in London doing something for her father, and she has a
few days spare before going home so decided to come and see
Lindisfarne for herself.'

And you, I bet...

'After all this time? Doesn't that strike you as odd?'

'Not really. We were together a long time, and I probably bore
her silly talking about where I grew up, and the place I loved most
all the world.'

'Why didn't you bring her at the time?'

'Just never got round to it. I'd started working for her dad, she
was busy with the company and the wedding, and to be honest she
never seemed that keen to visit back then.'

And surprise surprise, now she is...

'I don't want her back, Ellie,' he said bluntly.

'And does she know that?'

'It never came up in conversation. I assume she knows that
already.'

'And does she know about me?'

'Yes, of course. I told her that we live together and that I'm very much in love with you.'

My heart managed to slow down slightly, but I bet it would still be in the aerobic zone of my fitness watch.

'And what did she say about that?'

'Not much, to be honest.'

'So, how long is she staying?' I asked, hoping he was going to say she was leaving on the next tide.

'Well, that's the thing. She has a few days spare and wants to stay and try and mend the bridges that she burnt not only with me, but with Aurora and Ma and Pa.'

'Why on earth would she want to do that? She hardly knows them.'

'I don't know, Ellie. Guilty conscience, or maybe she's just grown up and wants to put things right. I chose to run away from it all at the time. We never really spoke about things and I've always wondered if I should have stayed...'

My heart was now residing in my shoes, and he must have noticed the dejected look on my face.

'Not stayed as in to put things right with Beth. I knew it was over for us. I mean stayed to end it properly, not just with Beth but with her family too. They had been so kind to me, and I just bolted without a word of thanks for all they had done for me – they'd given me a job and a home. From the day I got on that plane from Brazil, Beth and I haven't spoken a word. I left all the negotiations about

272

getting my stuff back to Aurora. I basically buried my head in the sand.'

'And where is she staying?'

He went quiet.

'W-well,' he stuttered, 'the thing is... because it's May weekend there's nowhere left on the island for her to stay. Everywhere is full.'

'Do you mean to tell me she came all this way without making any arrangements?'

Because she assumed she would just be staying with you...

'So, I was wondering...' he went on.

'Not in a million years, never, NO! She is not staying with us.'

'Ellie! I wasn't going to ask that. Of course that wouldn't be appropriate. I was going to ask whether she might be able to have one of the rooms at the holiday house. Tara and Toby don't need them all now the others have gone.'

'Still no. How can you even think it's okay to ask if your ex can stay with *my* best friends? No Zen. Maybe I should just go and stay at the holiday house, and she can share the attic with you?'

He looked crestfallen.

'Ellie, the attic is *our* home, yours, and mine, and I hope neither of us is going anywhere. Please don't make this any more difficult than it already is.'

'Difficult? Zen, I'll level with you, I'm jealous. There, I said it out loud. I have enough little green-eyed monsters frantically tapping me on my shoulder to fill Luxembourg.'

'There's no need to be jealous. It's you I'm in love with. She'll be long gone – forever this time – in a few days, so please, let's not fight over this. I understand what it must feel like. I was the same when your ex, Matt, turned up over Christmas.'

'But Matt was gone from the island as quickly as he came, if you remember. Beth is going to be hanging around for days. You cannot really compare the two situations. Our lives have been disrupted enough over the past few weeks what with everything that's been going on. This is just the last straw. Can you not just tell her to go?'

'Beth does her own thing, Ellie. She always has, hence the situation I found myself in back then. She'll only leave when she's ready to leave and, short of kidnapping her and putting her on the next flight, somehow, we are just going to have to get through this. And far better that we do it on a united front.' He reached out and took my hand. 'I know this is asking a lot of you, but can we find her somewhere to stay?'

'Where is she now?'

'Still in the *Crab* as far as I'm aware.'

I pulled my phone out of my pocket and called Aidan. A few minutes later, it was all arranged. Aidan would collect Bethania and take her to her accommodation – a brand new, top of the range motorhome in our old yard, well away from us. If there was any joy to be gained out of this whole debacle, Beth being there would irritate the hell out of Isla. One thing Isla hated was competition, and beautiful Bethania would give her a run for her money any day of the week.

CHAPTER 46

e walked back to the attic in virtual silence, neither of us quite
owing what to say.

'She'll be fine over at the castle you know,' I said, breaking the
ence. 'There's lots of stuff going on, free food on tap, and you
ver know, she might get on the telly. Plus, she had that Barnaby
ap eating out of her hand.'

I looked at Zen's face to see if the idea of Beth and Barnaby had
ggered any emotion. It hadn't.

'I'm not worried about her, Ellie. Beth is more than capable of
oking after herself, but I would like to be able to meet up with her
fore she goes – with you and Aurora. Ma and Pa won't be able to
ave Greater Reef at this time of year, but I want to close this down
ad on this time, and I've got no secrets from you.'

'I don't have to be there. You and Aurora meet her if you like.
n, and Zen, if you feel you need more time with her on your own,
en go for it. I do trust you, just today was such a shock and it's
king me a little while to adjust to you having Miss Brazil as your
-fiancée. Matt was hardly Mr Universe by comparison.'

'Ellie, you're my partner and, for the record, you're every bit as
autiful as her, and more. I'd like you to be there with me. Just for
bite to eat in the *Crab* one night.'

'Let me think about it.'

Half of me was desperate to go and meet the woman who
uld have become Mrs Chambers, the other half was thinking it
as the stupidest thing ever to even contemplate it. I needed to

276

sleep on it, but not until I'd spoken to Sophie, so I went into the kitchen and closed the door.

'You what?' spluttered Sophie through the screen.

'There she was, large as life and twice as beautiful. Honestly Soph, imagine Sofia Vergara and you're not far off the mark.'

'She's Columbian.'

'She's also very sexy, and so is Bethania. They've both got that Ipanema beach vibe going on.'

'And how are things between you and Zen? That must have been really difficult.'

'It was. It is. Oh, I don't know. I just don't understand why she' come here other than the obvious – that she wants him back – and that scares me, Sophie.'

'And what does Zen say?'

'Oh, all the right things. That he's not interested, that he loves me, that he just wants to shut this down once and for all. He wants me to go with him and Aurora to meet her.'

'Sounds to me like he's trying, babe. He's in a difficult situation and it must have been a bigger shock to him. Auntie Sophie says try not to feel threatened. Go and meet her. At least you will get a better idea of what you are dealing with. If she's a nightmare, just set the Poison Pylon on her!'

'Talking of that cow, you should have seen her face when she saw Bethania at Maypole Saturday. It was hilarious. I can't wait to find out what happened when Aidan turned up at the castle with Beth and her suitcase. I bet Isla was far from happy.'

'Now that was a masterstroke. Well played, Ellie Nellie. I've taught you well!'

'Barnaby, the big cheese over there, was virtually licking her sparkly feet. With any luck she'll end up with him and we won't see any more of her.'

'When the caravan's a-rocking don't come knocking,' howled Sophie. 'Now tell me quickly before we go. How are Bert and Meg? Have they settled in with Granny Ethel?'

'They had a great day today. I've just spoken to Meg. Bert was feeling quite positive that his hip is getting better. While they are both still angry that they're not at home, I think they are enjoying being fussed over by everyone in the village, and they're content that all the animals are doing well. As from next week, we're going to be taking Bert over to the paddocks in the car. He's really looking forward to that.'

'Ah, that's good to hear.'

'And what about Tara and Toby? She said she had called you to tell you their news. It's fantastic.'

'Yes, she did. It's a gorgeous house. It might be fantastic news for you, but not so much for me. No, seriously I think the pair of them, and Bee Dee, will fit right into the island way of life. They almost already have. And at least there's going to be plenty of room for us all to come and stay. I know the boys can't wait to come back.'

'And I can't wait for you all to be back.'

'Okay, Ellie, got to go and get some sleep. You take care and try not to stress too much over Bethania. She'll be gone soon enough, and I know Zen loves you – I can tell.'

'I hope so. Nighty night, Soph. Love you.'

'You too, babe. Now go and get some beauty sleep.'

I cleaned my teeth then went into our bedroom. The light was off and Zen was already in bed. I climbed in next to him. He usually turned over and spooned me. He didn't move and lay rigid, but I knew from his breathing he wasn't asleep. I turned over, my back to his, and despite all that he had said earlier, and Sophie doing her best to raise my positivity, I felt like a gulf had suddenly appeared between us. I wouldn't be getting much in the way of any sleep, beauty or otherwise, tonight.

***

The next morning, Zen had gone to the roastery by the time I got up. When I went into the kitchen to put the kettle on, I saw a note on the table.

Sorry for being such a dick last night. I love you more than all the stars in the sky – and that's a lot of stars Ellie x

And *I* loved him, it should be as simple as that.

I was at a loose end as it wasn't my shift in *Love Lindisfarne* and Maurice was on animal duties, so I called Tara and arranged to meet her in the café for breakfast. A good talk with her would sort me out. Tara was the voice of reason. We settled ourselves at a table and ordered. Aurora was too busy baking scones for the day to join us, the aroma of mouth-watering home baking permeating the cafe,

hich would be quiet until the causeway opened later that
orning, bringing in tourists in search of refreshments.

'So, how did it go last night?' asked Tara.

'As expected, I suppose. Zen is trying his best, but I feel he just
eeds to tell her to... well, you know... do one, but that's not Zen, is
?' I told Tara about the conversation we'd had and how he wanted
e to meet with Beth.

'Ooh, that's awkward, but then why should it be? Many exes get
n after the event and it's not like it would be a regular occurrence,
er being on the other side of the world.'

'I'm thinking about it.'

I then told Tara about Beth going to stay in the motorhome, or
hatever it was, belonging to the television production company.

'Priceless,' she guffawed. 'I saw Isla's face yesterday, and that will
eriously rattle her cage. I'd love to be a fly on the wall.'

'You and me both. They're starting filming tomorrow. Pity them
orking with that self-absorbed cow—'

'Err Ellie,' interrupted Tara. 'I think you might need to make your
nind up about meeting Beth more quickly, because she's coming in
ight now with that Barnaby Big Bollocks from the show, and I'm not
eaving here until me and Bee Dee get one of Aurora's gorgeous
cones straight out of the oven, dripping in butter.'

I turned round to see Beth and Barnaby heading our way. Me in
ny old trackies, not a scrap of make-up, and my hair in a scrunchie,
nd there was Bethania in an off the shoulder crocheted jumper in

vibrant pinks and yellows, black leather flared trousers, her huge sunnies perched on top of her head.

'How can she look like that at nine thirty in the morning?' said Tara checking her watch. 'I can't even manage to look like that at nine thirty in the evening these days.'

'Me neither,' I replied miserably.

They sat down at the next table and Barnaby, a tall, thin, somewhat beige guy in his forties, extended his hand. 'You're Ellie? Aidan told me about you, and I've seen you mucking out the animals in the paddocks.'

'Yes, that's me, always up to my neck in shit,' I squeaked, conscious that Beth was watching me with intent. She suddenly jumped up.

'Elleee,' she squealed. 'You are Zen's girlfriend? So pleased to meet you.' She clasped my shoulders and gave me the full force of her pillow soft lips on both sides of my cheeks, leaving a waft of *Chanel No.5* behind.

'Err hi,' I managed to say, quite taken aback.

'Zen, he tell me about you. I am so pleased that he has found a new love after I break his heart, but I am a passionate woman and sometimes...' she tailed off.

I swear I saw beads of perspiration forming on Barnaby's top lip. She was exactly as Aurora had said. Captivating, theatrical, and exuding warmth.

'We meet tomorrow night with Aurora and Zen, yes?' she said, ssing her fingers, a large silver ring shaped like a coffee bean :ching the light.

'Err yes,' I squeaked.

'Good. And who is this with the baby cooking?' She smiled.

'Oh sorry, this is Tara, my friend.'

Tara then got the kisses.

'And this is baby Bee Dee,' said Tara, stroking her bump.

'You make beautiful mama,' said Bethania.

Barnaby's eyes were scanning the walls of the café, taking in the ant images of the Northern Lights taken from all over rthumberland.

'Wow. I love these. Are they for sale?'

'Zen took them,' I replied proudly. 'If you pop into *Love disfarne*, Imogen will sort you out.'

'Who knew Zen had such talent?' purred Beth. 'He was always od with his hands, erm, I mean so good with the coffee too. Come rney, let's go and sit outside. You tell me all about your ogramme, and that awful Isla woman that the lovely Lord Aidan ith eyes like the ocean at Copacabana Beach is marrying. He must , how do you say, bonkers?'

'He's not quite a lord,' I said smiling.

'But he must be bonkers.' Tara laughed.

'See you later, Elleee,' said Beth, blowing us both air kisses, hips swaying as she sashayed out to the garden, Barnaby's long thin legs in hot pursuit like a lovesick teenager.

Tara and I sat in silence for a few minutes, absorbing the exchange that had just taken place, before we both burst out laughing, interrupted only by Aurora who came bearing warm scones and homemade raspberry jam.

'Nice to see you laughing this morning, Ellie. What's got into you two?' She smiled, putting down the plate.

'We've just been Beth'd!' Tara laughed.

'See, told you so. She's hard to dislike, isn't she?' Aurora laughed, pulling up a chair and joining us for a good old island gossip.

n Monday morning, Zen and I drove Bert over to the paddocks for
m to assume his role of site foreman. We set up a camping chair
ext to the shelter of the storage shed, where he could see
verything that was going on, and dumped the bag containing a
ask and goodies inside. The sky was a leaden gunmetal grey, the
ind from the North Sea whipping over the island, but the look on
ert's face was one of absolute joy as he looked over the flat
crubland to the distant sea beyond.

'It's good to be back where I belong,' he said, surveying his
ingdom, and his charges, who had all appeared at their respective
ences waiting for their breakfast. 'Look there's the Kittiwakes,' he
aid, pointing up to the sky. 'It'll be a cacophony of sound on the
eef Islands at the moment; such an important time of the year. In
y younger days, I would have been over there helping.'

'You want to sit down, Bert?' I asked, Meg's words ringing in my
ars about taking care of him.

'Not yet, Ellie. I can walk a bit now. I may not be up to carrying
nything while I still need sticks, but I'm going to hobble my way
round saying hello to everyone.'

'Okay, we'll just get on with the mucking out before we do the
eeds.'

Robson, Nacho, Flo and Duchess were running around. In
airness, Duchess was undertaking more of an ambling gait, but
hanks to all the exercise she had been getting with us all walking
er for Ethel, she was much trimmer. She had settled into her new
ome as if she had always been there, and Ethel absolutely adored

her. It really was a match made in heaven, even though Duchess's flatulence problem had not gone away.

'Eeh, it's grand to see that old lass enjoying her life, isn't it?' said Bert, nodding towards Duchess. 'It's a shame Tri isn't here too to complete the gang, but he's out with Maurice and Nora. They've gone to Amble for the day and taken him with them.'

'Nora has really fallen for Tri. They both have. Do you think he might just stay with them long term?'

'Aye, Ellie pet, it crossed my mind. He could maybe stay until James and Grace get home because Tri and Robson usually live with them in their apartment as you know. Let's wait and see what happens. I can't tell you both how good it is to be back. I'd rather be up there mind.' Bert pointed towards the cinder path leading to the five-bar gate into the yard. 'But we'll be back home in a few weeks' time, all being well. As long as I get to come here, I'm as happy as a pig in muck. I'll be stacking bales by the end of the week!'

As we got on with the jobs in hand, Bert went from paddock to paddock telling us that Wilma needed grooming, Nanny needed her feet checking, Hannibal was getting too fat and Stout needed more love!

'Tea, Bert?' I asked, getting the flask out of the shed.

'Lovely, lass. You two come and sit with me. Put that invalid blanket Meg insisted you bring for me on the ground and sit on that. You're not wrapping me up like Waldorf and Statler.'

I spread the tartan woollen blanket out on the ground, and Zen and I sat with Bert. It wasn't exactly warm, but I leaned against Zen and snuggled up to him. He put his arm around me and kissed me

285

n the cheek, and I caught a whisper of his familiar scent. For the rst time in a couple of weeks, I felt totally at one with my gorgeous oyfriend. I had told him about meeting Beth in the café, and that I ound her really likeable, and whilst I was still unclear exactly what he was doing here, I would happily meet her with him and Aurora. felt as if Zen and I were back home where we belonged, a bit like ert.

The clouds danced across the Lindisfarne sky, the far distant ound of the tide ebbing and flowing a constant, and the birds ircling above us noisily trying to find a mate. The island was doing ts special thing of reminding us of the circle of life and the mportance of hanging on to those you loved.

'They're starting the filming today,' I said, looking up towards he yard.

'God help them,' said Bert, taking a sip of his tea. 'Hope they're etting well paid having to cow-tow to Lady Muck.'

'Did you two know that they've shut the castle today?' asked en.

'No! How come?' I gasped.

'Don't know, there was no warning. The volunteers due in this morning got an early text to say it was closed to the public today nd for the rest of this week.'

'You know what, I'm not surprised,' said Bert. 'Nothing that happens up there shocks me anymore.'

'You don't seem too concerned, Bert. I thought that would make you angry.'

'Pet, I've had my operation and come out the other side, I've got my lovely Meg, I'm quite enjoying convalescing in the village, and today, I'm back here,' he spread his arms wide. 'Me getting angry about what they are doing up there isn't going to change things. Any more tea in that flask?' He winked.

Bert was so wise; we could all do with being a bit more Bert.

'I'm going to go and have a look through the gate and see if I can see anything happening,' I said, getting to my feet.

I climbed up the track and peered through the gate. I couldn't really see much beyond the two massive motorhomes that were lined up at the back of the yard. There didn't seem to be many people about – probably all in the castle following the Queen Bee around. Then one of the motorhomes looked like it started to sway slightly. Maybe it's the wind, I thought, but the other one was rock solid. Sophie's words about caravans a rocking sprung into my mind. Could that be Beth's van and if so, were all of Barnaby's dreams about to come true? I didn't have long to ponder because I heard Beth's unmistakable throaty voice drifting out of an open window right next to the gate.

'I have wanted this to happen since my eyes saw you. I want you. Now. You are very naughty boy, but I like you a lot, and we are going to make beautiful love again and again...'

And as faint moans reached my ears and the movement of the van increased, I ran back down the hill, my cheeks blazing. I'd never make a voyeur – I could only imagine the smile that must have been on Barney's face at that moment!

CHAPTER 48

at evening, I picked up my bag and went into the living room
ere Zen was waiting for me. Nacho and Robson were curled up
the sofa together, both of them giving us the side eye, aware we
re probably going to leave them.

'You look beautiful, Ellie,' he said. 'You always do, but even
re so tonight. That shade of pale blue really suits you.'

'It was the dress I was wearing—'

'—for Aurora's wedding. I remember. Thanks for agreeing to
me tonight. I know it can't be easy for you.'

I didn't think it was going to be anywhere near as difficult as I'd
ought it would be since I'd heard what was going on in that
torhome. I hadn't told Zen. Didn't think he needed to know, but
told Aurora when I had popped into the café when I'd got back to
e village. She had nearly choked on her hot chocolate.

'Oh. My. God. Barney Big Bollocks got laid. Do you think he was
ming it?'

'Aurora! No. Well at least I hope not.'

'Maybe it's for another show altogether. Did you tell Zen?'

'No, do you think I should?'

'No, I don't. Let's see what she's like tonight, and if she's not
ce we can drop her in it.'

Bethania was already there when the three of us got to the
ab. She looked as stunning as ever in a fitted white dress which
nphasised her curves and complemented her tanned skin. A tiny

clutch bag and her sparkly red sliders finished off the outfit. Simple but so elegant. We were treated to the double kisses, and it all felt very natural, like four friends on a night out. We found a table in the snug where it was quiet, and Zen and Aurora went to the bar to sort the drinks.

'Zen is even more handsome now that he has become a proper man,' said Beth, watching him as he went.

I felt a slight rise in my heart rate. He did look extra gorgeous tonight in a fitted paisley shirt and black jeans, his wayward curls tamed for the occasion, the silver coffee bean twinkling from his neck as always.

'Elleee,' she grabbed my hands and looked into my eyes. 'Don't look so worried. I want to be honest with you. I did come here to the island wondering if Zen and I might get back together. I thought I still love him, but now I realise I don't, not that *special* kind of love anyway. I know now that I should never have treated him the way I did, but I'm a passionate woman Ellie—'

You can say that again. I heard you in action this morning...

'—but maybe I knew deep down that Zen and I were not meant to be married, so I meet other men. When Zen and I come to pub on day I arrived and we talk, I see his face whenever he mentions you. Then I knew there was no chance for us. I can see that he loves you, not me, in that *special* way. But I am not sad, I am glad for him. In fact, it may be good thing,' she said cryptically, smiling.

Yes, to give you more time to bonk Barney's brains out...

'I see the way he looks at you. He never look like that for me. We were young, Elleee, in real love, but not a forever love. I think at he has now found that with you. And me, well, I'm erm, how ou say, feeling filled?'

So, Barney Big Bollocks really does live up to his name...

'I think you mean fulfilled.'

She squeezed my hands and I smiled at her. I really did hope ne would find her happy ever after with Barnaby, because she was terally glowing almost radioactive with the magic sparkle the first me with someone special creates.

Zen and Aurora came back with a bottle of Prosecco, a pint of ndisfarne Lil and some menus. They were both looking at me itently as they sat back down. I patted each of them on the knee nder the table as a signal that all was well.

'Mmm, they've got chilli on tonight,' I said, glancing at the ishes of the day.

'I like my chilli hot and spicy, just as I like my men.' Beth winked t me and Aurora.

Zen's cheeks flushed pink, and we all burst out laughing. It ooked like it was going to be a fun night.

We finished our meal and were sitting chatting when Barnaby ame in. He did not share the glow that Beth was still emitting – in ct, he looked drained. He was carrying a bottle of red wine and ne glass.

'If anyone wants a drink, then please, I'm happy to take orders, ut this entire bottle is mine. I have had the day from hell.'

Ooh, scandal.

'You not have so good a day filming, Barney?' asked Beth, stroking his arm, but even that failed to lighten his mood. Things must be bad.

'No, I bloody did not. That woman...' he stopped. 'Confidentiality prevents me from saying any more, but suffice to say, it's been traumatic, and it's only day one.'

I went to the bar and got some more drinks.

'Here Barney,' I said, giving him a double shot of hooch. 'Try thi – guaranteed to make you forget your troubles.'

He downed it in one. Followed by a large glass of red. Ten minutes later, it had the desired effect. Barney was spilling the beans.

'That woman is a nightmare – and I have worked on *Love Island*. Isla is more demanding than all those wannabes in the villa put together. She refuses to take direction; she wouldn't wear what we wanted for the scene she was shooting. It was meant to be her talking to a caterer about the wedding breakfast and she was dressed as if she was in the royal enclosure at Ascot. We were supposed to be getting some shots of her and Aidan, and he was nowhere to be found. Don't blame the chap, I'd be running for the hills too. Any more of that stuff?' He hiccupped before going on. 'And she has no concept that time is money. We have virtually wasted a day's shooting which costs a fortune. The investors will be after my tail.'

'There, there, Barney,' said Beth. 'Will I kiss it better for you?'

Aurora and I glanced at each other and somehow managed to hold it together.

'What's the show called?' I giggled. 'Or is it top secret?'

'*Queen of the Castle*,' sneered Barney. 'Guess who insisted on that as part of the deal. I thought this was the one that was going to catapult me into Hollywood. American investment and loads of interest in the British aristocracy state side. Your amazing ancient castle, the stunningly beautiful island and all that rich history – the vikings, Christianity – I could go on – and all that vacuous bint is interested in is herself. Aidan seems like a nice bloke; I've got no idea why he would want to marry someone like her, but he'd better or I'll be up shit creek without a paddle.'

'Maybe the sequel can be called *Queen of the Divorce Court*,' said Zen, tongue in cheek.

'Sequel?' yelled Barney, his face scrunching up like a discarded crisp packet. 'It won't be me doing it. I'm going to sign up for something nice next time like *Gangland Gangstas*.'

'Ethel loves that.' I laughed.

'It would be a walk in the park after spending the day with Queen bloody Bee. I'd take them over her any day of the week!'

Later that night, as we lay in bed in our cosy attic, with only the sound of raindrops pitter pattering on the roof above our heads, I felt as relaxed as I had in weeks.

'Thanks for tonight,' said Zen, his arms wrapped around me so tightly that I wondered if my circulation might stop.

'I really enjoyed it. I do like Bethania. I can see why you fell for her. She's almost magnetic. She's like a colourful bird of paradise, and I'm more of a sparrow.'

'Stop putting yourself down. I like sparrows – they're my favourite bird! Bethania and I were little more than kids, Ellie.'

'Funny. She said that.'

'I loved her but not that *special* kind of love.'

'She said that too.'

He laughed. 'I promise Beth and I didn't get together and script this. Seriously, not for one minute since she arrived have I thought about getting back with her. I have found my forever love right here on Lindisfarne and I couldn't be happier – Bethania is very firmly in the past.'

'I think she's having a thing with Barney,' I blurted out. No more secrets.

He laughed so hard I thought he was going to fall out of the bed.

'You are kidding me, right? Bethania and Barnaby? Well, I'd never have thought that he was Beth's type, even though he's a television producer. She's no Isla. That kind of thing wouldn't interest Beth. He's a nice bloke but rather, err… beige…'

'Wait and see if I'm not right. Anyway, hopefully that's all the drama of the past few weeks done and dusted. Beth will be going home shortly, with or without Barney, Meg and Bert seem to have come to terms with their extended holiday and will be back to the castle in a few weeks, and Toby and Tara will soon become our neighbours. Life is good,' I said kissing him.

'Amen to no more drama. Life is good, and it's about to get a ole lot better right this very minute, so flap those wings Miss ntague, and get ready to fly...'

CHAPTER 49

A few days passed, blissfully drama free. Zen was catching up on *Island of Beans* deliveries so had been spending a lot of time on the mainland. Bert's hip continued to get stronger every day, thanks to his physio routine, and he was hoping that it wouldn't be too long before he would be able to drive himself across to the paddocks and do some light duties. After a morning shift in *Love Lindisfarne*, I had arranged to meet Tara, Meg, and Ethel for lunch in the café garden.

'It's blooming boiling today,' said Ethel, cooling herself with one of those battery-operated fan things.

'Stop complaining, Ethel. We only get a few days like this a year,' said Meg, adjusting her straw sun hat which looked like it had started off life as a fruit bowl.

'It's Ethel's,' she said, noticing me staring at it. 'Better than sunstroke, I suppose, but I look like a proper numpty in it.'

It was true, the weather was beautiful for May and we all huddled under the parasol out of the strong sun. There wasn't a cloud in the sky.

'It's global heating,' said Ethel. 'It'll melt this island eventually, I'm telling you. That young lassie on the telly has been trying to tell us since she was in junior school.'

'Well pet, we'll be long gone by the time it happens, so I doubt it will bother us,' said Meg.

'It's melting me now,' said Tara. 'Pregnancy and heat are like pineapple on pizza; they just don't go together.'

'Here pet,' said Ethel, handing over her fan. 'Have a blast of this. Anyway, you two young 'uns, what's been going on over at the castle? Heard anything?'

'Bethania and that Barnaby fellow?' gasped Meg, after I gave them the low down, missing out the bit about the rocking motorhome. 'Now there's a turn up for the book. He's a bit… err… dull.'

'She doesn't seem to think so.' I winked at Tara.

'I would,' said Ethel. 'If he would get me on the telly. I always fancied myself as an actress, you know.'

'Ethel! You're old enough to be his granny,' said Meg.

'You are so naïve, Meggie. Have you not heard about these places on t'internet where young men meet us more, erm, mature women? Cougars we are. Or Sugar Grannies.'

'Ethel pet, there's mature, and then there's God's waiting room.'

'You two should both be on the telly.' Tara laughed. 'Honestly, the cameras should follow you about. You'd be far more entertaining than…'

But before Tara could get the words out, the topic of her conversation came bursting into the café garden – Isla, with her face displaying its usual storm warning. It was just as well she'd had so much Botox it prevented her eyebrows from crossing over like a giant X in the middle of her face, such was her attempt at a frown. She was wearing a woollen Chanel suit. It was about a hundred degrees and there was Isla in cashmere *bouclé*. At least she was co-ordinated because her pink flushed face matched the suit.

She marched into the garden, Barnaby in very hot pursuit, followed by a guy with a camera, a soundman with what looked like a giant fluffy guinea pig on a pole, and various other hangers on with clipboards and mobile phones. They all shared one thing in common – horrified looks on their faces.

'Where is he?' she screeched.

'Who?' asked Aurora, coming out of the café to see what all the commotion was about.

'My fiancé, that's who. I bet she,' she rasped, pointing at me, 'has something to do with it. She still fancies him and I wouldn't be surprised if she's hiding him somewhere.'

'What the hell are you talking about?' I said, wondering if she'd had too much sun.

'Aidan is meant to be filming with me today and he's nowhere to be found. I expected him to be holed up in here or the pub.'

'Well, he's not, as you can see, so you'd better all leave. You're upsetting my customers,' said Aurora.

I doubted that as they all looked thrilled to be watching the drama unfold.

'What's all this anyway?' Isla pointed to our table. 'A pity party for poor little Ellie, is it? I told you he would dump you the minute that someone more on his level came along. I saw him this morning with Carmen bloody Miranda, going off in that rust bucket you call a campervan. Hope the pair of them are driving all the way to Brazil,

297

but unlikely seeing as it won't get beyond Alnwick before it breaks down.'

'What are you talking about, Isla?'

'Saint Zen and that Brazilian tart, that's who.'

'I think you need to go to Specsavers, Isla. Zen gave a lift to Harriet this morning. Remember her, you absolute cow? I told you to never mention my brother again. You're not fit to lick his left-over coffee grounds.'

The pair of them stood eyeballing each other, hands on hips, like a pair of wild west gunslingers. The tensions that had been bubbling for weeks suddenly erupted into life. Isla lunged at Aurora and the claws came out. From that point on, it was chaos.

Aurora grabbed Isla by the hair and found herself with a clump of over-lacquered hair extensions in her hand which she waved about like a trophy. Isla, not to be outdone, grabbed Aurora's ponytail, and twisted it. Ethel jumped up, took her straw hat from Meg's head, and began bashing Isla with it.

'Take that, you blooming bean pole. I've seen more fat on me hob than on you.'

Meg, Tara, and I sat motionless, as if we were participants in a competition to see whose mouth could open the widest and catch the most flies.

'Do something, Ellie!' shouted Meg, her mouth eventually catching up with her brain.

'Like what?' I said, noticing that the camera crew had suddenly come to life, their faces gleeful at the spectacle in front of them.

The camera was whirring and the guinea pig microphone was capturing every expletive being yelled.

'Oh. My. God,' said Barney, 'there goes my career right down the, erm...'

'I think the word you are looking for is crapper, pet,' said Ethel helpfully.

I had to do something, so I picked up a glass of cola and threw it all over Isla's mega expensive Chanel suit.

'Oh my God!' I heard one of the crew say. 'That cost thousands and it's on loan. Does anyone know how to get stains out?'

'That should cool you down, you witch,' I said, before wedging myself between her and Aurora and getting an elbow in the eye for my trouble. But all the ice-cold cola did was enrage Isla even further.

Then I saw Bethania come through the gateway into the garden. She was wearing the tightest Lycra exercise leggings and matching cropped top, which showed off a beautifully toned midriff. If she had been glowing the other day, she was now positively radioactive. Seeing her was like a red rag to a bull to Isla, who leapt forward and grabbed Beth's top, pulling her into the melee.

'And as for you and your giant arse that's big enough to block the bloody sun, how dare you come to *my* castle and walk around like you own the bloody place?' she yelled at Beth.

'Jealousy is such a terrible trait, Isla,' I shouted. Then quickly shut up because it really was a case of pot calling kettle black.

'It was Aidan who invited Beth to stay over there, and it's not *your* castle,' shouted Aurora.

I don't know who stumbled first, but the four of us all ended up a tangled heap on the grass with Ethel continuing to bash us with the fruit bowl hat.

'What the hell is going on here?' boomed Aidan as he came into the garden. He grabbed Isla by the stained jacket and yanked her to her feet, which were now missing a pair of Louboutins. Beth was lying on her back, laughing like a drain, her cheeks flushed and eyes sparkling.

'Ooh, me and my giant bum enjoy that.' She grinned.

If she had a giant bum, my name was Kate Moss…

Aurora and I helped each other up. Her blouse was ripped, and I could see a scratch on her neck.

'You okay?' I asked.

'Think so. You're going to have a lovely shiner later, Ellie.'

'Never mind that now. Look, we've been filmed by the crew, and all of the customers have been taking videos. We're probably online already. Zen will not be impressed.'

'Jack will think it's hilarious! There's no such thing as bad publicity. Well, except if you are supposed to be making some genteel programme about an aristocratic wedding that is.'

'Anyone want to tell me what this is all about?' asked Aidan, looking furious.

'Ask her,' said Meg, pointing at Isla. 'She came in here full of hell with a face like a Bulldog chewing a wasp. We were minding our own business, and she was the one to start it. She was looking for you so, if you don't mind me saying so, it's really your fault.'

'Me?'

'Where were you?' yelled Isla. 'I've been looking all over for you – you're like the Scarlett bloody Pimpernel at the moment.'

And as I looked at Aidan, waiting for him to answer, I noticed a surreptitious glance pass between him and Beth, and it struck me like a bolt out of the blue. He had that glow about him too, and I knew just where he must have been disappearing to of late. Maybe poor Barnaby Big Bollocks never did get to realise his fantasies with the beautiful Beth after all.

'Show's over,' shouted Aurora. 'Barney, get everyone out of here please. Aidan, take your pitiful excuse of a girlfriend and make sure she understands what the word barred means because she is. I never want to see her in my café again. It's a freebie for all you customers for your inconvenience,' said Aurora. 'If you must put something online, can you make sure you get the name of my café right, please. *Northern Lights and Bites*. And tell them that my scones are as legendary as my right hook!'

The drama was back – not that it ever really went away.

CHAPTER 50

'Ooh I bet that's painful,' said Sophie, squinting at my eye which looked like I was wearing a monocle. 'The pylon's elbow must be as bony as the rest of her.'

We were having our weekly inner circle online get together and there was only one topic of conversation.

'And this, it happen just today?' asked Stan, trying not to laugh.

'It did,' said Tara, 'and I had a ring side seat. Poor Ellie was just trying to help.'

'I wish I'd been there,' said Sophie. 'I'd have sorted her out with a few spinning hooks.'

'It's been bubbling under the surface for a while. I'm not proud of it, but now it's reached boiling point maybe it will all just quieten down,' I mused.

'And it was all because Aidan had gone walkabout?' asked Jake.

'Apparently,' said Tara.

'So, where was he hiding?' asked Aleksy.

Then seven pairs of eyes bored holes into me until I was in danger of springing a leak.

'Why are you all looking at me like that?'

'Because Adey's got a soft spot for you, and I bet he tells you things,' said Sophie.

'Not this time,' I answered truthfully, not about to tell them my theory about him and Bethania. Loose lips sink ships and all of that.

'Luckily, Lindisfarne's answer to Tyson and Tommy Fury didn't make it onto the internet.' Zen laughed.

'What a relief,' I sighed. 'Apparently, it cost Barnaby a fortune buying the silence of the customers in the café, none of whom wer particularly internet savvy, thank gawd.'

'Granny Ethel is devastated she hasn't made it on to Tikky Tokl as she calls it!' Sophie laughed. 'She rang me with all the gossip.'

'So, what's going to happen with the show?' asked Toby.

'I suppose it will have to go on,' said Zen. 'They've invested too much to pull out now.'

'Maybe Isla will just get a rap on the knuckles and be threatened with them pulling the plug if she gets up to anymore shenanigans,' said Jake.

'Or maybe Adey will just pull the plug on the wedding,' said Sophie.

'Erm, I don't think so,' I said, the eyes then all immediately returning to me.

'See, you do know something, don't you?' accused Sophie.

'No, I do not,' I replied, this time crossing my fingers behind my back. 'Right, who wants to hear about Zen's new coffee blend?'

***

Later than evening, I took Nacho, Robson, Flo and Duchess down to the beach next to our bench. There was someone sitting o it, the very cheek. As I got nearer, I saw it was Barney, looking out t sea, lost in thought.

'Penny for them, Barnaby,' I said, sitting down next to him.

'Oh, hi Ellie. I might take you up on that as a penny is going to be better than nothing, which is precisely what I'm going to have the way things are going.'

'Barney, I'm so sorry about earlier. It was a car crash, wasn't it?'

'It was indeed, Ellie, but hardly your fault.'

'Want to talk about it?' I asked.

'Maybe,' he said, 'but first tell me about the island in the bay. Since I arrived, I really haven't had much time to learn about this magical place. I did read somewhere that Lindisfarne was meant to be a balm for the soul, but I want a refund because the opposite has happened for me.'

'Well, that's Greater Reef, the largest of the Reef Islands and the only one of them inhabited.' I pointed to the small island in the bay. 'They belong to the Lindisfarne Estate and are in trust to ensure that they will always remain a conservation site for the birds and mammals who return every year to breed. The island isn't open to the general public, although if you want to visit, Zen might swing it. His mam and dad are wardens over there and have been for years. They're usually alone on the island but have volunteer wardens join them at this time of year.'

'I'd love that,' he said. 'It must be that time now, I suppose, judging by the amount of bird activity.'

'Yes, it is – the puffins are just starting to breed now. Everyone loves those. Their babies will be here by June, and then all of them will be gone by about August. The one thing this island does is remind you of the cycle of life.'

'I hope I will be long gone by June too. No disrespect, Ellie, but would love to come back as a tourist and experience the island properly, without the stress.'

'None taken, Barney, and seriously, if you ever do want to come back, just let us know. Let's swap numbers.'

'It is very beautiful,' he sighed wistfully, looking over the bay, which was cast in rays of golden light, the sun giving a last-minute push through light clouds which had begun to appear after a perfect day.

'It is. I've only been here myself a few months.'

'No… honestly, I thought you were almost a local other than your southern accent.'

'I feel like I'm a local already.' I smiled. 'That's all down to the warmth of the islanders.'

'I'm sorry the old couple got moved out of their cottage. I knew nothing about that.'

'They chose to go, Barney. It's a long story. Anyway, what's happening after the debacle of today? Are you still filming?'

'Yes, we have no option but to continue. It's meant to be a serious look at an aristocratic union. If it had meant to be a typical reality show where everyone bickers and fights, it would be TV gold, but as it is, it's lacking. I've seen more love between two garden gnomes than those two.' He sighed, closing his eyes, pale eyelashes ntly shut against his sad face. 'And then, here I am in this nderfully romantic place and there's...' He stopped mid-sentence.

'Beth?' I said gently.

'How do you know?' His eyes snapped open.

'Just let's say I've seen the way you look at her.'

'She's the most vibrant woman I've ever met, Ellie, and so autiful. I've fallen for her, but sadly, it's not reciprocated – like she uld ever go for anyone like me.'

'Hey, don't put yourself down. You're a hotshot television oducer and I can tell after talking to you that you've got a kind art. Beth is, well, just Beth, a beautiful bird of paradise who will ver be tamed.'

Or maybe she already has been...

'Don't mind me,' he said. 'I haven't been in a relationship since fiancée broke things off with me and the instant I saw Bethania I s hooked.'

And you're not the only one...

I got up to go while calling for the dogs. 'I hope the rest of the ning goes well. I meant what I said. If you fancy coming back to e island, please give us a shout.'

'I will, Ellie, and thank you. I'm sorry that awful woman gave u a black eye, but if it's any consolation, Aidan gave her such a essing down about it – pity we can't film that kind of thing and ake a sideline show.'

'*Queen Bitch of the Castle*?' I laughed.

'Perfect,' he said. 'I'll pitch that one soon!'

CHAPTER 51

The next couple of days passed peacefully, like life on the island should be. There had been no sign of anyone from the castle in the village, and it remained closed to visitors, so we had no insider information trickling through to the local grapevine. I had called to see Meg and Bert at Ethel's. The weather had held, and I found the three of them sitting in the back garden along with the chickens.

'Hello, Ellie pet. No Zen?' asked Meg.

'He's just on his way back from deliveries.'

'And in the blue corner, it's Cassius Clay!' Bert laughed, pointing my eye.

'Who?'

'An old boxer, Ellie, you won't remember him. My, the colours of your eye remind me of a halo around the moon on a winter's night,' said Bert.

'Err, thanks, I think. Sounds very poetic, anyway.'

'No sign of a rematch with the wicked witch?' cackled Ethel.

'No sign of anyone,' I said. 'They must be filming inside the castle. It's still shut.'

'Aye, that's a travesty,' said Bert.

'Has Bethania gone back now?' asked Meg. 'I haven't seen her about.'

'Not heard anything,' I said.

The gate creaked open and in strolled Zen. He was wearing his old Brazil tee shirt and a pair of board shorts; his usual pale skin was now golden thanks to the sunny weather, and his wayward dark curls escaped out of a baseball cap as he pulled it off his head. I felt my tummy do a triple backwards somersault at the sight of him – he looked like a surfer dude from Bondi Beach, and what I wouldn't have given to be able to just take him home right then and do some horizontal surfing of my own!

'Hey, something's going on at the castle,' he said, helping himself to a glass of Meg's homemade lemonade. 'Quite a few of the people carriers passed me heading towards the mainland as I was coming back on to the island.'

'Maybe they've got a few days off?' pondered Ethel.

'They don't get time off until they're finished, and that's not due to happen for another couple of weeks,' replied Zen.

'Maybe Barney's just given them a night off. They've been cooped up on the island with Isla for long enough,' said Meg, her face twisting into a scowl.

'Er, look,' said Zen, pointing towards the road out of the village which you could see from the back of Ethel's garden. 'Isn't that one of the motorhomes?'

'Those things all look the same to me. Could be though,' said Bert, squinting into the distance.

'Zen, I reckon the dogs need a walk. I think over to the castle sounds like a plan. We can check on the animals while we're there.'

'And spy at the same time. I like your thinking pet!' Ethel laughed.

We walked up the cinder path to the gate to look into the yard. The motorhome that had been occupied by Beth was gone, giving a full view of what was going on. The place was a hive of activity with people scurrying about packing things into the vehicles. The shutters on the catering van were closed, and there was no aroma of the frying bacon which had permeated the air for days.

'What the...?' I said.

'They're packing up to leave,' said Zen. 'Remind me, when's the wedding?'

'Still about two weeks away yet.'

'Then maybe there isn't going to be a wedding anymore,' said Zen.

There was no sign of Barnaby, Aidan, or Isla, but Cyril and Rosa, the housekeepers, were walking down the yard carrying their suitcases. They stopped by the catering van, opened the door, and loaded their luggage into the back.

'What the heck? 'Cyril, Rosa!' I yelled, waving at them from behind the gate which was still padlocked. They came across to see us.

'What on earth's going on?' I asked.

'Aidan has left. Miss has gone mad; she's screaming like a banshee and smashing all his stuff looking for her ring.'

Her ring? Nice to know she had her priorities right.

'Yes, we think Aidan take it with him.'

'Where's he gone?' asked Zen.

'We don't know,' said Cyril.

'And what about you two? Why are you putting your things in the catering van?' I asked.

'Barnaby has given us a new job. We're going to do catering for the production company. Mary, the lady who was running this unit, has taken early retirement,' said Rosa.

Probably working with Isla finished her off...

'And you're happy about that?' asked Zen.

'Delighted. We get to see new places and don't have Miss yelling at us. We'd better go – we're off to Scotland. One of the units there is doing a documentary about finding the Loch Ness Monster. It will be far less scary than Miss if they find it.' Cyril smiled.

We wished them well then looked at each other.

'What the hell? No Aidan, no wedding – no wedding, no show. What a mess,' I said.

'Look on the bright side. Bert and Meg, and this lot,' he gesticulated down towards the paddocks, 'get their homes back.'

'Shall we go and see if we can find Barney?' I asked.

'Yes, but before we do, let me see if I can find Beth.'

'Erm, Zen,' I stuttered. 'I think Beth might be halfway to Heathrow by now... with Aidan.'

You could have cut the silence with a Viking Seax. Even the ds seemed to stop their relentless calling for a few seconds. The ressions on Zen's face changed quicker than the Lindisfarne ather, until it broke into a huge grin. Then he burst into raucous ghter, deep belly laughs that were infectious.

'Aidan and Beth,' he eventually squeaked as he managed to ow a few words together. 'I thought you said she was having a g with Barnaby?'

'I think I got my wires crossed.' I grinned, wondering if the last gh was going to be on me when it transpired that I'd got rything wrong, and Beth wasn't with Aidan at all.

'You mean the pair of our mutual causes of jealousy have got ether and run off?'

'It seems likely.'

Zen threw his arms around me, picked me up and spun me und before putting me back on the ground and kissing me firmly the lips.

'And even better, Isla gets her comeuppance.' He smiled.

'I hope so. She's earned it.'

I drew him towards me, wrapping my arms around him and joying the feel of him against me as we hugged, only to be errupted by our phones going off in tandem.

'Aidan' I said glancing at the screen, 'I bet yours is—'

'Beth,' he replied.

CHAPTER 52

I walked back down the cinder track as I talked to the Scarlett Pimpernel.

'Aidan, where are you?'

'I'm at Heathrow with Bethania.' He stopped, waiting for some kind of murmured surprise from me, but when there wasn't one, he carried on.

'You knew?'

'Just let's say I guessed.'

'Ellie, I am besotted with her. It's like nothing I've ever felt before and even if it had meant giving up everything, I would have still gone with her. Listen, I haven't got much time and we can speak more soon. We're flying to Brazil, then who knows? I wanted you to know that I've spoken to Pa, who has in turn spoken to James, and everything is sorted. I think the castle is going to be in very capable hands soon, so you are not to worry.'

'How? Who?'

'All in good time, Ellie. Isla has been told she has to leave today otherwise some of the staff will come over from Bamburgh and help her to move, but I thought you might want to go personally and get Meg's key's back. I think they might need them.'

'Yes, I'll do that with pleasure. But Aidan, what about the trust fund and the financial difficulties?' I asked bluntly.

'Ellie, my old friend Sebastian, along with the help of your friend, Jake, have been amazing. They drew me up a financial plan,

313

sically a get out of jail card, and with their help I've managed to coup quite a lot of the money I borrowed from the company.'

'Jake helped you?'

'He did, Ellie. Fantastic guy for a West Ham supporter.'

'He secretly supports Newcastle.' I laughed. I felt immensely oud of my bestie's fiancé. He was indeed a top geezer.

'I've come clean to Pa. He knows everything and whilst he's not ppy, he's seen that I've made attempts to put things right. In lation to the trust fund, I'm only going to get half as I won't be arried by the time it's my birthday, but who cares? As much as I uld marry Beth immediately, we need to get to know each other d not be too hasty…'

Who was this new Aidan and what had they done with the old e?

'I also followed your lead, Ellie. Remember when you got the g back from that awful ex of yours at Christmas? Well, I retrieved at ostentatious rock that Isla insisted upon, and I've given it to Pa take back to the jewellers in London. I told him to put the money wards my remaining debt. I'm a free man, Ellie elf!'

'Aidan, that's brilliant. I really am delighted for you. I didn't ant to like Beth for obvious reasons, but I do, she's great, and I ink you and her are well matched.'

'Turns out my parents really disliked Isla. My brother knew all out her past and had filled them in, but they thought I loved her kept schtum. Anway, my dear old papa concedes that I am not ely to be the next winner of the *Apprentice* anytime soon. I'm not

314

totally off the hook. I'm on a sabbatical from the business, but maybe one day Beth and I will be back, and we would both love to see you and Chambers. Take care, Ellie, and tell that bloody hippie to get a haircut. Oh, and before I go, I've left a donation with Pa for the charity in honour of Duchess. She's a great little dog.'

The line clicked off and Zen came running down the bank towards me.

'Well?' he said.

'You first!' I laughed.

'Oh, just that they are going to Brazil, and then maybe travelling, and she really likes him and she really likes you. That's about the size of it.'

I told Zen what Aidan had said. 'I'm so curious as to how they've resolved the estate management so quickly. He was very cryptic.'

'Me too, but it will all come out in the wash as Meg would say,' said Zen.

'Yep, and at least she'll be able to hang it out to dry!' I laughed 'Anyway, let's go and get Meg's keys back and see if we can catch Barney before he goes.'

We bumped into Barney in the yard as we approached the stairs to the castle.

'Ellie, Zen, I was going to see if I could find you before we leave The shit has hit the industrial sized fan over here...'

'We know. We spoke to Cyril and Rosa.' I didn't mention Aidan.

'Aidan's done a bunk. Seriously, I think I would have done the same with the prospect of having to marry her.' He pointed up the stairs. 'I can honestly say she is the most difficult person I've ever had to work with, and the way she treats people is deplorable.'

'But are you going to get into trouble? Will you get the sack? Be able to get another job?'

'No. No and yes.' He smiled.

'Cruella has broken the contract; it's got nothing to do with the crew or me. The production company will get the legal eagles on it and try and recoup some of the investment.'

'So will Aidan be held responsible too?' I gulped, thinking he'd just got out of one unholy financial mess. But then a thought popped into my head. He had told me a while ago that this was Isla's baby and she was the one to sign the contract. He was having nothing to do with it, other than being paid for his time.

'No,' confirmed Barney. 'The only name on the contract is Isla's. I hope she has a good lawyer. Do either of you two know where Aidan is? Beth's motorhome was cleared out yesterday too. Did she say goodbye?' he asked, a faraway look in his eyes.

'Barney, she's gone off to Brazil... with Aidan.'

He looked sad, for about a minute, before grabbing my hand and kissing it.

'Ellie, I think I might just have thought of a new show to pitch. Watch this space!'

We left Barney packing and climbed the stairs to the Lindisfarne's apartment. Isla was alone, sitting on a chair and staring into space. She looked dreadful. Her face was puffy with crying, the usual immaculate hair like a bird's nest, and whilst she was wearing couture lounge wear, it was so crumpled it looked like something she might have acquired from a market stall.

'Come to gloat, have you?' she sniped.

'No. Just to get *Meg's* keys back,' I said. 'You won't be needing them.'

'And how am I supposed to lock up? I'm waiting for my father t come with his car to collect me.'

'Zen and I will just wait downstairs in the yard until you go and we can lock up after you. We'll be changing the gate code the minute you leave.'

'You've both always hated me, haven't you?'

'Not without good reason,' I said. 'You made a rod for your own back. Try being a nicer person, it really does help,' I said, but deep down I doubted she had it in her.

'And I bet you know where he's gone, with MY ring,' she spat.

'Your ring? I think Aidan paid for it, and now that you are no longer engaged, maybe he had the right to return it.'

'How could he do this to me? We're supposed to be getting married in two weeks,' she wailed.

'Isla, we all know that you and Aidan weren't marrying each other for love,' I said.

'He loved me. He did. Why else did he propose?'

I wasn't the one to tell her about the trust fund, and though like her as I did, I couldn't pour salt onto her very deep wound.

'And did you love him?' asked Zen.

'Yes… well…' She faltered. 'We were good together.'

'Really? I don't think so,' said Zen.

'Anyway,' she went on, 'I bet you know where he's gone, Ellie. ↓ and him always were as thick as thieves. You'd better watch her ↑ny, but if you ever find yourself at a loose end…'

'My name's Zen,' he bristled.

'I do know where he is as it happens, Isla. On his way to Brazil. ↑h a woman who is everything you are not, and I hope they are ↑y happy together.'

'That tart? Her with the arse as big as Lindisfarne? Oh my ↓d…'

It was the final straw for Isla and she began flinging things ↑out the room like a woman possessed. Luckily, none of it ↑onged to James and Grace.

'Isla,' tried Zen, 'smashing things is a waste of—' as a photo ↑me came flying by his head.

I grabbed Meg's keys off the coffee table, Zen held out his hand ↑d we left her to it, hoping Gordon wouldn't be too long, ↑erwise she might wreck the place completely.

We waited on the bench, watching the last of the production ↑mpany get ready to leave.

'What do you think will happen to her now? It's so difficult to feel any sympathy towards her,' I said.

'She's a survivor, Ellie, but it's going to be difficult to wriggle o[ut] of this one. She's lost everything. The money, the title, the chance [of] fame, and then there's the contract to deal with. I wouldn't be surprised if she just disappears where no one can find her.'

'Sounds good to me,' I said. 'Right, as soon as they're all gone, let's lock up and go spread the good news. Meg and Bert are comi[ng] home!'

e next day it was if there had never been a television production mpany in the yard. They had left it exactly as they found it, and it as lovely to see the cottage door open, Meg singing away to her ow tunes as she gave the place a bit of a clean. The first load of ashing was already hanging on the line, which was stretched out ross the yard. The dogs were running around and happy to be ck too.

'Get the big table and some more chairs out of the shed – put em up at the five-bar gate in the sunshine, Zen,' shouted Meg om the door. 'I've got the kettle on and you'll all want a break.'

A few of us had come to open up the stalls and get them ready r when they were needed. Zen was going to bring the chickens d turkeys back the next day.

'Eeh, it's grand to be back, Ellie lass,' said Bert, leaning on the te, surveying his kingdom. 'Will you bring Stout and Han up after e've had some tea? Give them a spell in their stable and a bit of a oom.'

'With pleasure. We'll get them all up over the next few days d we can give them the once over, eh? Pacino and Murray are in ed of a trim for sure, and we must get the kids to do a few more paca walks with them, or they'll be in the huff. Oh, look over wards the sea, Bert. The number of birds increases every day. reeding season is in full swing now. This is my first time of seeing

The sky seemed to be alive with birds, circling, swooping, and oking like they were having the best of times.

'Yes, next year's guests to the island are already being created right now. Isn't nature just wonderful? We're right in the midst of eider nesting at the moment, and you can see the arctic terns arriving. Just you watch the divebombing antics by the end of the month as they protect their colonies. I always think of them as being like a constant stream of holiday visitors who stay a few weeks then leave – it's the same with the birds. By next month, the cliff edges will be packed with all kinds – that's like the height of the holiday season. Just you go on that Google thing you young ones all use like it's the Encyclopaedia Britannica, which, me dear, was a huge book of knowledge that we had to look things up in, and that me mam used to use as a step!'

'And the puffins, Bert? Everyone wants to see those.'

'You'll be able to see the adults, but it'll be a few weeks yet before the baby pufflings arrive. Even then, you'll be lucky to see any because they bury deep down in burrows away from prying eyes.'

'Aw, I do hope I see at least one. Zen showed me photos and they are super cute.'

'Anyway lass, come on, let's get that tea otherwise Meg will have our guts for garters. I can't tell you how happy she is today, and if my Meg's happy then I'm happy too.'

I linked arms with him as we made our way to the table and took our seats. The door set into the gate opened and in piled the Crafty Lindisfarners with their trusty Tupperware boxes and cake tins.

'There'd better be sausage rolls in yours, Dora lass,' said Bert.

'And scones in yours, Muriel.' I smiled.

'Welcome home, Meg and Bert. We're going to miss you in the village, but it's good to see you back where you belong,' said Linda, taking a seat. 'Ethel's just following. Duchess doesn't do speed.'

'Where's Tara and Toby, pet?' asked Maurice. 'Thought they would be joining us.'

'They would have, but they've had to pop back to London to sort some stuff out. They're back tomorrow. You haven't changed your mind about the house, Muriel?'

'No, I'm happy to go at their speed. They can rent it for now until they're sorted.'

'We're going to have a get together in the *Crab* tomorrow to celebrate Meg and Bert's return, and the departure of the wicked witch, so make sure you invite them.' Linda laughed.

Ethel came across the yard and let Duchess off her lead to waddle around with the other dogs.

'Eeh, me feet are like a couple of ripe haggis,' she groaned, sitting down and taking her shoes off.

'They smell like it too!' Zen laughed.

'Well, who'd have thunk it?' said Ethel. 'Aidan and your Beth.' She looked at Zen, raising an eyebrow.

'She's not my Beth anymore, Ethel. That was a long time ago and I'm fine about her and Aidan; I hope it works out for them. There's only one woman in my life now,' he said as he grabbed my hand, 'and I wouldn't swap her for the world – maybe for a new van though.' He laughed. 'Poor old Ravi the camper's on his last legs.'

I punched him gently on the arm.

'So, who's the new Estate Manager – do we know yet?' asked Linda, no doubt collecting gossip to pass over the bar counter.

We all shook our heads.

'No one knows, but hopefully we will find out soon. That castle's been closed long enough and needs to re-open,' said Bert.

'It's possibly someone from Bamburgh. Maybe even Lord B himself.' I laughed.

'Funnier things have happened.' Bert smiled.

'Well, whoever it is, it surely can't be anyone worse than Isla Thompson,' said Meg.

'She's going later today,' said Dora. 'I was over at the hotel earlier and you could have cut the atmosphere in there with a butter knife. I don't know where she's going, mind, just that Gordon's taking her to the station in Berwick. To be honest, I think him and Elspeth have had enough of her too.'

'Good bloody riddance,' cackled Ethel.

'Anyway, enough of her,' said Meg. 'I want to thank you all for coming. It's lovely to see our friends, and family.' She smiled at Zen and me. 'Bert and I love the bally lot of you. Now get stuck in and let's just be thankful that we are a step closer to normal service resuming on our wonderful island.'

***

323

'That goes there,' said Meg, standing in the middle of the living
[roo]m of James and Grace's apartment and directing us like a traffic
[wa]rden as we brought all of their things from storage to reinstate. 'I
[wa]nt this place put back exactly how it was and bottomed for when
[Jam]es and Grace eventually come home. I'll be coming in every
[we]ek to do my normal clean, even though no one is going to be
[livi]ng in here. Just dump any of the stuff belonging to you-know-
[wh]o in that cupboard and I'll tell Elspeth to come and get it.'

'Hoy, Lord Toby, put that lump of rock over there on the
[boo]kcase,' said Bert. 'Don't think you're too grand to be told what
[to] do!'

'I'll have you know that is a piece of prehistoric rock art.' Toby
[lau]ghed.

'I still can't believe it,' I said, looking at Toby. 'You, the official
[cus]todian of the Lindisfarne Estate until James comes home.'

'Me neither,' said Tara, sitting on the sofa and watching
[pro]ceedings. 'Me, married to an honorary honourable.' She
[lau]ghed. 'Does that make me Lady Tara by default?'

When the pair of them came back from London, they broke the
[ne]ws to us that Toby had met with several of the Lindisfarne Estate
[tru]stees, and James, via video link, and that Toby had agreed to
[acc]ept the job of Estate Custodian.

'James knows of my work,' said Toby, 'and after meeting with
[hi]m recently, perhaps I was on his radar. I am absolutely thrilled to
[ha]ve the opportunity, and I'll be working hard to get this castle up
[an]d running at full speed from Monday. Are you looking forward to
[sta]rting your new job Ellie?'

'I am.' Toby had reinstated me as Team Leader of the staff and volunteers even though I'd never had chance to start the job when was first offered to me. 'We're going to get this show on the road and make sure we keep Lindisfarne's place at the top as one of the best places to visit in Northumberland.' I grinned. 'And are you bo looking forward to living temporarily in my old apartment, Tara?' asked.

'We are, although we are also so excited to finalise the purchase of the holiday house and move in when James and Grace come back.'

'Toby, you'll do a grand job. I know how much passion you ha for our history and I can't think of anyone better to steer this ship, said Zen.

'Well, as long as we can change the Henrietta Room into a *Game of Thrones* experience,' joked Tara.

Zen smiled. 'Over my dead body.'

n and I stood at the top of the lighthouse on Greater Reef looking rough binoculars at the puffins, which were clumsily waddling ound the grassy area at the top of the cliff.

'They're such funny little birds.' I smiled.

'They're very clever,' said Zen. 'They come back and prepare eir burrows, making a fresh nest for their offspring, then they lay e egg – it takes over two months for it to incubate. If you look at at one over there to the far left, looking like it's sitting in a hole, ere'll be an egg under there, and when the time comes, the baby ffling will emerge and eventually waddle off to be introduced to e sea for the first time.'

'Can we come back and see if we can spot a puffling?'

'Of course we can. This is *our* lighthouse, remember! It's been a eird few months, Ellie, since we were sitting in this very spot and aring our first ever kiss.'

'You can say that again. I feel like we've been through so much r a couple starting out at the beginning of their relationship.'

'What doesn't kill you makes you stronger, though, and we're rong aren't we?'

'Like cast iron.' I smiled, drawing him towards me. 'And we're all one, at the top of a lighthouse, *our* lighthouse, and we never did...'

'Ellie! Ellie! Come quick.' Zen's mum Simone yelled up the hthouse stairs, interrupting our very sexy smooch.

The first baby puffling had been spotted and I was not going to miss such a special moment. The other special moment would have to wait. We raced down the stairs laughing.

'So, you would rather see a cute ball of fluff than spend alone time with your boyfriend in *our* special place? I know where I am in the pecking order, but later, Ellie Montague – non-negotiable.'

'It's in the diary and I don't care if a Tyrannosaurus Rex is spotted on the island, it's our time now and I cannot wait. I love you, Zen Chambers.'

'And I love you too, Ellie Montague. More than ever.'

And as we hurried across the island to witness nature at its very best, I once again thanked the universe for the life I now shared with such wonderful people on Lindisfarne and beyond.

vo months later...

Baby Farne Butler Dunne made his way into the world in early
ly. He was the first baby to be born in the castle for over twenty-
ve years, and the bells of All Saints rang out across the island to
erald his arrival. Mother and baby were both doing well. Amelia, of
ourse, already knew he was going to be a baby boy and had made
m a welcome to Lindisfarne card with a reminder of his
rthcoming appearances in things like the nativity, the Easter
lebrations, and all the other events in the island calendar. We
ere expecting the gang to arrive to 'wet the baby's head' as Ethel
ut it. Ethel had already wet Farne's head regularly since his arrival.

Toby had settled well into his job, as had I. The castle was once
gain humming with the throng of visitors, who had the added
onus of seeing some of Toby's initiatives on local history taking
hape. Visitors could now also get a cup of tea or coffee, but not
om inside the castle. Ravi, the campervan, had indeed given up
he ghost, so Tara, Aurora and I had come up with the idea of
urning him into a refreshments van and *T.E.A. at the Castle* had
ecome a welcome addition. Zen was not at all happy that it had tea
ather than coffee in the title, but it wasn't our faults that our
itials were Tara, Ellie, and Aurora, and made for the perfect name.

James and Grace were still in California. Grace was now out of
he rehab centre and making progress. They were living with their
aughter in the sunshine and planned to return to the island after
aving a year out to rest and recuperate.

Aidan and Bethania were very much in love. Thanks to Barnaby, they are about to embark on a tour of the world's best beaches. *The Lord and the Girl from Ipanema and other Beaches,* a forthcoming new show, was already creating huge interest, thanks mainly to the promo shots of Beth in a bikini. Of course, the title was factually incorrect on both counts: Aidan was not a Lord and Beth was not from Ipanema, but since when have things like the truth mattered in the world of reality shows? We had told Barney that if it really was a celebration of the world's best beaches, then they would have to make an appearance at Bamburgh beach because that was the best ever, but whether it would be warm enough for a bikini…

As for Isla, there seemed to be regular rumours floating around about what she was up to. 'She's on the bones of her backside working in a chippie in Blackpool' – doubtful. 'She's hooked up with a gangster and is running a crime empire in Marbella' – possible. 'She's married a 93-year-old Texan billionaire and is waiting for him to pop his clogs' – highly likely. The consensus was that as long as she stayed away from the island, then nobody really cared.

All was well in Courtyard Cottage. Bert's hip was indeed bionic and he was back on full yard duties. The animals were fine; Nanny's milk supply had just about dried up, which Meg was delighted about. The only blot on the horizon was that Colonel Sanders, the cockerel, had turned up again and was waking Meg and Bert up at stupid o'clock. Tri, the greyhound, was still with Maurice and Nora, but Robson was back with Flo at the cottage. Duchess was smothered in love by everyone, especially Ethel.

And as for Zen and me, we were blissfully happy in our tiny attic with tiny Nacho. I think it's safe to say we had caught up on our

neymoon' period after all the drama, and maybe one day, we'd
e an official honeymoon, the kind that follows a wedding...

E END.

AUTHOR'S NOTES

I hope you enjoyed your trip to Northumberland via the pages of Love Beyond Lindisfarne. The story and characters are of course fiction, but the settings are all real. Whilst there are no Lords of Lindisfarne or Bamburgh, the castles exist and are stunning, and open for visiting, as is Chillingham Castle:

www.nationaltrust.org.uk/visit/north-east/lindisfarne-castle

www.bamburghcastle.com

www.chillingham-castle.com

Whilst the Reef Islands are fictional, you can visit The Farne Islands:

www.nationaltrust.org.uk/visit/north-east/farne-islands

Or pop to Seahouses Harbour to find various sailing options.

You can also visit Hadrian's Wall and Vindolanda Roman Fort and Museum:

www.english-heritage.org.uk/visit/places/hadrians-wall

www.vindolanda.com

And for general information on visiting Northumberland:

www.visitnorthumberland.com

Plus, there are loads of groups on social media promoting this wonderful county. Whether you visit Northumberland for the spectacular views, the wildlife, the history, or just some time to recharge the batteries then you won't be disappointed. If you are visiting the island – don't forget to check the tide times first!

ACKNOWLEDGEMENTS

Writing this book was an unexpected joy as I hadn't planned it, but after the fantastic feedback on Love Lindisfarne it felt right to continue the story. So, my first acknowledgment is to YOU, the reader, who came with me, a new author probably unknown to you, and joined me on my first steps into publishing. Wow, you were so very supportive and kind, and I want to thank everyone who took the time to message me, leave a review or a star rating or joined me on social media for a banter – it warms my cockles just thinking about some of the wonderful things you said, and makes the hours of sitting chained to a laptop all worth it.

Talking of social media, I'd like to acknowledge the support I've had from a couple of special Facebook groups. The lovely, funny bunch on The Friendly Book Community which is exactly as it says on the tin, and Chick Lit and Prosecco Chat Group where I've made some lovely author friends. A big shout out especially to Chrissie Parker who has patiently helped me through the mire of self-publishing even though we haven't even met – thank you Chrissie - I can't wait to read your next book!

Thanks also go to every single business who took a chance on me as a new author and stocked Love Lindisfarne. The book ended up in locations all across Northumberland and it was great to work closely with other small independent businesses and support each other. I'm in awe of you all battling away despite everything conspiring to take away our high streets and village shops – long may you all reign.

To my team behind the cover, editing and graphics – Sarah, Helen and Rachel, I couldn't do this without any of you and wish you all continued success in your own creative careers.

To my writing buddies at Northumbrian Writers who once again have supported me through yet more questions and melt downs, with special thanks to Jo Mabey who helped edit the book and boosted my confidence along the way. Jo, I can't wait for your work to be published – it deserves to be.

To all those book bloggers and readers out there that take their craft very seriously and work tirelessly to support authors, old and new, you do a fantastic job.

Finally, to the northeastern authors I have met along the way. I'm proud that our region has some fantastic writers. It's often a little more of an uphill struggle being from 'up north' especially for those of us who are self-publishing, but I reckon we collectively do our region proud and the best of luck with your future writing endeavours.

ABOUT THE AUTHOR

Kim was born in Corbridge in Northumberland and still lives in this gorgeous corner of the world. Passionate about the area, Kim tends to set her work in the northeast, and why not, considering the wealth of stunning scenery, and the warm-hearted locals who are often keen to have a bit of a natter and share anecdotes that give her inspiration!

Kim is now the author of two books and has a part share in a third! None of this feels real to her considering it has all happened about 8 months.

Kim's debut Love Lindisfarne was released October 2023 and from its first cover release on social media, went like a hot stottie and took Kim totally by surprise. Kim had been advised not to release a debut novel into the very busy Christmas romantic comedy market, but she just wanted to share the story that had been with her for a while and is so pleased that she chose to go with her instinct as readers seemed to enjoy their visit to the island.

Kim finds most of her inspiration mooching around cafes across the Northeast where she 'overhears' some of the funniest and warmest things which she stores away for future use (anonymously of course!) If you see her, buy her some cake, then she promises never to write about you!

Say hi to Kim on social media:

Twitter - @kim_adamsWriter

Facebook – Kimberley Adams-Writer

FB Page – Love Lindisfarne

Instagram – love_lindisfarne

Reviews for Love Lindisfarne can be found on Amazon – and I thank each and every one of you who took the time to write one or give the book a star rating – you lovely Lindisfarne lovers are a very special bunch indeed. If you enjoyed this one please pop on Amazon and leave me a review, you can do this as a customer without even buying the book from them and it really helps the author.

Milton Keynes UK
Ingram Content Group UK Ltd.
UKHW020230180524
442616UK00004B/22